'More than thirty-five years ago, our church was blessed by prophetic leaders who really understood that the Jesus we follow is not just Lord of an hour or two on Sundays, but truly Lord of the rest of the week too. He is Lord not just of church structures and organisations, but also of the whole earth – and it came as a profound and life-changing revelation that God's commission to Adam in Genesis 2:15 was to work – and to care for the earth is our commission too. Anything less misses the point entirely and diminishes the gospel.

'The result of this teaching has been a faith adventure in computer software, video production, holidays and facilities management, and with them the opportunity to partner with God in some exciting and fruitful ways – and to see how he uses us for His divine purposes. Your faith adventure will lead to different roads – but serving the same Lord of all.

'Here is a clear, well-explained, faith-building prompt for others to come into such a fullness, for churches to recognise and honour those in the workplace. Not just because they want the cash, but because genuinely Jesus cares passionately for all aspects of the world He created, the world (cosmos) He died to save – and the world in which He has planted us in the twenty-first century. That is what we were created to do. That is the kingdom that is now – and is to come.'
David Dorricott, CEO, AFD Group, Isle of Man

'Steve is a man of gravitas, character and vast experience, who has lived his life embracing workplace mission. *His Kingdom My Business* is filled with wisdom, practical advice, good theology and memorable stories; this book is a must read for Christians searching for answers and encouragement in their workplace mission field.'
Jill Garrett, Executive Director, Tentpeg Consulting

'Having journeyed with Steve for more than twenty years, it is perhaps not surprising I found myself in complete agreement with the central message of this book. I also found myself re-

energised by the challenge Steve brings. As a skilled facilitator and communicator, when Steve speaks to you, not only does he give you the opportunity to respond, but he also asks the follow-up questions which will ensure you are actively engaged; it happens in conversation, and it happens in this book.'
Richard Nicol, Finance Director, Nicol and Co

'A deeply practical, committed analysis of the place of work in holistic religious practice. Developed from within an evangelical–social activist tradition, and regularly illustrated with practical challenges and dilemmas, Steve Botham's argument addresses the dual responsibilities of citizenship and discipleship in the complex multicultural urban environment of the twenty-first century. True to the gut-wrenching turmoil of the workplace, but full of encouragement and wisdom, the book provides an energising blend of theological reflection, practical psychology and personal testimony that will stimulate any reader to reflect afresh on their approach to work and its place in their understanding of themselves.'
Professor Alastair Ager FRSE, Director, Institute for Global Health and Development, Queen Margaret University

His Kingdom, My Business

Partnering with God in the workplace

Steve Botham

instant
apostle

First published in Great Britain in 2022

Instant Apostle
104 The Drive
Rickmansworth
Herts
WD3 4DU

The views and opinions expressed in this work are those of the author and do not necessarily reflect the views and opinions of the publisher.

British Library Cataloguing-in-Publication Data

A catalogue record for this book is available from the British Library.

This book and all other Instant Apostle books are available from Instant Apostle:

Website: www.instantapostle.com

Email: info@instantapostle.com

ISBN 978-1-912726-52-3

Printed in Great Britain.

Contents

Foreword
Roger Sutton

This book is a very welcome addition to the growing global library being developed by the unity-based city transformation movement. All across the world in cities and towns, from Durban to Dallas, Chennai to Charlotte and Berlin to Brisbane, Christians are waking up to the realisation that if they are to have any lasting kingdom effect of transformation across their places, they will need to operate as the whole body with the whole gospel for the sake of the whole city. Operating as one body is fundamentally a new and emerging paradigm shift in thinking and activity. It is a re-forming of the Church and its role in humanity to bring about a new flourishing.

The old paradigm of silo working, competition and suspicion, divisive theological fights and at times blatant selfishness and ego-building are on the way out. They are a fact of the past and not the hope for a new future. The new paradigm emerging is one of friends across the Church of the city working in harmony, supporting each other through the struggles, working strategically and in an orchestrated way to minimise duplication and maximise effectiveness. This beautiful sunrise has the kingdom colours of humility, gentleness, forgiveness, kindness and sacrificial love. This new warmth is then permeating other wider relationships between the Church and the public, voluntary and private sectors and then between them all. Things work better in all contexts where there is a shared vision for human flourishing with shared kingdom values of operating in a culture of servanthood. Families, friendships, businesses, communities, sports clubs and workplaces operate better in this atmosphere, as do all human relationships.

However, as this book explains, this new paradigm shift is not only about Christian churches and charities operating in a new structural way, it's also about each of us as ordinary people being part of this expansive God-infused city-changing initiative. At its very core is the understanding that in order for anything outside ourselves to be transformed we must first ourselves be open to the transforming movement of the Spirit of God in our own personal lives. We can't preach to institutions about taking their place among others in the greater kingdom quest without first knowing ourselves better, knowing our own calling and our own place on the transformation bus. Moving from self-interest to selflessness is primarily a personal journey: living the gospel is to be worked out in my own relationships, realised on my own street, with my own neighbours, and lived out in my own workplace.

This reformation of the Church is a root and branches transformation from the very top structures of how we operate to the ground level of ordinary Christians being city-changers in their own homes, streets, communities and workplaces. We have seen over the last twenty-five to thirty years that much progress has been made in the top level structures that enable strategic and coordinated unity; a new paradigm is being lived out in more than 150 cities and towns across the UK that are part of Gather Movement (www.gathermovement.org). Based on friendship, sustained prayer and holistic mission, church and charity leaders are operating as one body across a place with one phone number and one website, linking effectively with their civic authorities to serve the city and respond to the challenge of the recovery (www.movementforrecovery.com).[1]

---

[1] www.movementforrecovery.com (accessed 23rd November 2021) is helping churches in towns and cities come together to work with civic authorities and bless their place.

The major challenge ahead of us now is to focus on the ground-level transformation and the releasing, discipling, encouraging and supporting of ordinary Christians to be the transformation needed in our schools, art studios, hospitals, neighbourhoods, offices, bin lorries and boardrooms. But again, this is a fundamental shift in how Church operates and what it's there to do. The former model of success for a church leader was about bums on seats, finances in the bank and the new building project, and in later years we've added a raft of social action projects to the success criteria. Not that any of this is wrong, it's just that we've lost the core reason for being the Church, and that is to produce followers/disciples of Jesus. Men and women who look more like Jesus every day, people who live the Jesus way and love their neighbour and their city as themselves.

In these days as we emerge out of the Covid crisis, this paradigm shift is being accelerated. Church leaders are reassessing the model they've been working to, and the disruption of the pandemic has caused us all to re-evaluate what we are doing and what we want to do with our lives.

This book is part of a growing cry to realign the Church around its age-old calling, to set free the people of God into places God has called them to serve. To release, train and support people to be great neighbours, exemplary nurses, artists, businesspeople, civil servants, carers, grandparents, shop assistants, friends, parents and teachers. A city is changed by a host of city-changers, an ordinary but determined group of people who want to follow Christ and be part of his exciting mission. A church's ultimate success will be in its ability to make these city changers; these new disciples – to see the fruit of their work not ultimately in how many people attend or how much is given or how many ministries they have, but in how effective the people of God are in the world that Jesus loves.

Roger Sutton Founder and joint CEO, Gather Movement

Introduction
The Fresh Call

Have you ever had a great call? It might have been that call for a job interview that changed your life, it might have been a boss saying, 'We want you to consider leading this project,' or the time you were selected for the football team, or the netball side, or called to play in a band or that first date that changed your life.

I believe it is time for the fresh call. You may already be well into this call, you may be exploring it. It's the call to be an integral part of God's great plan. The call to be a player, not a spectator. *God wants to bring His kingdom into our workplaces.* One of the great features of our God is that where He calls He also provides. More than that, the more we understand His call the more we make sense of all that has happened in our lives. God has shaped us.

God has a great plan. It is announced by Jesus when He gives His apostles authority and sends them out to proclaim, 'The kingdom of heaven has come near. Heal those who are ill, raise the dead, cleanse those who have leprosy, drive out demons. Freely you have received; freely give' (Matthew 10:7-8). 'Your kingdom come'[2] (Matthew 6:10) is dramatic, incredible, life-changing. Jesus continues, 'As you enter the home, give it your greeting. If the home is deserving, let your peace rest on it' (Matthew 10:12-13). As we are sent out we have authority to

---

[2] Note all future references in the book to 'Your kingdom come' will be from Matthew 6:10.

bring shalom, the deep peace that God gives us as we walk with Him.

This is my central message. God is calling millions of us to take His kingdom out. This is a transformational call, because God's desire is to do a great work in us, so He can do a great work through us. The Covid-19 pandemic has changed much. One of the key changes is that God has taught us to value more the Church sent out. Five per cent of our time and energy is spent on church, but real fruit and impact comes from the 95 per cent we spend in the world – where God has sent us.

I want us to be excited about our call. We will see God created us to be masterpieces. We will see He calls us to be His witnesses and His instruments for change and blessing. Jesus wants to work through us as we meet people, in the Zoom meeting, as we email, as we shape our day. The workplace is a place where heaven touches earth. There is a heaven-sent wake-up call. 'Go – I am with you.' 'Be confident – I have called you.'

The New Testament is full of incidents, miracles and wonders that happened in the marketplace. They also happened in many people's homes – and these were their workplaces too. Paul the apostle was certainly a wonderful thinker and intellectual, but he was used to working with his hands as a tentmaker and to meeting and selling to potential customers. His day-to-day call was to flourish in a place and with its people. So is ours.

We will see examples of people being 'pastors' in the workplace, making a real difference to colleagues' lives. We will hear stories of how people have learned that praying for friends and sharing faith can flow very naturally. We will see miraculous interventions and answers to prayer. We will see those who have used their workplace skills to bless and impact their local communities. The apostles brought peace to the places they entered; that is our call as well. We take the things of the kingdom – shalom, mercy, justice, righteousness, compassion and forgiveness – into our meetings. Each one of us is a kingdom person.

God's heart is for more, much more. His kingdom is our business, His kingdom is to be released with ever-increasing impact into our workplace or business. 'Arise, shine, for your light has come, and the glory of the LORD rises upon you' (Isaiah 60:1). Wherever your business or workplace is, God's light is there, because you are.

The big picture

I am part of a global adventure called Movement Day. It started in New York in 2010 with a vision to gather people ministering in the church, marketplace and non-profit spheres. They were passionate about their cities and the opportunities for the gospel that came through greater denominational, ethnic and geographical collaboration.[3] It developed rapidly into a global movement as we became aware that God is doing something remarkable in the cities across the world. We started to build deeper relationships and shared vision across denominations, ethnicities and churches within and across our cities. The shared vision is seeding bold initiatives to transform cities and to address issues around poverty, broken families, education, racism, etc.

At the same time, the gospel is at the centre – a vibrant city is where the Church and its people are growing not just numerically, but also in their faith and capacity to personally impact their city, town or village. Central to this book is the belief that we are a sent-out people and the workplace is key. I am convinced that God wants to move much more powerfully in us and in our workplaces. He is shaping our skills and experiences and enabling the whole people of God, working together, to transform their city. As part of that there is a growing global momentum to bless the workplace.

I want to challenge some well-established mindsets that often hold us back. One of those key mindsets is the picture we

---

[3] www.movementday.com (accessed 12th October 2021).

have in our heads when we talk about church. Our picture will normally be of a Sunday, of a church where the action is happening upfront, where a small number of people are ministering to the congregation or 'spectators'. It might be a very traditional picture with candles and vestments and choirs, it might be guitars and clapping, or via our computer screen. We may have a picture of church as an institution doing youth work, old people's work, Sunday school, all within church premises.

While this is true, there is a bigger picture! Can I ask us to replace our picture of church with a picture of a typical working day? We might be sat in an office, standing by a machine, driving a car, talking to our colleagues or customers, engaged in a Zoom or Teams call. We need to change our pictures from that constrained view of the church gathered, with us as spectators, to the church scattered where we stand at its centre, ministering to the people we work with and live near. *We are the Church.*

This is an identity challenge. Who do we think we are? We often focus on what we do – our job title or role description. The kingdom way is to focus on call; that call may be released through a job title, but the call comes first. Joseph has a call to rescue Egypt and Israel, David has a call to lead, Peter has a call to bring radical change, Paul has a call to make sense of that change. What's our call? Beyond the job title we may be a pastor, or an enabler, an encourager, a problem solver, an innovator, etc. This is a call based on who God has made us to be. It's His kingdom shaping our identity.

I believe the army of Christians in the workplace can be incredibly powerful. We have seen it in past revivals, perhaps most notably in New York, then the wider USA, then Ulster and elsewhere in the late 1850s. This revival[4] was started in

---

[4] Known as 'The layman's revival', it started with a great call to prayer with ever-increasing numbers of workers praying together. One million people came to Christ in the USA. Joel Mosier, 'Revival History – Jeremiah Lanphier and the Prayer Revival', Bethel Life, 29 April 2009, https://bethellife.wordpress.com/2009/04/29/revival-history-jeremiah-lanphier-the-prayer-revival/ (accessed 25th November 2021).

Manhattan by praying people from all strands of working life – by accountants and mechanics, lawyers and lamplighters who prayed for their friends to come to Christ, and hundreds of thousands saw their prayers answered. This is what happens when the workforce stands in its divine calling. In simple terms, it's when the workforce moves from being spiritual spectators into spiritual players. There are many current, up-to-date examples of it happening globally.

Our call to restore

I love the book of Nehemiah; it is full of so many great lessons. At its heart is the remarkable story of restoration. God has rejected Israel and Judah. They broke His heart with their widespread worship of other gods. But His promise repeated in Isaiah, Jeremiah and Ezekiel is for a double restoration – He will restore the burnt-out ruin of Jerusalem and He will restore His covenant relationship with His people.

Ezra is called to rebuild the temple first and given a remarkable resource of treasure and materials and people to do this work. As prayer, worship and hearing God's Word are restored to the heart of the nation, the rest of the rebuilding can be done. Nehemiah hears that Jerusalem is still in ruins and is distraught. He seeks the favour of the king and, like Ezra, he is commissioned and resourced to rebuild a city that has been in ruins for many years.

He calls all the people to rebuild. The goldsmiths and perfume makers, the priests and officials (Nehemiah 3:1-32). He puts them in teams to work together and to support each other. They rebuild near where they live. As a leader, Nehemiah's task is to inspire them and allocate tasks. He tells them, 'We can do this thing!' He gets them to build in the area they feel most passionate about – near their homes. They have a local focus but a city-wide vision, and God does something remarkable: this long-prophesied rebuild in the ruins happens incredibly quickly, despite opposition. 'So the wall was completed on the twenty-fifth of Elul, in fifty-two days' (Nehemiah 6:15).

How does this link with our call to restore?

- We are not restoring walls; our cities need jobs and innovation; we might be rebuilding people's confidence and mental health, or their families. We are restoring shalom, integrity and justice in our workplaces. We might also be called to rebuild in other spheres – our communities, schools, health service, etc.

- We build where we are passionate – this will normally be our workplaces, where we meet and interact with many people who need that kingdom touch.

- God can do remarkable things. He can change a toxic environment, He can restore relationships, He can inspire you to bring fresh ideas and breakthroughs to your work.

- We are temples of the Holy Spirit. At the heart of the rebuild is our ongoing prayer, worship, studying the Word and fellowship. God sends us out with the authority and resources we need and people to stand with us.

A time for change

Pastor Adam Hamilton from the Church of the Redeemer, Leawood, Kansas, surprised his congregation one day when he delivered his sermon from behind a desk with a phone and stapler and other office resources. He had done some calculations. Between the ages of twenty-five and sixty-five, people would spend 2,266 hours in the church's pews – and roughly 96,000 hours in work.

'The workplace,' Hamilton concluded, 'is the primary place where we live out our faith.' He continued, 'Your five-day-a-week job has sacredness; it has value to God. It is innately good.'[5]

The people rebuilding Jerusalem with Nehemiah clearly had a kingdom call, a Holy purpose. So do we.

Many people in the workplace feel unsupported by their church. There is a tension. I believe God is doing a new work. It needs churches that are actively encouraging and equipping the saints for the work of ministry *outside* the confines of a building. Churches should be *obsessed* with equipping the whole body of Christ to flourish. The congregation needs teaching that understands both the challenges and the opportunities in the workplace.

You may hear the phrase, 'I am in full-time ministry.' But the vital truth must be that if we are thinking kingdom instead of church, we are all full-time. We don't suddenly stumble out of God's presence or purpose when we attend that planning meeting, or meet a client, or unload the bins, or paint someone's kitchen. God wants to use us in the workplace just as much as He wants to use our church youth leader or pastor. We are equally called and valued.

This is another key mindset issue. We may carry the message in our heads that what we do is not important. We might not talk about our job and calling to our Christian friends. But this needs to change. Let us see ourselves standing under a 'divine spotlight'. Jesus loves our gifts, the values we take to work, the skills we use and the conversations we have. We are *not* unimportant. We need to understand that we are all in full-time, highly valued ministry and Jesus loves us passionately. We are integral to His kingdom purposes.

Here are some important ways I suggest we may need to change our church thinking about kingdom calling:

- Mission is for everyone.

<hr>

[5] Amy L Sherman, *Kingdom Calling* (Downers Grove, IL: IVP, 2011), p114.

- Ministry is everywhere.

- Jesus loves to restore situations, lives and communities in the big, wide world.

- We are all servants, but each of us will serve in different ways that reflect who God has made us to be.

- We must release the talent in the church to impact our community. We are blessed with planners, carers, developers, community activists, artists, strategists, mechanics, repairers, change agents, housing specialists, finance specialists, etc.

- *Each church should have a map of where its people are working and studying – to celebrate the kingdom lights impacting the community.*

- We can spend lots of time trying to get our congregation to give and to serve in the church – let's invest at least as much time discovering and celebrating the remarkable talents and resources God has given His Church to bless our community.

- Church should send us out inspired to bring God's kingdom.

- Teach the congregation to respond with kingdom wisdom to the relational and ethical dilemmas they face in the workplace

- Keep teaching about the kingdom – its features, its values, its aims.

- Constantly think, 'Your kingdom come,' to impact your village, town or city.

- Leaders must understand the workplace and spend time there.

- The small group system is called to enable each other to flourish. We must understand each other's call – as neighbours, parents, colleagues – and hear each other's stories.

Hear Jesus' words spoken as He taught us as the body of Christ at the Last Supper: 'You did not choose me, but I chose you and appointed you so that you might go and bear fruit –fruit that will last – and so that whatever you ask in my name the Father will give you' (John 15:16). God prays a prayer of fruitfulness on Israel and its leaders constantly in the Old Testament. We need that regular refreshing, and consecrating, because Jesus calls us to be fruitful. Let this be our constant prayer: make me fruitful today, 'Your kingdom come' into my workplace. Jesus' word – 'whatever you ask in my name the Father will give you' – can be applied to every part of our life, including our work.

Paul in 2 Corinthians 5:19-20 says this: 'God was reconciling the world to himself in Christ, not counting people's sins against them. And he has committed to us the message of reconciliation. We are therefore Christ's ambassadors, as though God were making his appeal through us.' We all have a ministry, we have a message, and we are appointed as ambassadors from the kingdom of heaven to Johnny Bloggs Electrical Retailers, to Scratchit and Checkit's Accountants, to the cheese counter in a local supermarket or to a graduate trainee in a law firm.

Let My people go – to work

I believe God has started a major reset for His Church and our individual callings. It is time for a significant spiritual breakthrough. It is a 'let My people go'[6] moment. We are shaped by low expectations because the enemy[7] has successfully held us

---

[6] Exodus 5:1-11. Moses repeatedly asks Pharaoh to let God's people go.
[7] Satan, the devil.

back. Let us acknowledge that God loves our city, town or village and the people we work with so much that He has positioned people across our land who are equipped and called to be a remarkable blessing. Covid-19 proved that a model that relies on people coming to our buildings is no longer fully fit for purpose. But Jesus is restoring His original plan – to equip us and give us the authority to be *sent-out kingdom people.*

As we become more confident in our call, we become more confident in God working through us. When we become confident in God working through us, we are more naturally Christian, we trust God in challenging times, we pray regularly for our work and our colleagues, because this is our call.

Here's another mindset change – where a church leader's highlight is a great feeling of joy that comes every time people leave the church building (or the online gathering) and move out to flourish in their Monday to Saturday calling. The Anglican closing prayer is right. 'Send us out in the power of your Spirit to live and work to your praise and glory. Amen.[8] Church leaders need to passionately inspire that sending-out through their love for their city, town, the local school, the hospital and the many workplaces.

This book will look afresh at our understanding of Church. We are not a building. Scripture repeatedly tells us we are Jesus' Ekklesia[9] – a moving, dynamic, decision-making assembly with authority to change where we live and work. We have lost this truth and it has held us back. This makes us rethink the Great Commission – Jesus sends out *all* His Ekklesia with His authority to change the world (Matthew 28:18-20). It was always

---

[8] www.churchofengland.org/prayer-and-worship/worship-texts-and-resources/common-worship/holy-communion-service#na (accessed 10th February 2022).
(accessed 28th January 2022); taken from *Holy Communion Service 1,.*
[9] We will look at the frequent occurrence of the word Ekklesia in the Scriptures rather than the word 'church', eg Matthew 16:18, where Jesus says, 'I will build my Ekklesia.'

part of a great divine plan that *all* God's people are sent to bless and called to minister reconciliation.

I have met many Christians who bring integrity, peace, compassion and capability into the workplace. It's in their character and nature – and it is 24/7. They make their workplace and the workplace culture better just by being who God has made them to be. We will share some of their stories in this book. We have many examples of ordinary people bringing Christ to those around them.

We have been chained, constrained and held back as Christians in the workplace. We are like old King Théoden of Rohan in *The Lord of the Rings* who has become rusty and covered in cobwebs, incapable of action. He needs setting free from the lies whispered into his ear. We have fallen into a state of thinking that has emasculated us; we have been taught to think about ourselves as spectators watching the match rather than as players on the pitch. We have heard the message that we are unimportant, that our prayer is weak and that the workplace is no place to show Jesus. But God calls us to be like the Church in Acts – let's break free of the cobwebs!

There will be many other lies the enemy has given you – 'you don't do enough', 'you work too hard', 'nobody listens to you', 'financial ruin is round the corner'. We listen to his voice too frequently. His job is to undermine us. There's a simple response to this: 'Is God saying these things to us?'

What God is saying is a powerful truth that will indeed set us free.

- We are His masterpieces, God's very own handiwork.[10]

- Nothing can separate us from the love of Christ (Romans 8:39). He loves us so much – Paul tells us it is difficult to really understand the height and depth and breadth and

---

[10] Ephesians 2:10 says, 'For we are God's handiwork' ('masterpiece' in the NLT) 'created in Christ Jesus to do good works, which God prepared in advance for us to do.'

width of the love of God (Ephesians 3:18). We live a life continually finding out more and more about that love. God watches over every breath we take in the workplace.

- He delights over us (Zephaniah 3:17) – He consistently takes pleasure in watching as we encourage someone else or use the skills He gave us in problem-solving or building a great plan. We are not hidden away or forgotten in our workplace.

- We get stuck thinking about what we can't do or say in the workplace: we should be released by the long list of kingdom things we bring to work with us – shalom, mercy, justice, righteousness, compassion and forgiveness – they shape our behaviour and make us a blessing.

- God wants us to rediscover His powerful Ekklesia.

- Church is not measured by its meetings, its numbers or even its pastoral support. It is measured by its impact.

- Jesus' final words on earth are the Great Commission 'to go and make disciples' (Matthew 28:16-20) – to work as a mechanic or dentist, a shop assistant or a jeweller, an auditor or a security guard. His heaven to earth cry is, 'Look at My boy; look at My girl! They are empowered by Me. They're doing wonderful things.'

- 'The kingdom of heaven is like yeast that a woman took and mixed into about thirty kilograms of flour until it worked all through the dough' (Matthew 13:33).

We are the yeast of the kingdom. I believe God is calling, equipping and releasing people across our workplaces. It won't be easy; no important spiritual shift ever is. That is why we need each other, why we are not just our brother and sister's keeper (Genesis 4:9); we are their cheerleader, their champion, their encourager. There will be times when we feel unsupported, but we must overcome that feeling. Jesus is with us, He delights in the way we encouraged people in yesterday's team meeting, He loves the insight we had looking at the budget, He is thrilled at the time we gave to someone whose children are struggling. Are we being everything He has called and equipped us to be? Are we flourishing? His kingdom is our business – go out and be fruitful!

Steve Botham

Chapter One
Answering the Call

Introduction

We are in a time of incredible change. All around us we can see chaos and uncertainty. As followers of Jesus, we might make bold declarations about building on the rock (Matthew 7:24-27), but for many the reality is we feel like we are standing in a thick fog waiting for someone else to sound a foghorn or shine a bright light because we don't know the way forward. Many are uncertain about what lies ahead.

It is not dissimilar to the nervousness that must have faced the hundreds of thousands of Israelites as the warriors and their families waited to cross the River Jordan into the Promised Land. God speaks to their leader Joshua and tells him repeatedly to be 'strong and courageous' (see Joshua 1:9). Do you feel strong and courageous as you look at the challenges facing you? Joshua orders the officers to tell the people, 'Get your provisions ready' (Joshua 1:11). It is nearly time to move. Like this large group of Israelites, we are people on a mission, mobilised and resourced to move forward, to be together and to take land. There is a light shining ahead of us because God has a clear plan and purpose.

The story in Joshua moves on.

After three days the officers went throughout the camp, giving orders to the people: 'When you see the ark of the covenant of the LORD your God, and the Levitical priests

carrying it, you are to move out from your positions and follow it.'
(Joshua 3:2-3)

It is a simple but powerful message – *we are following Jesus*. This is our great distinctive in life's journey. Jesus has a plan for us, our families, where we live and where we work. That is what should give us confidence and cause us to be strong and courageous. The officers by the Jordan continue, 'Then you will know which way to go, since you have never been this way before' (Joshua 3:4). It is a powerful statement – Jesus is our heavenly GPS, keep our eyes firmly on Him. He is our good shepherd (John 10:14), leading us into places where we can be refreshed and fed, but He also leads us through places that may seem as awful as the 'valley of the shadow of death' (Psalm 23:4, ESV). Even there we are not lonely, we are not abandoned, He is with us, He is for us.

Finally, I want to pick up Joshua's short words of encouragement to the assembled men, women and children: 'Consecrate yourselves, for tomorrow the LORD will do amazing things among you' (Joshua 3:5). How do we respond to God's prophetic word through Joshua: 'I am going to do amazing (or extraordinary) things among you'? It is easy to be dismissive. To say that was for another very special time. But we are also called to consecrate ourselves because we walk with God, we are in His presence, and He is always extraordinary.

Nervous starts

Starting a new job is a nervous experience. It is like entering another country, we don't know the language they speak or the customs they follow. We don't know if they are going to like us and make best use of our skills and experience. As we discover more about the new job and how little we know about the new context we are working in, everything can feel intimidating. Like crossing the Jordan.

My first job was working on a farm. In a few short months I learned to milk cows, throw hay and straw bales onto a trailer, drive a tractor, shovel cow poo out of the winter sheds and spread its mucky, smelly contents onto the fields. I nearly killed myself once in my tractor but also learned how to have authority over cows (the nearest I ever got to a superpower!). My next job was as a stripper, at a cardboard factory! As if poo shovelling wasn't bad enough, this second job was dangerous because it involved stripping excess cardboard from layers of cardboard sheets so they could be folded into boxes. My fingers were sliced with paper cuts and we all secretly admired the worker who wore pink marigolds while the rest of us were too image conscious to protect ourselves!

There have been many subsequent starts. Getting to know the car industry and eventually working for a manufacturer, for a distributor and for car dealerships, a fairly unique experience. I also got to know financial services industry, a complete change of culture and way of working, not least because of tight regulations and a range of mergers and acquisitions. Eventually I found myself as a leadership and change consultant working with a wide range of clients where each one was again like entering a different country with its culture, history, characters and values.

I would highlight three key things that were important to me in navigating my new countries as I went into the lands.

- Consecrate yourself – it's not easy. The workplace is challenging, from sexual temptations to integrity temptations, to office and team politics, to covering things up. We can feel lonely and isolated. We need to commit ourselves to remain holy.

- Build relationships – for fun and for support. My wife and I found some older couples to help us, to share wisdom and to keep talking about spiritual issues. We also had peers on similar journeys, and we often spent hours sorting out life together. Alongside that it is important to build a range of work-based friendships. Build trust, show compassion and contribute well.

- Prayer – I have always valued prayer. In my early working years we had many amazing prayer adventures where huge situations turned around because people prayed together. God built our prayer muscles.

Following Jesus

We may struggle with the concept of servanthood; it seems strange in our very individualistic era of human rights and personal freedom. But the story of Joshua is of a people trusting God to guide them. The Hebrew word for 'work' is *avodah* – it is a rich word meaning worship, work and service. Our work, our talents and our calling, and the people we work with, can be offered to God as worship. As we worship, we hand things over to God.

Our God is the same God who did great things on that historic day when the Israelites entered the Promised Land after so many years. Our God placed this story in the Scriptures for our benefit and encouragement. Our God kept His promise to the children of Israel – as they followed and served Him, they saw extraordinary things. They saw the Jordan river part, they saw the walls of Jericho tumble, they saw their ferocious enemies vanquished and saw the promise of 'a land flowing with milk and honey' (Exodus 3:8) fulfilled. This is our God, the God of promise and the God who delivers.

Joshua tells the children of Israel to consecrate themselves, to prepare themselves, because entering the land of promise is a holy action. God has a great plan for the Jewish people; God's hand is seen as they occupy the land. But it is true for us also: we are people of promise; we are part of God's great plan. Heaven can come to our workplace.

So let us set our GPS for our destination – to move fully into God's call on our lives. Along the way we have set some destination markers:

- To understand our personal calls.

- To understand our unique identities – because God has known us from the beginning, and He likes what He has made!

- To understand that this call is not about task; it is about relationship. Jesus really does want to be our best and closest friend.

- To be prepared to go deeper – we are in demanding and challenging times, but God is with us.

  It is time to unlock kingdom identity, kingdom authority, and kingdom ministry. It is time to unleash the power of everyone, everywhere, everyday so that the church begins to fill every city: every industry, and every family with the beauty and the story of Christ.[11]

Who do you think I am?

We need to start with some theology. My passion with this book is to set God's people free. I want us to understand our calling and our equipping. For those of us in the workplace, and every other walk of life, this is the heart of God's plan for us – and the people around us. The theology helps us understand why – and why our previous understanding may need a bit of a shake-up!

Six months before His crucifixion and resurrection, Jesus takes His disciples on a road trip. They go north to Caesarea Philippi (Matthew 16:13). This is a remarkable place to go and may well have made His disciples deeply uncomfortable. This was a pagan region, and Caesarea Philippi had been built by Herod's son, Philip the Tetrarch, to bring attention to himself and to honour Tiberius Caesar. Caesar was acclaimed as a god;

---

[11] Alan Scott, *Scattered Servants* (Colorado Springs, CO: David C Cook, 2018), p14.

the town contained a temple where people could worship him. But the real place of worship, established for many centuries, adjoined Caesarea Philippi. In Jesus' time it was called Paneas (nowadays known as Banias). It is a spectacular place at the foot of Mount Hermon. The Jordan emerges as a bubbling stream running through attractive sun-dappled woods. On the towering cliff face you can still see the remains of the temple and shrine to Pan.

Pan was the god of fertility. He was half-goat, half-man. Behind him was the entrance to a deep cave known locally as the Gate of Hades. Local belief was that Pan and other demons entered the cave in the winter and would emerge in the spring if their followers carried out a range of occultic, and what Jews called 'detestable', practices (see for example 1 Kings 14:24), including prostitution and sex with goats. The Paneas cult centre had been built through Greek influence 300 years earlier. It was built on a place of ancient spiritual darkness.

Further back in time this area had been known as Baal Gad. Baal is called 'the Lord' and is also associated with fertility and promiscuity. Baal is referred to frequently in the Bible, including the great conflict in 1 Kings 18 where the priests of Baal confront Elijah. The people watching are unsure who to support. God shows His power and Baal's impotence and the people of Israel fall prostrate and declare, 'The LORD – he is God! The LORD – he is God!' (1 Kings 18:39). Throughout the Old Testament there is an ongoing battle as God speaks against the children of Israel following Baal and engaging in 'detestable practices'. Ezekiel prophesies, 'You will suffer the penalty for your lewdness and bear the consequences of your sins of idolatry. Then you will know that I am the Sovereign LORD' (Ezekiel 23:49).

So this is no ordinary location. Jesus has chosen it on purpose. This is a confrontation – it is every bit as great a battle as that between the priests of Baal and Elijah on Mount Carmel – with the same outcome, the revelation of God.

As we look at Matthew 16, we see this dramatic confrontation unfold as Jesus asks the disciples a key question, 'Who do people say the Son of Man is?' (v13). We can imagine the nervous looks from one to another; they were feeling uncomfortable enough with their setting and now the rabbi is asking them a challenging question. They have a half-hearted attempt, suggesting John the Baptist (although they have seen the two men together), Elijah, or even Jeremiah (v14). Then the tipping point moment happens. This is a heaven to earth moment; we can imagine hosts of angels listening transfixed to what happens next. Matthew tells us:

Simon Peter answered, 'You are the Messiah, the Son of the living God.'
Jesus replied, 'Blessed are you, Simon son of Jonah, for this was not revealed to you by flesh and blood, but by my Father in heaven.'
(vv16-17)

Jesus is the Messiah, the Christ. He is not a reincarnated prophet. He is not just a good teacher or gifted rabbi. He is the Christ. All of Jewish history leads up to this moment. The Christ has come. He is the anointed one, the promised one, the Messiah. This is a historical shift – the Messiah has come and is literally standing among the people gathered in Caesarea Philippi. Peter has a revelation from God about who Jesus truly is.

I am sure it took weeks for this to sink in and was then shaken and refined after Jesus' crucifixion and resurrection. Here was an astounding fact: these men, and eventually so many others, could be in a living, breathing, walking, eating, joking, praying, listening relationship with the Messiah. And so can we. It changes our whole life story – because the story of what we do is not ours; it is God's story. Just as for the disciples, our lives are closely integrated with the story of Jesus. It is the story that the Christ walks with us in our workplace, where we live, where we have our leisure. It is Christ, the Messiah, who moves through us and in us.

A key feature of revival is the restoration of our intimacy with God. Intimacy allows us to draw close, to come into heavenly places – the courts of praise, the seat of judgement, the place of government. The disciples standing together intimately with their friend and teacher have this great revelation – this is the Christ, the pivot of history. This is the King, building His kingdom.

A new identity

Jesus gives Peter a new identity. This is a powerful analogy for us, because when we understand the revelation that Jesus is the Christ, He gives us a new identity too. We may be familiar with the story and the wordplay between Peter and Jesus. Peter in Greek is *Petros*, which means a small stone, and *Petra* is rock, a solid immovable object for building on. Jesus says, 'You were Simon or Simeon (which means he who hears) and while you are a small stone, I will build My Church on the solid rock (*Petros*) of your declaration' (see Matthew 16:18). It is the declaration that is key.

We see a similar identity change with Gideon, in the Old Testament. At first, he is hiding in a winepress to thresh wheat. Much to his surprise, an angel appears, and then astounds him even more with his declaration that Gideon is a 'mighty warrior' (Judges 6:11-12). Through God he becomes what was promised, he is remembered through time for his military victory with just 300 soldiers, following God's plan to the letter, bringing destruction to the camp of the Midianites and Amalekites.

Gideon is hiding, his land has been invaded, and he is protecting his crops. He has every right to be annoyed that an angel with an odd sense of humour has turned up. The last thing he feels like at that moment is a 'mighty warrior': he is hiding in fear. But the angel is making a faith declaration. He is issuing a call to Gideon.

Maybe you are used to hiding yourself away in the workplace, maybe you feel intimidated by your colleagues. But the angel knows what he is doing – he is revealing Gideon's true identity and calling. Just as Peter becomes a rock. What is your identity in Christ? Is it more than you currently understand? Is the angel beside you going to call you a mighty auditor? Or workplace pastor? Or a person of compassion? Or a woman of great integrity?

We will look at the issues around identity as we progress through the book. But the starting message is this – what you believe about yourself may be wrong! The story of Caesarea Philippi is central to God's plans and purposes. The enemy aims to emasculate the people of God, to bring disunity and to stop us from becoming all God wants us to be. He has made us lose sight of the enormity of this moment in Scripture. God has raised us to be mighty, to be rocks, to be builders – and the enemy wants us to be confused about our identity and call.

Our identity has been narrowed down. I remember my church doing a course on our gifts. I had some expertise in this area, being responsible for some pioneering work in British industry on using psychometrics so we could better understand our different personalities. Disappointingly, the programme was all about how we used our gifts to serve the Church. But Jesus call on Peter was for something much bigger.

Introducing the Ekklesia

Let us go back to Caesarea Philippi and this dramatic setting for a major moment in the disciples' teaching programme. Jesus was preparing this small group of fishermen, tax collectors and zealots to change the world. Jesus has responded to Peter's dramatic declaration that He is the Christ, the Messiah. He has given Peter a new identity. Now He gives *all* His followers a new identity, a new calling and a clear authority.

> I tell you that you are Peter, and on this rock I will build my
> church, and the gates of Hades will not overcome it. I will
> give you the keys of the kingdom of heaven; whatever you
> bind on earth will be bound in heaven, and whatever you
> loose on earth will be loosed in heaven.
> (Matthew 16:18-19)

Familiar words – but the wrong words: they are not what Jesus
said! In fact, if Jesus had said these words the disciples would
not have understood Him because they did not know what a
church was. The English word for church is taken from the
Greek word *kyridakos*, which does not appear in the Greek
manuscripts of the New Testament. The large team that worked
on the King James Version of the Bible made a number of
translation errors; some errors were to keep their royal sponsor
happy, others were owing to a lack of understanding of some
key words in the original. It was a mistake that was copied by
most subsequent translators. The critical word they missed here
was Ekklesia (the Greek word – *ecclesia* in Latin). Significantly, it
is used more than one hundred times in the New Testament but
is improperly translated as the word 'church'.

In Jesus' time this term would be clearly understood. It was
a very well-established word; the book of Ecclesiastes was
actually known as the book of Ekklesiastes. It refers to the
Teacher of an assembly – the author describing himself as 'the
Teacher' (Ecclesiastes 1:1). An Ekklesia was an assembly called
to listen and make decisions. At national level, that may have
been decisions to go to war or make fundamental changes.
Locally, it may have been to engage in decisions about
expenditure, judicial decisions or appointments. It is used in the
Old Testament to describe the people gathered together. It
comes from two words: *ek*, meaning out of, and *klesis*, meaning
calling or gathering. But it clearly has a government and
decision-making purpose. It was, for example, the name for the
periodic meeting of the Athenian citizens for conducting public
business and for considering affairs proposed by the council.

I remember talking to a Swiss member of Agape[12] some years ago and she described the Ekklesia process still happening in her town, where the whole town would gather for decision-making meetings. The council had proposed that taxes remain the same as the town's income was good. The gathering argued there were many people currently being left unsupported and, much to the council's surprise, they voted to raise taxes. The gathering had the authority to make high-impact change.

Jesus' words to Peter have been misinterpreted. He says, 'on this rock I will build my church [Ekklesia]'. Some argue this is about building the Church on Peter himself, the leading apostle. Clearly Peter had a pivotal role in founding the early Church. But we need to move away from Church again and remind ourselves that Jesus is building His *ekklesia*. The rock foundation on which He builds is Peter's declaration that Jesus is the Christ. Only Jesus is the heart of the Ekklesia. He resources it and guides it, and sometimes challenges it.

What do we know about being the Ekklesia?

- We have an authority from Jesus to make decisions as an assembly (Matthew 16:19).

- The gates of Hades will not be able to stand against us (Matthew 16:18).

- We are powerful. When a small number of the Ekklesia – only two or three – agree, we can bind and loose in prayer and create this wonderful link between heaven and earth (Matthew 18:18-20).

- We work together to make decisions. This is a group that listens to each other because it is acting on behalf of the local community with its diverse issues.

---

[12] www.agapeeurope.org is the Western Europe part of Campus Crusade for Christ International a global Christian missions organisation (accessed 20th November 2021).

- We are called to govern – in our workplace, neighbourhood, town/city and nation.

Joel 2:15-17 gives us a further insight:

> Blow the trumpet in Zion,
> declare a holy fast,
> call a sacred assembly [Ekklesia].
> Gather the people,
> consecrate the assembly [Ekklesia]; …
> Let them say, 'Spare your people, LORD.
> Do not make your inheritance an object of scorn,
> a byword among the nations.
> Why should they say among the peoples,
> 'Where is their God?'

Here is a critical moment; a terrible judgement is coming upon the land as a horde of hungry locusts is going to ravage the nation. But God is calling His Ekklesia to pray. He is giving them a remarkable authority to change this national disaster as they repent, rend their hearts (Joel 2:13) – a powerful picture of intense anguish and passion – and ask God to relent.

A holy confrontation

So, one final trip back to Caesarea Philippi, and let us look again at Jesus' holy confrontation. This is the gunfight at the OK Corral, the Avengers against Thanos, David v Goliath. At the place many believe to be the literal Gate of Hades, He wants His disciples to know that these gates cannot stand against God's Ekklesia. Indeed, He is giving us, His people, the 'keys of the kingdom of heaven' (Matthew 16:19). It is a shout of authority over Pan, Baal, Caesar and any other entity that claims to be divine. There is only one God. Across history, Jesus brings His Ekklesia together at national, city-wide or local level. He teaches them to hear His will and use His authority to pray for change. It may be for revival, it may be to turn a plague or sickness around, it may be in the face of great danger, it may be to release blessings and fruitfulness. Jesus works with His Ekklesia.

Jesus is also Jehovah Sabaoth, the Lord of Hosts.[13] Here again is one of the ways the Church is disempowered. We have lost sight of who our Jesus is. He is Yahweh Sabaoth. Many are familiar with the compound names of Jehovah – Jehovah Jireh (the Lord, my provider), Jehovah Shalom (the Lord, my peace). The phrase 'Jehovah Sabaoth' is an important one and is used more than 250 times in Scripture. It is often translated as the Lord Almighty, but this loses sight of the Lord of Hosts with His vast angel army ('ten thousand times ten thousand' says Daniel 7:10). Jesus is not a penny-pinching God, with meagre resources and a reluctance and inability to act. He has vast angelic forces at His disposal. Angels can undo chains and set prisoners free (Acts 12:7), confuse and terrify huge armies (2 Samuel 5:24).

Do we have a vision for angels unleashed in our workplaces? Can we see a need in our workplace, in our team or with an individual colleague for peace, or for hope? Where is there a need for breakthrough and fresh ideas? Where is there a need for protection? When it comes to spiritual warfare, one of the reasons God's people often lose is because they don't get into the battle. We have authority to use heaven's amazing resources to bring peace to tense team meetings, to pray for our colleagues' marriages, to bless their children. It does not have to be complex; simply praying, 'Lord, bring Your peace,' can change situations.

David defeats Goliath – 'in the name of the LORD of hosts' (1 Samuel 17:45, ESV).God has given him peace and courage to face the giant that had turned more experienced soldiers' hearts to the wobbliest of wobbly jelly. David did not come in strength; he came trusting in God.

---

[13] 1 Samuel 1:3, 'This man went up from his city yearly to worship and sacrifice to the LORD of hosts in Shiloh', NKJV.

Our God is a God of justice, in the workplace as well as elsewhere. James tells rich people to weep and wail because they 'have hoarded wealth in the last days. Look! The wages you failed to pay the workers who mowed your fields are crying out against you. The cries of the harvesters have reached the ears of the Lord [Sabaoth]' (James 5:3-4: I have replaced the NIV's use of 'Lord Almighty' with the proper translation of Sabaoth.) Doesn't a verse like this show the great relevance of the scripture today? Workers' wages are still abused, and people are still crying out for financial justice – and the Lord of Hosts cares about it. You may not have responsibility for people's wages but can pray for justice and for God to change minds.

All authority

God has given us the power and authority to be like a lion, but we wander about like domestic cats. He has empowered us to be like a sleek sports car, yet we appear like worn-out, scratched and battered old vehicles that we are ashamed to park outside our front doors. We need to better understand, and use, our authority.

Authority comes from God. He tells us to move mountains (Matthew 17:20). He tells us to heal the sick (Luke 9:1). He tells us to bring peace (Luke 10:5-6). Alongside this He tells us to apply these things where we are. In Acts 3, we read that Peter and John were walking to the temple, they were open to God, and when they passed a man who was lame, they felt they had the authority to tell him to walk. The man was astounded and started to leap about and dance because he hadn't been expecting his life to be turned around that day!

Jesus tells the story of the ten minas given to ten servants (the equivalent of two to three years' average wages). He gives them authority to put the money to work. We know one of the servants hides his single mina in a cloth and is told he is a 'wicked servant' for not doing anything better with his mina (Luke 19:22). Look what happens to those who use their authority well – the king says, 'Well done, my good servant! ... Because you have been trustworthy in a very small matter, take charge of ten cities' (v17).

Early in my career I had responsibility for graduate recruitment for a large motor manufacturer. We generally received about 3,500 applications annually, and part of my job was to sift through them all and select those people we would invite to assessment. I well remember Friday nights sat with 100 at a time putting them into 'Yes', 'No' and 'Maybe' piles. I developed a capacity to work through the application forms and select those people I wanted based on how positive their comments were. If people said, 'I started this initiative ...' or, 'I took responsibility for ...', I was much more likely to select them than if they said, 'I was part of the team that...' or, 'While I was in the club we won...' In hindsight, I was looking for authority, for those who were most likely to make things happen.

Here are some challenging words on our authority. 'What is mankind that you are mindful of them ...You made them rulers over the works of your hands; you put everything under their feet' (Psalm 8:4, 6). We are destined to rule, not in our strength, but because God has given us authority.

Let us look at what Peter (*Petros*) has to say: 'But you are a chosen people, a royal priesthood, a holy nation, God's special possession, that you may declare the praises of him who called you out of darkness into his wonderful light' (1 Peter 2:9). The royal priests get access into the presence of God. Hebrews 12:22-23 reinforces that access: 'You have come to ... [the] joyful assembly, to the [Ekklesia] of the firstborn'. When you are going through difficult times in the workplace, you have authority to come into God's presence, and the heavenly Ekklesia, and know He will hear you.

Authority means you can do things! A king or queen of England gives authority to a wide range of people to represent them and undertake tasks on their behalf. The 'King of kings' (Revelation 17:14) gives us authority as His children in a wide range of areas. We can bring peace into a situation at work, we can pray for wisdom for significant decisions and pray for breakthrough when we need change. We have authority to bless other people and situations.

> We have settled for building churches, rather than using our authority to bring life to cities. And yet Jesus was exceptionally clear: 'I will build my church; [ekklesia] you have the keys of the kingdom' – in effect He invites us to take the keys of our authority into the community and introduce it to its divine destiny.[14]

We are like the twelve sent out in Matthew 10:6-8 to preach, heal and see miracles. These were not mature, theologically sound, highly educated men – they were ordinary workers used to mending nets, catching and selling fish and collecting taxes (and facing abuse). Jesus gave them authority. Stories abound from around the world today of healings, people being set free, miraculous occurrences, or getting wisdom in difficult situations. Every believer has spiritual authority. We may struggle but our God is able. Let us be hungry to live in our authority and use it more.

The Great Commission is for the Ekklesia – Jesus tells us to go, not in weakness but with authority:

> All authority in heaven and on earth has been given to me. Therefore go and make disciples of all nations, baptising them in the name of the Father and of the Son and of the Holy Spirit, and teaching them to obey everything I have commanded you. And surely I am with you always, to the very end of the age.
> (Matthew 28:18-20)

The call is to go. This must be our mindset. This is the call of the Ekklesia – we are sent out; yes, we do things when we gather but our prime calling is to go. We need to see our workplace as

---

[14] Scott, *Scattered Servants*, p49.

central to Jesus' plan and purpose. He sent us, and He gives us His authority.

Your kingdom come

Peter was stepping up into his leadership call at Caesarea Philippi. He goes further on the day of Pentecost as he stands in front of thousands and announces the birth of the Church/Ekklesia. He has entered more fully into his apostolic ministry, as have his colleagues. It is interesting that Jesus calls them 'apostles' (Luke 6:13). It is not a religious term. It comes from the Greek *Apostolos* (meaning a delegate or envoy). In Roman times an apostle might lead a mission to change the culture in a given nation to better reflect Roman ways and values. Jesus appoints envoys who will go and bring about change. They are announcing a new kingdom – just as Jesus did. They are changing the culture around them – just as we can do in our workplace.

Church Growth teacher Ed Silvoso writes:

> Something extraordinary is going on all over the world. Ordinary people are doing extraordinary things that are radically transforming schools, prisons, cities and even nations.[15]

Ed has written extensively about God calling Christians to the marketplace, as priests, as signed up members of the Ekklesia. 'Many already know that they are called to play a vital part in the establishment of God's kingdom on earth. They believe they are ministers, and they have turned their jobs into ministerial vehicles.'[16]

Ministry might be protecting people as a security guard, bringing peace and compassion to the shop floor, or asking God to give you the way forward on a major business breakthrough. My friend Steve shares his story later in the book – he is in a

[15] Ed Silvoso, *Transformation* (Ada, MI: Chosen Books, 2010), p11.
[16] Silvoso, *Transformation*, p11.

high-paid, demanding job changing transport systems, and sees his call as being a pastor to his workplace. Matthew runs workshops and training sessions where he asks God to give him words of knowledge and holy wisdom for the attendees.[17] Another friend is given mathematical formula that give him breakthroughs on social media.

Ministry is praying for the presence of God in every situation. It is listening to God when He holds us back from sending that stinging email that lets everyone know how frustrated we are. It is Aquila and Priscilla building a business together with Paul in their home in Corinth (Acts 18:1-3). Paul the apostle and culture changer was also Paul the tent seller. In a bustling trading place like Corinth, this gave the opportunity to meet and impact many people.

It is time to go!

We have already referred to the Great Commission given to the disciples by Jesus just before He ascends to heaven. It is His last word; He wants them to remember and act on what He tells them to do. 'The Great Commission was never given to a *kuriakon* or *church*. It doesn't have the tools nor the DNA. No, the mission of Christ uniquely requires the ekklesia to arise.'[18]

So we are called to go; the Ekklesia is a movement of generous sent people:

- To go to the nations of the world;

- To go into the homes and marketplaces as they did in the book of Acts;

---

[17] Paul says 'there is given through the Spirit a message of wisdom, to another a message of knowledge' (1 Corinthians 12:8) as he describes the gifts of the Spirit.

[18] Dean Briggs, *Ekklesia Rising* (North York, ON: Champion Press 2014), p121.

- To go to broken cities that need rebuilding and hope;

- To go and build strong relationships with others, so they can hear our stories, find out about Jesus, be freed and blessed;

- To go and serve both those who are literally and those who are spiritually hungry and thirsty;

- To go in authority because He goes with us.

This is a big step of faith. Sometimes we end up in situations or places that are not of our choosing, but it is pretty certain there will be people in that situation who need hope and compassion and love. The Bible is full of people God chooses to partner with, from Adam in the Garden of Eden through to the farmer and businessman Boaz who works righteously, as we see in the book of Ruth. In the beginning of the book of Acts, 120 people (Acts 1:15) are gathered to wait on God. They have just seen the resurrected Jesus, and everything in me would have cried out, 'Let's go and tell the world what we have seen!' No one in history has seen what they have, and yet they are told to wait (v4). Because on their own they could do something, but with the promised Holy Spirit God powerfully equips them.

Rick Warren says, 'a church is measured by its sending capacity, not its seating capacity'.[19] Alan Scott, in his book, *Scattered Servants*, talks of the huge growth their church in Coleraine, Northern Ireland, experienced when they realised that God's call was not to plant churches but to plant people. People were sent everywhere. In Doxa Deo church in Pretoria, South Africa,[20] they have fully grasped this; they literally

[19] Rick Warren, 'Multiplication: The Most Important Thing Your Church Will Ever Do', 9th January 2017, pastors.com/the-most-important-thing-your-church-will-ever-do(accessed 10th February 2022).

[20] For more details on the Doxa Deo story read Alan Platt, *City Changers: Being the Presence of Christ in Your Community* (Colorado Springs, CO: David C Cook, 2017).

commission people. They have wonderful and powerful moments when they get all the people working in the health sector at whatever level to stand, and they pray for them. The church lovingly gathers round those being commissioned, to hear from God words of scripture, prophecy, wisdom and encouragement. Another week they commission all of those in the business sphere, or education or the arts. This is the Great Commission at work – Jesus commands us to go.

Doxa Deo is a church of incredible contrasts, the wealthy and the poor, the young and the old, male and female. There is a range of ethnicities and languages. One of the hard challenges for any church like this is to welcome all, irrespective of wealth, health, history or prospects. Its Great Commission focus is anchored in the belief that everyone is precious to Jesus. Jesus did not discriminate when He gave His life for everyone. They give intense focus to the pain of their city, the large numbers of homeless, the jobless, the addicts, those with mental health issues, those thrown out of their homes. The Old Testament regularly tells us to focus on the widow, the orphan/fatherless, the alien/foreigner and the poor (Zechariah 7:10). So their 'go' commission is not just to a workplace; it is with a heart for the poor and for their city.

> We must go out to our communities and immerse ourselves in our world in order to make a difference. The question, 'How big is your church?' should be replaced with 'What impact and influence does your church have in your community?'[21]

Call to action

Much of what we will take from this chapter – and from this book – depends on our level of faith, and how it leads us to action.

---

[21] Platt, *City Changers*, p148.

- Do we believe with all our heart and soul that Jesus is the Christ? If we truly believe Jesus is the Christ, He can build His Ekklesia.

- Do we believe we are fully appointed and anointed members of His Ekklesia? Many are unaware. Let faith change our mindset. We are a long way from powerless; we have Jesus' authority.

- Our calling is not on the sidelines of a church; it is right at the frontline of the Ekklesia. We are not spectators; we are key players.

- We are sent out – the Great Commission is for you and me. It is a living call, not a historical event. Jesus calls us to go – now. That call is to the workplace, to the marketplace, to our cities.

It is time to see ourselves in a different light. This does not happen overnight. It takes determination to move from a spectator to a player – but it is God's plan. He is for us!

Application

I encourage you to stop for a while to reflect and pray. Here are three things to reflect on. Maybe have a conversation with others and certainly pray about this.

- 'Your kingdom come' (Matthew 6:10) – what could that mean for your workplace?

- What signs do you see of churches/Christians you know acting as an Ekklesia?

- What more needs to happen? If you are part of a small group, could you discuss what acting as an Ekklesia would mean for you all?

Prayer

Thank You, Jesus. You have called me, changed my life. Use me to bring peace, to be a blessing, to be your instrument. Amen.

Terry's story

Terry Boatwright lives in Eastbourne, where he was a head teacher looking after four schools and 3,000 pupils. Following his retirement, Terry became the educational leadership consultant for his county council. He has advised government on school improvement and served as chair of Anglican School Heads National Committee.

Terry was a reluctant head. His wife spotted an advert for a 'Practising and committed Christian' for a headship at a Church of England school in Eastbourne, East Sussex. It did not fit with Terry's thoughts about the future, and he discovered the school was the worst achieving in the county. The Church of England had considered pulling out of it, and it was so unpopular that hardly anyone wanted to go there.

Terry writes:

> I remember telling my wife that I 'did not feel led to apply'. It was then that my ever-patient, and prayerful, wife pulled her killer punch. Totally unfairly she suggested that we pray about it! After prayer I reluctantly agreed to apply and that, if I was offered the job, I would take it as guidance that I should accept it. I have never put less effort into an application in my life. Yet I was called for interview and offered the job! So started the most amazing and fulfilling eighteen years of my life. I saw miracle after miracle and many lives transformed.

He later discovered a prayer group from different churches in Eastbourne had been persistently praying for the school: 'God had given them a vision that the school would become a beacon, a model, for other church schools up and down the country and of God's light shining far and wide from it.'

Terry continues:

If I were a betting man, I would have backed flying pigs over the chance of that particular 'vision' becoming a reality. Who could have imagined that over the next five years the government would name the school one of the most improved in the country; and it would become oversubscribed? I found myself shaping government policy for church schools as a member of the National Executive Committee of AASSH (the Association of Anglican Academy and Secondary School Heads); and, most significantly, the school would be one of three researched to be [the] subject of a book about successful church schools. The school literally did become a model church school and God's light did shine across the whole country, including featuring in a national newspaper article entitled, 'On a mission: Can a headteacher with strong religious faith really make all the difference to a failing school?'

Reflecting on his career from young teacher till now, Terry says:

What has impacted my work, and life, even more has been demonstrably walking step by step with Jesus. As a Christian, I believe it is not a holier-than-thou attitude that changes the world, but when the world recognises that we serve a God who walks with us each day and following Him is the most exciting and fulfilling thing we can ever do.

He gives some great wisdom on being a Christian in the workplace:

I want pupils and colleagues to realise that a Christian is someone who has a personal, loving, honest and incredible relationship with the God of the universe who loves us immensely. Of course, that affects our values and how we live our lives, but, I believe, there is a danger if we get those things the wrong way round.

Jesus is the key driver!

The school continued to thrive, winning numerous awards as the most improved school in the country. The story attracted national newspapers and writers to learn about its success. Here is part of *The Guardian*'s interview with Terry:

> When I first arrived at the school, the children would say to me, 'We're rubbish. The school is rubbish. Everyone thinks the school is rubbish.' But as a Christian I believe we are all of supreme value, and that became one of the planks of our mission statement. Drawing up a mission statement was one of the first things I did when I arrived, and I've got it plastered all over the school – it's a vital document, and we all need to be reminded of it all the time. The important thing about the mission statement,' says Boatwright, 'is that it's something we all sign up to, and we can all be brought to account because of it.'[22]

Eventually there was talk about Terry becoming a 'super head' with some struggling secondary and primary schools. Terry was travelling to a meeting and realised he needed to discuss this with Head Office! He recalls thinking, 'God, I'm sorry I haven't prayed properly about this. You know that I really, really don't want to do it. However, if You really want me to do it, please make it very, very clear. I won't do it unless You get someone from government to take me by the arm and directly ask me to do it, personally.'

> It wasn't my best prayer ever! The good news for me was that the whole meeting happened without anyone mentioning anything about taking over struggling schools.
>
> The bad news was that as I was leaving the room, one of the top government officials grabbed me by the arm, yes literally(!), and specifically asked me to take over three incredibly tough schools in a town down the coast from me!

God is good at getting our attention!

> That was the beginning of an incredible period when I and my church school were brought in to support a number of

---

[22] Joanna Moorhead, 'On a Mission', *The Guardian*, 8th May 2007, used with permission.

struggling secondary and primary schools. None of them was a church school, some far from it, and yet each school knew of my Christian faith and appreciated the support.

I would never have taken that path if the choice were mine. However, yet again, the God of Joshua 1:9 – 'be strong and courageous' – walked step by step with me and the journey we went on together was amazing.

Terry's headship was incredibly demanding but brought great fruit. He was supported by colleagues and by a number of prayer groups in Eastbourne. Prayer has constantly opened doors and given wisdom and direction as needed. Terry retired from headship and is now team minister at Gateway Church, Eastbourne.

Chapter Two
My Call

You are unique!

In the past I have run many workshops helping people to understand their strengths, normally in the workplace helping teams work better with one another but occasionally in churches. In churches we often hit the situation of people who felt uncomfortable about being there. They did not think they had any strengths and were quite happy to be in the background. We would want to engage them, to ask them what it was they enjoyed doing, when they felt fulfilled. Many times, the people we engaged with were introverts; they felt fulfilled sitting on their own doing complex tasks like stamp collecting or reading detailed materials. We would explore their gift of concentration, their ability to handle details, their accuracy and precision. That is the person God made them to be, and God is very fond of them. We can fall into the trap of thinking God wants upfront heroes but actually He wants servants, and each one of us has gifts to offer Him.

The key message for this chapter is that God has made you, He loves what He has made, and He has made you unique. Don't look at others; look at Jesus and see His delight in you! Paul captured that uniqueness when he talked about the body of Christ. The parts are very, very different from one another; some have a higher profile than others, others are supportive, but working well together they achieve great things.

Paul tells the Ephesians, 'We are God's handiwork, created in Christ Jesus to do good works, which God prepared in advance for us to do' (Ephesians 2:10). This is a little goldmine of a verse. 'God's handiwork' is translated by some sources as His 'masterpiece' (see NLT). God makes beautiful waterfalls and coastlines, the glory of a Mediterranean sunset or an African night sky, butterflies and tropical fish that are stunning artworks, amazing, delicate, multicoloured flowers and the wonders of spring. But *you* are His masterpiece. *You*. No mistake, it's *you* He looks at you with deep pleasure and affection. Many of us spend too much time focusing on what we can't do and on our inadequacies. God wants to shine the light on what He has made. He is very pleased. Who we are is shaped by our relationship with Jesus; the closer it is the more He shapes our values and character. Employers recruit us for our work-related strengths and experience. But those who love us appreciate the complete person, and they like what they see.

More than that, He has created you, His masterpiece, 'to do good works'. You, in your uniqueness, with your very particular skills and capabilities, and the things that energise and excite you – what good works can you do? They might be massive in scope or intricate in detail, they might make thousands of people's eyes light up or focus compassionately on one person in pain. They might be very practical or gloriously creative. God in His wisdom made us all different so that His universe can be filled with many good works.

Here's a perspective from the Christian novelist (author of the Lord Peter Wimsey detective novels) and playwright, Dorothy L Sayers (1893–1957) from the 1940s:

> The Church's approach to an intelligent carpenter is usually confined to exhorting him not to be drunk and disorderly in his leisure hours, and to come to church on Sundays. What the Church should be telling him is this: that the very first demand that his religion makes upon him is that he should make good tables.[23]

---

[23] Dorothy L Sayers, *Why Work?* (Scotts Valley, CA: CreateSpace Independent Publishing Platform, 2014).

We know what we have been saved from, but that's by no means the full story. We must also know what we've been saved for – God has a purpose, that wherever you go, His kingdom will come. So we need to know, what is our particular servant call? Yes, there are times our hands and our ability to put out chairs or serve at tables or welcome newcomers are good. But God knows us as a specialist servant, with specific skills that can bless our workplace and our colleagues but may also give a breakthrough to a local charity or community organisation or school. God knows our specialisms; He knows how our engineering, or marketing, or children's social care, or social media skills can be well used.

But the final golden nugget is this – He prepared us 'in advance' to do these good works. There is no randomness to what we do. God has a plan. It is not an autocratic plan, and sometimes we will wander away from the heavenly GPS, but He continually wants us to be in a place where He can show His masterpiece off.

That Tony Bennett moment

One of the memorable moments in my life was seeing the singer Tony Bennett, by then in his late eighties, perform in the Birmingham Symphony Hall. He paid a huge compliment that night, saying the Symphony Hall was one of only two places in the world where the acoustics were so good that you could hear clearly from the back of the hall what was sung on the stage without the sound system. So he demonstrated for us, and sang his famous song, 'I Left My Heart in San Francisco', with no microphones as a present to Birmingham. He needed the sound support in every other global venue – but for us, from his heart, was a special intimate moment when he seemed like he was singing to each of us personally.

I hope we have all had similar masterpiece moments: a play that gets us standing to acclaim the performers, a piece of art that takes our breath away, a child singing, a great and inspiring sporting moment. But I also hope we have had many masterpiece moments where we know that God has prepared this time and space for *us* to do good works. I hope you have seen the hand of God on you in the workplace. It may have been a wise decision that had great consequences, a new initiative, or a wise and timely word that made all the difference to someone struggling. God said to go into the world and do good works.

These are the moments we feel God's pleasure; there is a peace, or joy, or deep satisfaction. He has made us as we are so that through you and me the world can see the hand of the Master Craftsman. He invests in His masterpieces, so they become instruments that can change the world. Our spiritual development is one of His great passions.

You are wonderful

Not convinced that we are masterpieces? Look at Psalm 139:13-16:

For you created my inmost being;
you knit me together in my mother's womb.
I praise you because I am fearfully and wonderfully made
… all the days ordained for me were written in your book
before one of them came to be.

One of the most important skills for the workplace is self-awareness. Over the years, I have coached many senior business and public sector leaders. A key starting point is to understand their strengths and look at their impact on others. Our strengths give us a particular view of the world, they shape our values, they determine what we are most likely to be doing in our job. We need to appreciate our uniqueness more – very few people see, or can contribute to, the world in the special way we each do. We can get frustrated that others don't get it – actually, we are underestimating how 'fearfully and wonderfully made' and unique we all are. It could be that only we see things that way – it is our unique contribution, and we have to help others to understand our perspective. One popular psychometric tool estimates that we are so unique that only one other person in every 32 million will have the same profile as us![24]

You are different

Here is a simple set of measures – where do you think you sit?

| People Centred | Task Centred |
| Slow paced | Fast paced |

We have positive and negative reactions to these simple scales depending on our preferred way of acting. Here are some positive words we use to describe them:

CARER	**People focused, slow paced** Caring, loyal, reliable. Looks out for others, listens, team focused, gives time to people.
PRECISION	**Task focused, slow paced** Careful, excellent with detail, risk averse, thorough, monitors processes and rules well.
FLAIR	**People focused, fast paced** Seen as someone who initiates things, finds new approaches, inspires others, articulate.
ACTIVATOR	**Task focused, fast paced** Drives performances and results, gets past barriers, commands, works to clear deadlines.

This is a very simplistic look at four styles, and we may be wholly like one of these boxes or find some characteristics we share with other boxes. But here is a simple insight into human nature.

---

[24] www.gallup.com (accessed 24th November 2021) for The CliftonStrengths Assessment, previously known as StrengthsFinder.

I have put positive descriptions above, but we could see the carer box as over-fussy, gets easily distracted, time-consuming. We may see the precision person as obstructive, slow to get going, needing too much information. Others might see the flair person as all hot air but no substance, or going off in all directions. The activator person might be seen as insensitive, or not giving clear directions. This is where self-awareness comes in – knowing where our strengths can become someone else's irritation!

We can overplay who we are because we feel so strongly that our way is best. There are lots of tensions in the workplaces – self-awareness helps us understand our impact on others, and how we will respond in different situations. Having different approaches from others makes us complementary – look at the apostles John and Peter: carer John is asked to look after Jesus' mother (John 19:26-27); activator Peter is asked to look after Jesus' mission (John 21:17)!

All of us need to manage our impact on others. For some, our role involves having an impact on a wide range of people. Others are less bothered about their impact and think people should accept us as we are. But managing our impact is important, for most of us, especially as Christians.

One of the more insightful but scary questions at an interview is, 'How would your colleagues describe you?' Essentially it is asking us to think about our impact on others. I floundered badly in an interview once when I was asked the much more intimidating question, 'How would your wife describe you?' Given my propensity to honesty over fantasy I did not say, 'Like the next James Bond,' but said, 'She probably thinks I'm an idiot.' Well, it was certainly an idiotic response to a job interview question!

You probably know that others will see some aspects of who we are better than we see them ourselves. They may see the strengths that we need to build on if we are to grow our confidence. They may see those things we need to address to be better at our job.

One great technique is the feed forward question. Instead of feedback, which is also valuable, feed forward gives us some good opportunities to help us grow and change our approach. Questions like, 'I need to get back about 10 per cent of my time. I know I am not being as effective as I should be. What do you recommend I do?' Or, 'I want to raise motivation in the team – what do I need to do differently to help that?'

I am in the activator box; that has a big effect on my impact on others. It was made very evident to me when I was going through a planning session with my team. I did genuinely want to include them and get their thoughts, but it was a plan I believed in. 'Standing in front of your plans, Steve,' said a colleague, 'is like putting yourself in front of a turbo-powered bulldozer.' I guess he felt it was not a pleasant experience! I am pleased to say that that former colleague has contributed to this book, so it can't all have been horrendous. But if you talk to me about my achievements, they will all be tasky: they will be about delivering change programmes, and projects.

Here are some simple questions to help you understand your particular call:

- What would you describe as your top three achievements in the workplace?

- What does a really great day at work look like for you?

- What does that tell you about your personality and your strengths?

- In the past six months, where have you made a very positive impact on your colleagues – what strengths were you displaying?

But we need to remember that we never operate alone. We bring our gifts and personality and put them on the altar. 'Offer your bodies as a living sacrifice, holy and pleasing to God – this is your true and proper worship' (Romans 12:1). Depending on who we are, we may worship God with our thoroughness, our creativity, our ability to drive things to completion or our deep compassion. My spiritual offering is different from yours, but I want to ensure that I put them on the altar. Paul tells the Philippians, 'I can do all [things] through him who gives me strength' (Philippians 4:13).

So success is a combination of my unique gifts and personality and His Spirit and strength. This is a faith place. Faith is hearing God's direction and following it. The more we 'consult' and listen to God the more we exercise faith in our calling.

We continually have to apply what we learn to our unique characters and situations. For example, people pray in all sorts of ways, from the very structured and organised to the creative 'in the moment' prayer or to the 'I hardly pray at all unless it's an emergency' approach, and lots of points in between. Self-awareness is key to effective learning – you need to find those gold nuggets that apply to you!

My values

Our values have a big impact on what we do and how we do it. We see a great example of values in the story of Solomon. The Lord appears to the young king in a dream and says, 'Ask for whatever you want me to give you' (1 Kings 3:5). Solomon lets his values shape his answer:

> Now, LORD my God, you have made your servant king in place of my father David. But I am only a little child and do not know how to carry out my duties. Your servant is here among the people you have chosen, a great people, too numerous to count or number. So give your servant a discerning heart to govern your people and to distinguish between right and wrong. For who is able to govern this great people of yours?
> (1 Kings 3:7-9)

His values are people values; they are seeking the good of the people of Israel.

What are your values? What is important to you?

Some people will be very driven by justice and fairness. Others look for integrity and trust. Others will value good order and process, while others value an open environment where people can speak freely. Here again we have a range of things that are important to us. Some of us can become emotional in the workplace: we wear our values on our sleeves; everyone knows when we are frustrated or annoyed. Others may be more rational and calmer and reasoned but will then get to a tipping point where something is just plain wrong, and no sane person could possibly agree with it!

What frustrates you in the workplace? This can also be a good indicator of your values

Of course, the Bible helps to shape our values. This verse always causes me to pause and ask, 'Am I doing this enough?':

> He has shown you, O mortal, what is good.
> And what does the LORD require of you?
> To act justly and to love mercy
> and to walk humbly with your God.
> (Micah 6:8).

Peter reflects this call to humility:

> All of you, clothe yourselves with humility towards one another, because,
> 'God opposes the proud
> but shows favour to the humble.'
> Humble yourselves, therefore, under God's mighty hand, that he may lift you up in due time. Cast all your anxiety on him because he cares for you.
> (1 Peter 5:5-7)

We can choose to walk in humility. It gives us a teachable spirit, a generous attitude to others and a constant push to depend on Jesus. So we carry this mixture of values that are shaped by our past and spiritual values that are shaped by following Jesus. One of life's great challenges is how we combine the two wisely.

Look at Jesus' values-driven response to Zacchaeus in Luke 19:1-10 when He spied him up in a tree. Tax collectors were deeply unpopular, being seen as helping the Roman occupation and swindling people. Jesus does not criticise him; instead, He is 'countercultural' and honours Zacchaeus, inviting Himself to go and dine at the tax collector's house. It is a challenging example of countercultural values, not doing what the majority expect, and giving honour to a despised person.

There is a lot of teaching about money in the Scriptures, reflecting God's concern that money can corrupt. We are told in 1 Timothy 6:10 that 'the love of money is a root of all kinds of evil' – the correct attitude to money is to steward it well, letting it serve us and others. This is shaped by our values and God's call to generosity.

One of the clearest examples of values shaping the world was Martin Luther King Jr's 'I Have a Dream' speech, given in the tumultuous years when black Americans were fighting for fairness in a hellishly constraining voting and justice system, with prejudice and lack of opportunity. His dream was that his four children 'not be judged by the color of their skin, but by the content of their character'. As he himself announced, Dr King did not have a plan and a strategy – he had a dream.[25] That is a powerful picture to take into the workplace – I have not got a plan for my values to bless where I work, but I do have a dream!

I was a governor at an inner-city school in Birmingham. It was a school that really helped girls, primarily from poorer Muslim backgrounds, to improve their life chances. It tapped into some values for me. It was a technical college for girls, and I had previously worked in a job where encouraging girls into

---

[25] www.rev.com/blog/transcripts/i-have-a-dream-speech-transcript-martin-luther-king (accessed 10th February 2022). Delivered in Washington 26 August 1963.

engineering was an important value. So I took it into the school. Many of the girls were from struggling families with small aspirations – we raised their aspirations, and many became the first generation in their families to go to university. I was especially concerned about pastoral support for the girls, as there were increasing issues with mental health and personal identity.

Those values shaped my contribution and my long-term commitment to being a governor. In the later years we hit some very challenging personnel issues. It was hard work, but I wanted righteousness. I stepped down after eighteen years and was very moved to hear the head say I had been the moral compass of the school. I did not set out to be that – I just wanted to serve the school my daughters attended – but our values shape our contribution. I hope my impact was always positive, but it was always important that we did what was right.

The wonder of righteousness

As a student, I remember trying to act wisely when a fellow student who was on the cusp of becoming a Christian asked me what righteousness meant. I confidently said, 'It is where we are being righteous.' Unfortunately, the student pursued the point and asked what 'righteous' meant! I stumbled on, 'It... er... means being righteous, searching after righteousness.' Fortunately, a friend stepped in and said something sensible.

In truth, 'righteousness' is a beautiful word and calling.

Pastor and author Timothy Keller spoke on Proverbs 11:10: 'When the righteous prosper, the city rejoices.' The Hebrew for the righteous is *tsaddiqim*. Keller said the righteous:

Are the just, the people who follow God's heart and ways and who see everything they have as gifts from God to be stewarded for His purposes. The righteous in the book of Proverbs are by definition those who are willing to disadvantage themselves for the community while the wicked are those who put their own economic, social and personal needs ahead of the needs of the community.[26]

It is a beautiful concept – as the righteous flourish in their call, the city rejoices. 'Because the *tsaddiqim* view their prosperity not as a means of self-enrichment or self-aggrandisement, but rather as a vehicle for blessing others, *everyone* benefits from their success.'[27]

The *tsaddiqim* are bringing the things of the kingdom to the places where they live and work. As they prosper in shalom, they bring a deep peace with them; prospering in justice and mercy changes their culture and prospering in compassion brings deep, life-changing love. As they prosper, the change is so extraordinary that the city (town and village) rejoices.

The word Proverbs 11:10 uses for 'rejoices' is only used one other time in the Scripture. It describes ecstatic joy and triumph, like the cry of a people released from oppression. Imagine the streets of France, Holland and Italy as their liberation arrived in the Second World War. That's some rejoicing. We are the people called to bring such joy as God's kingdom comes.

God's favour

> With this in mind, we constantly pray for you, that our God may make you worthy of his calling, and that by his power he may bring to fruition your every desire for goodness and your every deed prompted by faith.
> (2 Thessalonians 1:11)

Paul's prayers are fantastic; he is such a great model, because he aligns with God's heart for us. We have these good purposes – in work, in our home, elsewhere; let us keep bringing them to God in prayer so He can show us His favour.

---

[26] Timothy J Keller, 'Creation Care and Justice' sermon, Redeemer Presbyterian Church, New York, 16th January 2005.
[27] Sherman, *Kingdom Calling*, p17.

He is the good shepherd (John 10:14). In Ezekiel, God says the shepherds have disappointed Him; they have exploited the sheep and not taken care of the flock:

> For this is what the Sovereign LORD says: I myself will search for my sheep and look after them. As a shepherd looks after his scattered flock when he is with them, so I will look after my sheep.
> (Ezekiel 34:11-12)

He goes on to promise to rescue them, gather them, move them to pasture, tend His sheep and make them 'lie down' (v14). In John 10, Jesus steps into this promise from Ezekiel to care for us: 'I am the good shepherd,' He says, who lays down His life for His sheep (vv14-15).

David knew that relationship with God, which is why he could write the famous words to Psalm 23:1: 'The LORD is my shepherd'. The Passion Translation picks up a deeper meaning:

> Yahweh is my best friend and my shepherd.
> I always have more than enough.
> He offers a resting place for me in his luxurious love.
> (vv1-2)

The reason for this translation is that the word most commonly used for 'shepherd' is taken from the root word *ra'ah*, which is also the Hebrew word for 'best friend'. Our best friend leads us and is prepared to die for us.

It is good to remind ourselves when we are in a tough meeting or challenging circumstances or up against tight deadlines that the Lord is a very, very good shepherd – and friend. We may not know the way forward, but we can know that He is leading us. In finishing, Psalm 23 tells us: 'Your goodness and love will follow me all the days of my life.' God is leading us, and God is pursuing us – I am surrounded by His love.

Our circles of influence

Paul tells us in 2 Corinthians 5 that Christ has given each of us a ministry and message of reconciliation, and this makes us 'Christ's ambassadors' (v20). What people see of Jesus and what they understand of Him is through what they see of you and me. I have heard colleagues talk of others, saying things like, 'She is supposed to be a Christian but...' It is likely they have said it of me as well.

But as ministers of the gospel, we have resources to help us do our job. Ministers and ambassadors have access to the presence of God; it might be through regular prayer times, it might be through a quick 'Help me, Lord' prayer, but God is with us. He gives us peace and wisdom. We can pray knowing we are aligned with God's purpose when we pray for justice, hope, life and integrity around us. We can better understand the people we work with as we reflect on their needs. We can bless them.

Alan Scott writes of his church in Coleraine, Northern Ireland:

> We could write several books of remarkable healings, signs and wonders occurring through ordinary believers in extraordinary places. All of them are scattered servants releasing the supernatural beyond the building. The sick are being healed in hospitals, parks, racecourses, public squares, swimming pools. Schools, factories, airports... everywhere.[28]

What are your circles of influence? They are a way to think about the people you minister to, the people who watch how you live and see Jesus at work. They may become the people you pray for regularly.

---

[28] Scott, *Scattered Servants*, p125.

- Level one influence – people who know us well: our character, our values. We interact regularly at home, work, in the community, etc. We are interdependent.

- Level two influence – people who know us: they have an opinion about us and interact regularly through the year. We have opportunities to impact their lives.

- Level three influence – people who know our name and a little about us: we may only interact a few times in the year.

- Level four – random connections: we might see them when we are visiting somewhere or interact very infrequently; they may not know our names.

Abraham Kuyper was Dutch Prime Minister between 1901 and 1905; he was also a noted theologian. He wrote:

> There is not a square inch in the whole domain of our human existence over which Christ, who is sovereign over all does not cry: 'Mine!' Your involvement and call will differ from mine, but it could be to anywhere.[29]

Once the light goes on in our dull minds that Christ declares 'Mine!' over 'all things' we begin to realise that He may be interested in slightly more than my own walk with Him, and my own church and its ministry. He declares His ownership over the street I live in, the shopping centre I visit, the health service I access, the policewoman I see, the coffee shop I sit in, the business I work for, the energy company I rely on, the road I drive down, the garden I sit in, the bank I withdraw cash from, the internet provider I use, the local council I moan about, the school I send my kids to, the village I adore, the town I come from and the city I am part of, and everything else besides. This is a big, wide, all-

---

[29] 1880 Inaugural Lecture, Free University of Amsterdam.

encompassing vision for every street, hamlet, village, town, borough and city across this wonderful nation and beyond.[30]

Kingdom values

When we pray, 'Your kingdom come,' for our workplace, we need to be alert to what might happen! Earlier we looked at the call to righteousness. It brings key kingdom values to our relationships with others. We will pick up some other key kingdom values below. These values significantly impact our behaviour and change the culture around us – they bring a heavenly culture to our team, and to our situation, because we choose to live a different way. A continued focus on praying for these values to 'come', to 'shape behaviour', will bring change in situations and individuals. Kingdom actions are countercultural, and they change the way people experience their workplace.

Shalom: is about a deep peace that impacts how we live day by day. It is an understanding that we are loved and always walking in an intimate relationship with Jesus. Shalom covers three key elements:

- Deep peace with God – at the Last Supper, as Jesus prepares His disciples for the new covenant between God and humanity, He declares, '[Shalom] I leave with you; my [shalom] I give you. I do not give to you as the world gives. Do not let your hearts be troubled and do not be afraid' (John 14:27).

- Peace with ourselves – we live in promise. Jesus has made us who we are. He has a plan and purpose; our futures are in His hands. Even during the sudden traumas that can blow us off course, we are in His hands.

---

[30] Roger Sutton, *A Gathering Momentum* (Watford: Instant Apostle, 2017), p22.

- Peace with others – peace with others comes when we pursue generous unity that wants others to excel.

Revelation 7 tells us we stand in peace with 'every nation, tribe, people and language, standing before the throne and before the Lamb' (v9). It's an eternal unity and we get to practise it now! Shalom comes when people feel safe; our community or workplace may be fearful – we can pray for shalom. We can look for shalom breakthrough. History is full of stories of people falling out and failing to find a way forward. We can see the workplace divide into an 'us' and a 'them'. Can you be a peacemaker? Can you break down the legends and myths that start to build up when people fall out?

Mercy: God's mercy is wonderful. Jesus died to take away our sin. But let's not fall into the trap of thinking that therefore our sin does not really matter. Sin grieves God's heart, it makes us compromise our behaviour and it can become addictive. The more we understand the mercy of God, the humbler we become, and the more we recognise our dependence on Him. God's forgiveness really does set us free, like a caged animal imprisoned by what the Old Testament calls our 'detestable practices' (Deuteronomy 18:12). Jesus releases us to run, jump, sing and shout. Mercy is wonderful, which is why we ourselves need to bring mercy into the workplace. People make mistakes; they have bad days – show them mercy. People may be selfish and hurt you – show them mercy too. People may struggle to keep up with you, to make time for you, or to hear your point of view properly – show them mercy. It is countercultural and powerful.

Justice: you may be in an unhealthy culture where gossip is rife and other people are constantly undermined or talked about behind their backs. There may be cheating or dishonesty or theft. Some people may feel oppressed, abused or coerced. There may be a sense of unfairness over pay or unequal opportunities. These feelings of injustice should inspire us to pray for the kingdom to come.

> So justice is far from us,
> and righteousness does not reach us.
> We look for light, but all is darkness;
> for brightness, but we walk in deep shadows.
> (Isaiah 59:9)

It does not have to be like this. There may be bigger issues of injustice in your community or city – inequalities, unfairness or deep hurts from the past. In all these circumstances we come to the God of justice. We can pray in His throne room (Hebrews 4:16) for kingdom justice to replace the world's injustices. We can look to Jesus who drove the moneychangers from the temple (Luke 19:45) and treated the Samaritan woman with respect (John 4:1-40), who reached out to the lepers and the disabled (Luke 17:11-19), and who treasures unity (John 17:21).

Compassion: Jesus feels compassion for the poor. The Greek word for 'felt compassion' is *splagchnizomai*, which means to have the bowels yearn. In these gut-wrenching moments, Jesus responds by healing, feeding or teaching those who have moved Him. This compassion moves through us; our challenge is to respond to it.

Forgiveness: Terry, our head teacher case study from Chapter One, was subject to a number of reviews after his school's rapid improvement started to draw national attention. He surprised people by saying forgiveness was a key feature. The school avoided expulsions, it gave troublesome pupils second, third and fourth chances. It supported and counselled the pupils. It believed in the power of forgiveness.

I am sure you will have come across broken relationships at work (and in churches). You may even hear one hurt party say, 'I can never forgive him for what he has done.' People make mistakes, we misinterpret other's motives and behaviours, and sometimes colleagues are just argumentative, untruthful or even toxic. The humble place is to admit we all make mistakes (I have made so many I could write a book about them – but that would be a mistake as well!). The forgiving place is to go beyond that. It is to bless those that hurt you, disrupt your plans, undermine you, deliver information you need too late, etc. Blessing should be tangible – it might mean a gentle discussion with the individual to find out why the issue arose; it might mean backing them up in their difficulties; at its heart is forgiveness. It's the rich gift Jesus gave us and a gift we can generously pass on to others.

Resilience and determination

Life brings challenges: the toxic job, redundancies, sicknesses, mental health challenges, financial struggles. Our level of resilience varies based on a wide variety of factors. Some people will be more emotional and the situation/challenge hits them quickly. Others respond more slowly until everything becomes too much. Others just lose energy and confidence and start to embrace every negative thought that comes their way. Some of us have people who support us, friends we can talk things through with and people who pray for us regularly. Others feel lonely and may not know where to turn.

There are plus and minus elements to stress and pressure, so it can be both a motivator and a demotivator. We will experience key stress points through major changes in our lives and when the changes stack up one on top of another. Some of us work in more stressful jobs than others.

One of the key stress points is whether we feel 'in control' of our job and the other situations we find ourselves in. One day the job may be straightforward, the next a row at home may make it feel impossible. If we are people-focused, what makes us anxious will be different from the anxiety for a results-orientated person. Indeed, we results-orientated people may be causing stresses for people who feel their colleagues are being asked to work harder and faster and are being put under too much pressure!

Jesus prepares for the challenges of His ministry by spending forty days fasting in the desert (Luke 4:1-13); we know the story and so tend to take it for granted, but this must have been a real endurance task. I am not sure I would last twenty-four hours, let alone forty days, in a desert place. What drove Jesus on was His desire to spend time with His Father and to pray about and prepare for His ministry.

It is clear that hope is a key factor in getting through horrendous experiences. It is worth reflecting on this for a moment. I have been through many challenging times in my work life, in a workplace with thousands of redundancies, a company takeover, the need to push my team to deliver extraordinary results in short time scales, etc. Knowing my good shepherd is always with me, wherever I go, makes a huge difference. I personally (after a few dramatic wobbles!) have felt a great sense of God's arms holding me up.

Of course, we can add unnecessary pressure to ourselves. We can spend too much time living in the past, not the present. If we look back too much to things we wish we could do differently, or even to a golden era when everything seemed better, it's a bit like self-harm. We reduce our capacity to live well in the present. Similarly, if we spend too much time worrying about the future, we become governed by uncertainty and fear – neither of which is a sign of being in God's presence or being led by a good shepherd!

Hope needs to be realistic. We can create a false optimism as Christians. God is not a prayer slot machine. David knew this; he knew that God could be with him if he walked 'through the valley of the shadow of death' (Psalm 23:4, ESV). God protected him when he hid in caves or was pursued by people who wanted to kill him. Our hope is that God is with us; our challenging situation may change, but it may not, and God is still with us. Health staff on the pressurised front line, people in grief, businesses struggling with funding, people who have become unemployed in an industry that is imploding – there are so many situations where relief is not close at hand. But God is. Jesus understands suffering and stress, and His love 'never fails' (1 Corinthians 13:8).

David knew great challenges and wrote:

If the LORD had not been on our side –
let Israel say –
if the LORD had not been on our side
when people attacked us,
they would have swallowed us alive
when their anger flared against us;
the flood would have engulfed us,
the torrent would have swept over us,
the raging waters
would have swept us away.
(Psalm 124:1-5)

God is with us in the fiercest storm. We see this literally as Jesus and the disciples decide to cross over to the other side of Lake Galilee. A fierce storm arises, and the disciples cry out to Jesus. Jesus knows He has a journey to complete. He has been called to the other side of the lake, so He calms the storm.

Then the wind died down and it was completely calm.
He said to his disciples, 'Why are you so afraid? Do you still have no faith?'
(Mark 4:39-40)

It is a challenge to us; we are often afraid but Jesus tells us, 'Have faith. I am with you until we complete the journey.'

You often hear the complaint, 'The job would be all right if it wasn't for the people.' Normally we want the people around us to flourish, but what if (through no fault of our own) the atmosphere is toxic? People don't trust one another, there is constant undermining and poison. The first psalm knew these workplace tensions, and says we are blessed if we do not 'stand in the way that sinners take or sit in the company of mockers' (v1). But there is a remedy that still holds true when our job is challenging:

> But whose delight is in the law of the LORD,
> and who meditates on his law day and night.
> That person is like a tree planted by streams of water,
> which yields its fruit in season.
> (Psalm 1:2-3)

It is a good thing that we are in a time of greater mental health awareness. It is talked about more frequently and people in the public eye are more forthcoming about the challenges facing them. We still need to move forward, and church often needs to be better at teaching on issues like anxiety, trauma and anger management because we need to learn how God equips us. Kintsugi Hope, founded by Patrick Regan, is an example of people doing wonderful work in this field. They provide great resources. They are finding that discussions about mental health are a wonderful way to connect with non-Christians – small groups are inviting friends to a twelve-week video-based training course.[31]

We know life is not always a bed of roses or a walk in bright sunshine. We get 'valley moments'. Scripture shows the incredible overwhelming grief of Job, the struggles in horrendous times heard from Jeremiah and Ezekiel, or David fleeing for his life from King Saul. Resilience is standing in a storm, and struggling to remain standing. It might be praising God through gritted teeth. It might be finding a friend who will listen to all the nonsense that is in your head. Never be reluctant to get help in difficult times; the body analogy is very important (1 Corinthians 12:12) – the body rushes to get resources to its damaged parts.

> God is our refuge and strength,
> an ever-present help in trouble.
> Therefore, we will not fear, though the earth give way

---

[31] www.kintsugihope.com/groups (accessed 14th October 2021).

and the mountains fall into the heart of the sea,
though its waters roar and foam
and the mountains quake with their surging …
He says, 'Be still, and know that I am God;
I will be exalted among the nations,
I will be exalted in the earth.'
The LORD Almighty is with us;
the God of Jacob is our fortress.
(Psalm 46:1-3, 10-11)

Distracted from God

An extensive five-year global survey by Michael Zigarelli looked at how we are distracted from God. As we consider our call, it is worth looking at his findings:

I think the problem may be described as a vicious cycle, prompted by cultural conformity. In particular, it may be the case that (1) Christians are assimilating to a culture of busyness, hurry and overload, which leads to (2) God becoming more marginalised in Christians' lives, which leads to (3) a deteriorating relationship with God, which leads to (4) Christians becoming even more vulnerable to adopting secular assumptions about how to live, which leads to (5) more conformity to a culture of busyness, hurry and overload.[32]

These 'secular assumptions about how to live' and 'conformity to a culture of busyness, hurry and overload' undermine our resilience. We live in a culture of individualism, which can lead to many selfish behaviours. Our issues of stress, anxiety and worry can go deep. We have to ask why we feel overwhelmed when Jesus tells us His 'burden is light' (Matthew 11:30). If we are more distant from God, we will struggle to know His peace

[32] See Michael Zigarelli, 'Distracted from God: A Five-Year, Worldwide Study',. www.christianity9to5.org/distracted-from-god/ (accessed 10th February 2022).

or to come with confidence into His presence to be built up by worship and prayer. This in turn impacts our resilience.

Many will say their worst moments, when love goes out the door, are when they are in a hurry. Do you resonate with that? When the stress builds up, we can block out love when we most need it. John Mark Comer writes, in much more depth and wisdom than I can, that we need to simplify our lives and in doing so come back to spiritual disciplines.[33] In a great irony, time invested in Jesus is not another time pressure; it is a release valve on what is shaking our worlds.

Call to action

There is a scene in the film about the Olympic runners Eric Liddell and Harold Abrahams, *Chariots of Fire*, which captures our challenge. Liddell, a committed Christian who later went to be a missionary in China, talks about his gift of running. 'When I run,' he says, 'I feel His pleasure.'[34] That's it – that's our challenge. Feel God's pleasure in His masterpiece. Feel His pleasure in your calling. He is building His kingdom, and the God who put the universe in place did not forget you! No, He has a plan and purpose, and He takes delight in it and in you.

Application

Spend some quality time looking at who you are and who God has made you to be, and let this thought fill you and fill you again.

- I am His masterpiece.

- I am created to do good works.

---

[33] John Mark Comer, *The Ruthless Elimination of Hurry* (London, Hodder & Stoughton Ltd, 2019).
[34] *Chariots of Fire*, 1981, distributed by 20th Century Fox.

- He is my shepherd – He leads me, and He pursues me.

- He is for me.

Who are you? What are you called to do?

Ask three close friends to give five words to describe you.

Create your own five words and compare the four sets.

Think about a time when you were in work in the past year and were really fulfilled, or feel you made a telling contribution. What skills and values were you displaying?

Who could you go to if you felt deep grief, trauma, anxiety or anger? Who can you talk to when it gets too much? If there is no one, ask God to help you find someone.

Prayer

Lord, You have made me who I am. You made me with love and purpose. You have led me through valleys of darkness and places of refreshment. Here I am. I bring my gifts, my values, my experiences and lay them on the altar. More, Lord, more of You working in my life, more of You in my job and in everything I do. Amen.

Mark's story

Mark has an extraordinary career history, moving (seemingly effortlessly) between the workplace and mission on numerous occasions. He has been CEO of an independent financial advisor (IFA), a church pastor and CEO of a missions charity. He is currently self-employed, working to build up a new business consultancy. This is a step-out-in-faith moment for him, as he has 'left the safety of a good job when most believed I was doing well in the role'.

This is part of a pattern of following God's call even when it means a big career shift. It has led to this current time where Mark has to really draw close to Jesus as he builds a new business with no customers during the Covid lockdown. He has written a book with some fresh thinking on teamwork and has really spent time asking God to shape his new work. He has seen God at work in many situations. Until recently, he led a Middle East missions organisation. 'We prayed many times for God to meet the budget we had set in faith for the year. When I took on the role, I had a strong conviction that if God "ordered the pizza", He would pay for it [the budget]. On at least two occasions we were significantly behind budget near year end and on both occasions significant and unexpected donations came.'

When applying for the CEO position with the missions team, Mark was aware that if he didn't get the job, he would need to leave the organisation, so it was a risk to apply. 'In praying this through I had a strong sense of God speaking to me out of Esther – "for such a time as this" [Esther 4:14] – which was both a command to step up and a confirmation of call. I am glad to say I did get the job and it was a significant time.'

He has extensive leadership experience, saying, 'I am looking to see people reach their potential and helping them see how that might happen, or directly influence it.' He is committed to working with honesty and integrity and to stand by his word, 'even if that costs me, which it has done on occasions'. Listening to people is an important leadership strategy: 'It gives people value, as I think all team members must know how they contribute to the team and believe their contribution counts.'

A key element to Mark's life has been to 'recognise that there is no secular/sacred divide. The only question is, where do we serve God? So praying equally for the missionary and the businessman, teacher, doctor, etc.'

Mark and I are prayer partners. As he describes it, 'I let my prayer partners know at the beginning of every week what I would like prayer for, and they me. They act as peer mentors whom I talk to regularly and pray with.'

I have known Mark well for many years; he is a man who is continually looking for God's will and purpose. It is a journey that has taken him from running a financial services firm to church growth in India, from equipping and supporting Christians working in very challenging countries to supporting team-building. It is a very broad portfolio, with his absolute commitment to Jesus at the core of his call to work.

Chapter Three
The Call to Abide

Getting to the roots

I have just been out looking at trees. I know it is a bit weird, but there is method in my madness. We have lots of mature trees near where we live. Our road is a beautiful avenue of tall trees towering impressively above us in our car headlamps on a winter's evening. They are even more glorious as they stand in the snow or let the sun shine through their leaves on a beautiful spring morning.

I have particularly been looking at roots. Many of the pavements are broken up by large roots that sustain and support extremely tall trees. When the winds blow, the roots hold them steady. When it is time to grow, the roots feed them the life they need for new leaves and branches. They fight for space; their mission is to keep their particular tree going, and council-laid pavement slabs or tarmac will not get in the way! The local pavement is cracked and full of hard-to-navigate dips and bumps made from growing roots.

How are our roots? I believe this is a critical question for each one of us. How deep do they go? Do they sustain us and help us grow? Do they enable us to be fruitful in the workplace, or are our leaves dying and our fruit decaying?

Paul tells the Roman Gentiles they have been grafted onto the Jewish olive tree. He writes, 'If the root is holy, so are the branches' (Romans 11:16). What happens if we have no roots? 'But since they have no root, they last only a short time. When trouble or persecution comes because of the word, they quickly fall away' (Matthew 13:21). The importance of having the right roots is reinforced by John the Baptist as he announces the coming of the kingdom of God: 'The axe has been laid to the root of the trees, and every tree that does not produce good fruit will be cut down and thrown into the fire' (Luke 3:9). This is the Bible's *kairos* moment[35] – the time is special; the kingdom is coming. But the axe is laid, not to the tree, as we might normally expect, but to its very root, because the root has lost connection with God.

We are called to 'abide', as it says in John 15:4 of the ESV version (the NIV has Jesus' words as 'remain in me') – to come into God's presence. It is the great privilege of our lives. The writer to the Hebrews captures it well:

> Therefore, brothers and sisters, since we have confidence to enter the Most Holy Place by the blood of Jesus, by a new and living way opened for us through the curtain, that is, his body, and since we have a great priest over the house of God, let us draw near to God with a sincere heart and with the full assurance that faith brings, having our hearts sprinkled to cleanse us from a guilty conscience and having our bodies washed with pure water. Let us hold unswervingly to the hope we profess, for he who promised is faithful. And let us consider how we may spur one another on towards love and good deeds, not giving up meeting together, as some are in the habit of doing, but encouraging one another – and all the more as you see the Day approaching.
> (Hebrews 10:19-25).

As we have seen, shalom is a great feature of God's kingdom. We have our deepest peace when we are walking with Jesus. Or as *The Message* version puts Hebrews 10:19, 'So, friends, we can

---

[35] *Kairos* is a Greek word meaning a timely or special moment. The New Testament talks about *kairos* more than eighty times, generally referring to the 'appointed time' for the coming of God's kingdom.

now – without hesitation – walk right up to God, into "the Holy Place."'

Put our roots down into this – we have confidence, without hesitation, to come into God's presence. How do we feel about that? Jesus has made the way clear, once and for all. There is a direct correlation between time spent in God's presence and fruitfulness. It is modelled by Jesus who constantly withdraws to be on His own with His Father. We look at people like the Welsh Revival leader, Evan Roberts, a key figure in the great move of God in 1904 that transformed his community, Loughor, the surrounding area near Swansea and the whole of South Wales. He made himself ready by years of prayer and time with Jesus as a teenager.

Can we see in this Hebrews passage the cry to continue meeting together? We often take this as a single verse but need to look at its context. If we want to come into His presence, to put our roots down, we must not neglect to meet with others. Again, we need to see the Ekklesia outworking of this. Can we find other Christians in our workplace or work sector to pray together? Can we cut across the denominational barriers, and create a group of two, three or four who will work to see lives transformed? Can we 'spur one another on' to good works, at work or in our local community? This support might come from our small group. There is a powerful Ekklesia concept in Hebrews – we should be encouragers and stand with those who encourage us to good works in our workplaces.

Busy, busy, busy

Life can be so busy it can be like finding ourselves standing in the middle of a fast-flowing motorway knowing we've got to get out of the way of all the traffic. The answer to the question, 'How are you?' often reveals a lot about us. My normal reply is, 'Busy.' That is about my driven, task-orientated personality. Others will feel they are 'surrounded by problems', 'trying to juggle too much', 'worried about the family, or my colleagues'.

Or just plain, 'Stressed.' Of course, there will be people wanting to get back onto the motorway; they are 'bored', 'hanging around'.

We live in a period when people work more, sleep less and try to double and triple task. We are in an important meeting while handling a demanding incoming text or email. We find ourselves having to be in two or three events at the same time. We complain we are in so many meetings we never have any time to get our work done. We dig into our weekend with work because we can dedicate more time, clear thought and attention to it.

We may be the people who like to say 'Yes'. We see a hand volunteering to take that piece of work forward in our team meeting and realise that hand was ours. We want to show everyone that we are 'responsible' and 'committed' and will meet every deadline.

But to add to this, we are in an era of distractors and time stealers. Many phones have a screen time feature in their settings; today's shows my average screen time is up 38 per cent on last week! We get caught up in Facebook, Instagram, Twitter – and if we don't keep up, we feel bereft. It grabs our attention. It is designed to do so; we feel good about the likes and shares and comments on our social media. We can show that although we are heavily pressurised at work, we still know that the prime minister just made an important statement about fishing and that there was an accident only a mile from where we live. Have you heard the latest management blog? The new sermon from Bethel or Times Square? The latest worship release from Elevation Worship? We are bombarded.

American pastor and author John Mark Comer shares his experience of realising he was swamped and taking on too much. He met his mentor. As he described his situation, his mentor gave him a very simple response (and book title!): 'You must ruthlessly eliminate hurry from your life.'

Comer's response was, 'Okay, what else?'

The reply shook his world; it may shake yours as well, 'There is nothing else. Hurry is the great enemy of spiritual life in our day. You must ruthlessly eliminate hurry from your life.'[36]

He makes a very profound claim and I want you to consider this carefully. *He believes hurry is the great spiritual battle of our generation – because Jesus is losing us.*

Hurry, distractions, busyness and worry squeeze our time and our energy. It's not just about work; it's also 'the other stuff'. We have time but we give it away to social media, to keeping up with the Netflix series, or the new release on Amazon. We can buy and research from home. We can look up who the actor is in the film we are watching. There is a psychological war going on. Companies, organisations and individuals are competing for our attention, they grab it, they reward us when we give them our time – a free offer here, a compliment there, a sense of achievement over here. We are literally being manipulated by experts.

You can imagine a modern conversation between C S Lewis' demons Wormwood and Screwtape:[37]

> Come up with whatever you can do to distract the humans. There is so much to choose from! They love to be distracted. Fill their heads with stuff and they will abandon the enemy. There were times when they used to have disciplined quiet times and give time to prayer and reading and contemplation. I believe for many of them this is almost non-existent now. I am pleased to see they are becoming almost powerless.

The tree is fed through its roots. If the roots are not accessing what is needed, the tree becomes vulnerable in the storm and fails to bear fruit.

This links to our sense of call. If we feel what we do is unimportant and low on God's radar, why bother with 'spiritual

---

[36] Comer, *The Ruthless Elimination of Hurry*, p19.
[37] The characters of Screwtape and Wormwood are found in C S Lewis, The *Screwtape Letters* (Grand Rapids, MI: Zondervan, 2001).

fuel'? We only need a sermon here, a worship song there and the occasional small group and we will be OK. Yes, that is fine for a low-impact existence, but this is not Kingdom Living. Kingdom Living is recognising that God has called and appointed us to where we are. He is with us twenty-four hours a day; what we do is always important to Him. He is calling us to be a blessing, a blessing that flows naturally out of us when we live a life abiding in Christ.

Walking righteously

We looked at God's call for the *tsaddiqim* (the righteous), mentioned more than 200 times in the Old Testament including fifty times in the Psalms; they are important to God! If we follow God's heart we abide with Him, we are sensitive to His voice, we are listening for Him to speak. For the real *tsaddiqim*, Jesus is their absolute centre, the true north for their compass. But it's our great spiritual battle. We will often have to admit that God has not got our attention when we allow other undermining accusations to influence our feelings and confidence. Thoughts like:

- It does not matter if God has not got my attention – I need to give my time to sorting my finances out, my family, work projects, etc.

- I'm a spiritual foot soldier, pew fodder; all the spiritual stuff is done by others.

- What's the point of 'investing' in myself spiritually? I'm not doing something important like 'full-time ministry', or a nurse, teacher or social worker.

- I have not got the time to be more spiritual.

- I need to get by with less spiritual gas in my tank!

These are all lies! There is one truth – God has called us; He has a plan and purpose for us.

Look with a different perspective on Peter's first letter. Here he is telling his hearers about the impact they should have on the marketplace, in other people's homes, with their neighbours and in their workplaces. Incredibly, he tells us we are:

A chosen people, a royal priesthood, a holy nation, God's special possession, that you may declare the praises of him who called you out of darkness into his wonderful light … I urge you … Live such good lives among the pagans that, though they accuse you of doing wrong, they may see your good deeds and glorify God on the day he visits us. (1 Peter 2:9, 11-12)

A priest (yes, you are called to be one), a person belonging to God, comes into God's presence regularly to:

- **Look upwards.** 'Be still, and know that I am God' (Psalm 46:10). We can sit quietly in God's presence wherever we are. We may pause as we travel to work or enter a meeting. A quiet 'Here we are, Lord' pause: 'You and me blessing the workplace.'

- **'Walk humbly'** (Isaiah 38:15). We are dependent on God in all circumstances. Life is not about our fulfilment but God's glory. This is very countercultural when we have so many messages about striving, achieving, consuming and living a life for ourselves. We are praying for His wisdom, His favour, His blessing. We want His presence.

- **'Enter his gates with thanksgiving'** (Psalm 100:4). We often have this strange relationship with Jesus when we come straightaway into His presence with our things to do/prayer list. Thanksgiving and praise remind us of who God is, how much He loves us, how much He has compassion on those around us. Prayer Houses[38] speak of

---

[38] There are many Prayer Houses across the UK and other countries, such as Beacon House of Prayer in Stoke, www.beaconhop.org (accessed 21st November 2021).

spending hours just praising and worshipping Him and then find that what was on their 'prayer things to do list' seem to have been answered.

- **Have 'clean hands and a pure heart'** (Psalm 24:4). Ezekiel 18 is a full chapter on the subject of righteousness. The prophet says we all have an individual responsibility to choose righteousness. Ezekiel describes what is 'just and right' (v21). He does not follow idols or chase after adultery, he does not 'oppress anyone' or rob. He 'gives his food to the hungry' and clothes to the naked (v7), he lends money generously and judges fairly between two parties. He faithfully follows God's law. There are times when we may be faced with righteous dilemmas – to cut corners, to fiddle figures, to undermine colleagues. We may face sexual temptations. But we are working for the Lord, not people. We are able to be at work and be in God's presence. 'Who may ascend the mountain of the LORD? Who may stand in his holy place? The one who has clean hands and a pure heart' (Psalm 24:3-4).

- **Lose ourselves in Jesus.** It really is all about Him. It is much more about listening than speaking, and sometimes it is just resting in His deep shalom. I like to just imagine coming and sitting on a bench with Jesus, spending time quietly and bringing the day to Him.

- **Surrender**. Contemplative prayer is like sitting with our hands open asking for wisdom, asking for peace, asking for favour, maybe asking for patience. This can happen in the workplace, in that stressful and tense meeting, as a big plan needs to be put together, before that negotiation with a possible customer or as I enter my office. I am not going into this situation alone – I have company!

- **Fulfil our calling**. This book looks at different aspects of our call – to dream, to lead, to disciple, to serve our community and city. This all links back to our roots going down into the presence of God. If we lead, we want His wisdom, we have a responsibility to pray for our teams that God will bless them. We should want to help build disciples. We bring our concerns and challenges to Jesus, and He leads us into the right situations and conversations.

- **Remember to ask!** It's strange how often we forget to ask. Jesus told people, 'You may ask me for anything in my name, and I will do it' (John 14:14). There is an 'as it is in heaven' (Matthew 6:10) element to every prayer, as we seek what Jesus is doing and releasing. Repeatedly Jesus responds to people's faith. By exercising faith we are acknowledging our dependence on God, but we are also exercising our right to come into His presence and make our desires known.

- **Know that God's word is a lamp to our feet.**[39] I used to read chapters of the Bible because this was my task to do (and it wasn't done frequently enough); it was like ticking off an action on my things to do list. Now I read it in awe and wonder; this is the Word of God and I expect it to inspire me, instruct me and bless me. As a lamp it prepares us for what lies ahead. We read in God's presence, seeking to hear His voice. So I read much more. There are so many promises in the Scriptures. We literally stand on the Word of God; it is like a rock under our feet (Psalm 61:2). I wish many times in my work experience that I had stood on the promise that *He is always with me* (Matthew 28:20) rather than getting annoyed, distressed, perplexed about a situation facing me.

- **Action!** 'To be the tsaddiqim, then, means to care about justice for the poor – to care with a deep, gut-level compassion, that energizes personal, sacrificial

---

[39] See Psalm 119:105.

commitment.'[40] We are called to 'do justice', to defend the poor, vulnerable, aliens and widows. This may be the Eastern European worker who is undermined behind her back, it might be the newly divorced mum struggling to juggle her hours, it may be those the rest of the office ignores. Many struggle in work: can we give time and grace to them? I know as a task-orientated person I can miss the signals of need and avoid people I think are going to soak up my time. I need to ask the question, 'How are you doing?' and really want to know the answer!

- **Persist**. Jesus tells us to persist (Luke 18:1-8) – again, it raises our faith and strengthens our spiritual maturity when we keep asking. I remember a prayer battle for my daughter who had a debilitating pain that stopped her studying for and then taking her GCSE exams. I had prayed constantly, but breakthrough came as I was driving and praying and realised I needed to hand this over to Jesus and trust His love for Rachel. I was in floods of tears as God broke through. In important prayer issues we keep going, spending time with God and talking through our frustrations and expectations. We are not hesitatingly going to the headmaster's study; we are climbing onto our Father's knee.

Be fruitful

The Galatian church is seriously distracted, and Paul writes to get it back on course. It is clear some people have been telling the followers there to get back to following the whole Jewish law. They argue that the law gives them what they need to live life, a framework for living. Who would not want that? It does mean you need to be circumcised, and that's painful, but that pain is a doorway to a better way of living (Galatians 4:8-20). It's a trap we all might fall into: 'Give me some rules, give me

---

[40] Sherman, *Kingdom Calling*, p52.

some guidelines. Life will be much more straightforward with fewer options and worries about whether I am doing things the right way.' Just as we are distracted by all the noise and 'wisdom' of the world today, the Galatians were distracted by the pull of the old legalities.

Paul is rigid in his opposition to this because there is a much better way. In chapter 5 he reminds them; 'You, my brothers and sisters, were called to be free … For the entire law is fulfilled in keeping this one command: "Love your neighbour as yourself"' (vv13-14). Let's not overcomplicate things! Then Paul makes a key comment for us as we consider this call to abide: 'So I say, live by the Spirit, and you will not gratify the desires of the flesh' (v16).

We have looked at the importance of spending quality time with Jesus, but living by the Spirit is more than this because the Spirit is always talking to us. He is constantly prompting us. He is leading us in situations that will surprise us.

Paul gives the Galatians (and us) some more key words for the workplace. He tells us the more we rely on the Spirit, the more we abide in Christ, and the more fruitful we will be (vv16-18). Our workplace, the people around us, will be changed and blessed because we take fruitfulness to the front line (with respect to Mark Greene who has written brilliantly about just this!).[41] 'But the fruit of the Spirit is love, joy, peace, forbearance, kindness, goodness, faithfulness, gentleness and self-control. Against such things there is no law' (vv22-23). Abiding with our roots deep in listening to the Spirit produces wonderful fruit!

Change my life

When God moves powerfully, He brings conviction of sin to Christians and non-Christians. We hear of people falling to their

---

[41] Mark Greene is the mission champion at the London Institute of Contemporary Christianity and has written extensively about life in the workplace, including his book, *Fruitfulness on the Frontline* (Nottingham: IVP, 2014).

knees in the fields and the workplaces as God moves. They crowd out the churches. They cry out for Jesus. They turn from (and are set free from) addiction, pornography, corruption, etc. Forgiveness is a wonderful, life-changing gift.

Conviction is a sign of a very intense move of the Holy Spirit. It gets people mobilised and they head out each evening with hundreds of others to the Welsh chapel to sing the songs of revival, they walk for miles to hear the gospel, or throng to million-people rallies in Africa to find out more about Jesus. Christians will describe having a God-given conviction to give up their job, to challenge a particular issue or to increase their giving and, in response, they find fulfilment.

I want to ask us to reflect – is God convicting us about how we manage and use our time? Are we in too much of a hurry? Do our lives get interrupted, maybe even controlled, by constant distractions and interruptions? Do our phones have a better chance of getting our attention than our families or even Jesus? We are in the distracted generation.

Without the roots strongly established in the ground, our tree becomes unstable.

Change is not something that happens just because we hope for it or have nice, warm feelings about it. We need to be deliberate. That's why conviction is so powerful. The work of John Mark Comer and others on returning our eyes to Jesus has caught many people's attention. He argues that we 'need to be deliberate, we need to put some disciplines into our lives'.[42]

We can fall into a false compartmentalisation where God has little impact on our work. But Jesus stands at the door and knocks (Revelation 3:20) – it would be madness not to let Him in. He wants to partner with us, stand with us and bring His love, peace and wisdom into every challenge, task, conversation and meeting.

A key habit for many of us to rediscover is to set aside to be time with Jesus. When I was a young Christian, the wise elders

---

[42] Comer, *The Ruthless Elimination of Hurry,* p110.

encouraged us to have a quiet time. I sort of did and sort of didn't. I knew some people who were better than me at setting time aside. I did some of my quiet time in the car, with praise and prayer. I would utilise times when I was waiting for a train, or a meal, or a phone call. It was 'tick-box Christianity', squeezing in actions when I could. I needed more time listening, not doing, being still, not doing faith on the run.

Paul goes back to the roots in one of his wonderful passages to his friends in Ephesus.

> I pray that out of his glorious riches he may strengthen you with power through his Spirit in your inner being, so that Christ may dwell in your hearts through faith. And I pray that you, being rooted and established in love, may have power, together with all the Lord's holy people, to grasp how wide and long and high and deep is the love of Christ, and to know this love that surpasses knowledge – that you may be filled to the measure of all the fullness of God. (Ephesians 3:16-19)

Here we are, back to our roots! The more rooted and grounded we are, the more we realise the width, length, height and depth of God's love for us – and flowing through us. These roots can overcome our challenges around time, distraction, work stress, work and personal challenges, etc, and remind us that our roots go deep into love. We enter the workplace loved, we go into one-to-one meetings loved, we interact with others as a loved person. Rooted and grounded in love. Amen!

The most successful people in life invest in their vision. This is described as 'the mastery point' when we have invested 10,000 hours in a subject and pass from being competent to being intuitively gifted. The Beatles did this by playing continuous shows in Hamburg, David Beckham did it with continuous work on his passing skills, Bill Gates was an early adopter of computers.[43] Invest. Look around you and see if you can spot

---

[43] Malcolm Gladwell, *Outliers: The Story of Success* (London: Penguin, 2008). Gladwell popularised the mastery research

the people who spend more time with Jesus. They love the Word, they love to praise, they love to pray and their lives operate at a different pace and reduced pressure.

If I want to turn more fully to Jesus, I need to make some things that have driven me become less important in my life. They will differ for each of us, but consider these issues and score them out of ten, with one being, 'This is not an issue', and ten being, 'This is a biggy: I am consumed and often controlled by this issue.'

- Competitiveness

- Task focus

- Busyness – I must fill my time

- Distraction

- Greed

- Worry and uncertainty

- Insecurity

- A sense of inferiority and worthlessness

- Anger

- Sadness and depression

- Criticism of others

- Desperation for others' approval

- Perfectionism

There are so many areas in all our lives where we do not hear the voice of God. We hear our uncertainties and the enemy's undermining. Jesus never tells us we are useless. He is our good shepherd; He leads us to 'quiet waters' (Psalm 23:2); He walks with us. There are times when He challenges, times when He asks us to do demanding things, times when our work or other situations crowd in on us. But even in the 'valley of the shadow of death' (Psalm 23:4, ESV), let alone a fast-looming project deadline, He is with us.

God designed us and designed the need for a break!

> Six days you shall labour and do all your work, but the seventh day is a sabbath to the LORD your God. On it you shall not do any work, neither you, nor your son or daughter, nor your male or female servant, nor your animals, nor any foreigner residing in your towns.
> (Exodus 20:9-10)

How do we react to these verses? I think for most of us it is a long way from our current experience, and yet, this is God's good will for us. He knows we need to rest (and we must not forget to let our servants have time off as well!). The Sabbath is 'to the LORD', or dedicated to the Lord.

The richness of Sabbath is not just rest; it is time to invest in our relationship with God. It is time for gratitude for our friends and family, it is time to build back our energy for the week ahead, and it is time to pursue God's presence. Not out of a sense of task but out of relationship, because God pursues our presence as well.

Next time your Sabbath comes along (recognising that while most people look to Sunday, some will use Saturday and others put another day aside to be their Sabbath), can we simply pray, 'I dedicate this day to God'? Can we consider what dedicating the day means? Rest is walking and spending time with friends. Look for God in that walk, in our friends, talking to our family about what we have to be thankful for. Maybe have communion. Slow down. When I was a child, we sort of observed Sunday as the Sabbath and it became a day we did not look forward to – the television was off, the ice cream van was ignored, we had to amuse ourselves. This is not a call for, 'Let's make at least one day a week a miserable day.' No, this is letting sap rise through the root of the tree. This is investing in our lives; this is recognising that the call behind Sabbath is a good call.

Sabbath is:

a spirit of restfulness that goes with you throughout your week. A way of living with 'ease, gratitude, appreciation, peace and prayer.' A way of working from rest, not for rest, with nothing to prove. A way of bearing fruit from abiding not from ambition.[44]

An instrument

This book talks about our call into business and the workplace as part of our call to serve Jesus. Jesus called the apostles and then the seventy-two to go out and prepare the way for Him. His instructions were clear: 'Do not take a purse or bag or sandals; and do not greet anyone on the road' (Luke 10:4). In other words, when Jesus sends you, travel light. Trust Him on whether you will be fed, watered and given shelter. He wanted them to walk by faith, and He wants the same for us. Walk into that supplier today, welcome people on the Zoom call, catch the bus or the train knowing that Jesus is with you.

Let us hear Jesus' sending-out instructions: 'Heal those there who are ill and tell them, "The kingdom of God has come near to you"' (Luke 10:9). God does not necessarily call us to be weird or to upset colleagues in the workplace, but He does call us to hear His voice (John 10:16).

As we have seen, living the kingdom values of shalom, mercy, justice, righteousness, compassion and forgiveness will make our behaviour and character distinct. I think offering to pray for someone is a wonderful gift. I understand there are HR policies and the need to respect other beliefs. But in many circumstances we can offer the gift: 'I'm a follower of Jesus, that means I pray – it's in our job description, we just do it! If you don't want me to, that's fine. If it's helpful and you want me to

---

[44] Comer, *The Ruthless Elimination of Hurry*, p172.

pray about some specific things, I would be glad to do that.' You need to sense whether you pray with words or silently. The kingdom of God is near all our colleagues in the workplace – through you. 'The kingdom of God is in your midst' (Luke 17:21).

Here are some other brief thoughts about being an instrument for Jesus and travelling light into the places He puts us:

- Do some dreaming. Spend some time with Jesus thinking about your call, talk about your concerns, ask Him to equip you.

- Use the heavenly GPS! Asking God to direct our feet, we will find He often prompts us to think and pray about certain individuals or situations.

- Listen to others well. This is like 'double listening', to the individual and to God. We all give away so much when we are talking, about our concerns and worries, aspirations and hopes. Listen to how they feel. Hear from God. He may tell you to listen more, ask some questions.

- Be confident in your Ekklesia call. He has positioned you to bless your workplace, to pray for its peace and prosperity, and to pray for God to move.

- Invest in relationships. God has sent you into situations and groups to seek people out, to make friends, to be a blessing. You have been sent to your work colleagues: expect God to move.

- Travel light. The world wants to intrude all the time. You can't stop it happening, but you can manage it. You might ration/control the times you keep up with social media. You might deal with emails at a specific time. Your things to do list might contain some compassion/caring goals like, 'Catch up with Amrick today,' or, 'Thank Rachel for her support in the meeting.'

I have learned to be content whatever the circumstances. I know what it is to be in need, and I know what it is to have plenty. I have learned the secret of being content in any and every situation, whether well fed or hungry, whether living in plenty or in want.
(Philippians 4:11-12)

Be content in the workplace, and in every situation.

Call to action

What is your fruit? In your work, home, church, community? That's not a heavy 'you must do more' challenge. Maybe you should do less. Fruit does not come by working harder but by listening to God more.

- Reflect: where do your roots go? Are they deep enough into Jesus?

- Can you practise abiding in Jesus (see John 15:4, ESV)? Not with a prayer list but just to spend time with Him, to strengthen your relationship and understand how much He loves you. Where is a good place to do this? How do you make time?

- Can you get more control over your use of email and social media? Can you have social media rest days? Can you put your phone on one side for Sabbath? Can you have TV-free days?

- Have you learned to be content? Think of some places and times where you have felt content. What do you do to hit that level of contentment?

Application

In the days of sailing ships, vessels were taken out of service periodically to remove the barnacles and other debris they had collected on their voyages. All this clutter was slowing them down and potentially putting them at risk. Imagine it's time to be put in dry dock for an overhaul. What is currently holding you back? What will give you the incentive to pursue God more, to spend more time in His presence, to look at the world from His heavenly perspective?

Prayer

Lord Jesus, be my heart's desire. Take my roots deep. Let me be fed, inspired and changed by You. Amen.

Matthew's story

Matthew works globally as a team coach and leadership development consultant and is also part of the leadership team for a multi-site church impacting his local community. Matthew and I were colleagues, and I value his wisdom and walk with God.

Matthew has a very distinctive understanding of his call; this has been honed over the years and really shapes what he does. He describes the call as, 'To relieve suffering and hurt and to help people and groups flourish.' His work enables him to create breakthroughs for people and groups. This is underpinned by his desire to 'treat all people with dignity. To be very transparent and open, and to seek excellence.' Matthew is committed to continually learning and finding ways to improve. This is shaped by his desire to bring real insight to his clients.

Matthew provides two inspiring prayer testimonies.

I had allowed a situation to gradually happen over five years, where a global energy company had grown to become 75 per cent of my business. I knew it was a problem, but I was finding it a difficult pull to resist. From June 2014 to January 2015, the price of oil dropped 60 per cent. In January 2015, my client cancelled all work with pretty much immediate effect.

Shortly after this announcement, I had a ninety-minute drive back alone. I began worshipping the Lord, and asked

God what He wanted to do in this situation. I felt the Lord say that He wanted to show me that He was my provider and was totally reliable and that He would hold me in His peace. As this was happening an SMS came in. A Christian friend had felt an overwhelming urge to text me this verse:

> Trust in the LORD with all your heart
> And do not lean on your own understanding.
> In all your ways acknowledge Him,
> And He will make your paths straight.'
> (Proverbs 3:5-6, NASB)

From that point onwards, I found it extremely difficult to get anxious. Against all the odds, enough work came in during the year. Financially, I had a comparable year to the previous one.

As a footnote, the energy company asked me to provide virtual classrooms to reduce costs significantly. Five years on and in the middle of a global pandemic, that experience of designing and delivering virtual workshops has kept me secure.

I was due to work with a colleague facilitating a one-day workshop for a global professional services firm. Beforehand she emailed me to say she'd had an accident and had severely damaged her shoulder and it would be in a bandage; she was going to need an operation. On the morning of the workshop, once we were set up and ready to go, I shared that I was a Christ follower and had seen numerous people healed that I'd prayed for, and gave an example. I acknowledged it wasn't for everyone but said if she'd like me to pray for her at the end of the event, I'd be happy to. I said that she would need to ask me, and I wouldn't mention it again as I didn't want to be pressuring.

At the end of the day, we packed up and as I said goodbye, she asked if I'd be OK to pray. I did and we shared a beautiful five or ten minutes. The peace of God was tangible. We saw improvement in her shoulder immediately. She did not need the operation. She was very grateful that I'd offered to pray and emailed me to tell me.

Matthew recognises that 'sharing your faith at work is becoming increasingly complex and fraught with challenges'. He describes being a Christian in the workplace as 'tricky territory' and has worked with many to help them think through their call and how they can see God move where they are.

Chapter Four
The Call to Wisdom

Keep learning!

Not surprisingly, the book of Proverbs, also known as the book of Wisdom, tells us to continually seek wisdom and understanding. 'My son, do not let wisdom and understanding out of your sight, preserve sound judgment and discretion; they will be life for you' (Proverbs 3:21-22). A key element in our spiritual walk is our commitment to learn.

We see this modelled in the disciples. Jesus was their rabbi – their learning mixed incredible wisdom and input from Jesus with many life lessons. He built His disciples' thinking skills. He asked, 'Why did this happen?' 'Who do men say I am?' and they also asked Him many questions. This was reinforced by parables, often around everyday issues like lost sheep and coins.[45] This was a key element in rabbinic teaching: a memorable story and the challenge to understand the key message within it. The disciples also observed Jesus doing extraordinary and countercultural things. Incidents like washing the disciples' feet, spending time with the Samaritan woman and bringing forward a child to bless all challenged the prevailing culture.

Jesus is, of course, the great role model. Paul is also a teacher, and he tells the Corinthians, 'Follow my example, as I follow the example of Christ' (1 Corinthians 11:1). The Amplified Bible translates this as, 'Imitate me, just as I *imitate* Christ.'

---

[45] See Luke 15.

Both Jesus and Paul repeatedly demonstrated their deep love and knowledge of Scripture; it inspired their thinking and their dedication to prayer. Both were empowered by their intimacy with God; they heard God's heart, they sought His guidance and wisdom.

So, spiritually, we learn from some key sources by:

- Soaking in Scripture with a hunger to hear God speak;

- Prayer: not just requests – as we have seen, prayer is often simply abiding in His presence. Let Him speak – it's a relationship;

- Being equipped by God with words of knowledge, the prophetic, spiritual insights and dreams (see 1 Corinthians 12:10; 2 Corinthians 12:1);

- Reading. There are thousands of Christian books;

- Social media. There are thousands of social media resources – for worship, teaching, preaching, etc.

Much of this is our choice – how much do we want to invest in our learning and growth? The power of learning gets released as wisdom when I apply it to my life, situation and workplace. Some invest years in professional development – lawyers, doctors, accountants, consultants, architects, etc. The old argument is the stronger you build the foundations, the larger the structure you can build on it. With so much choice, we need to determine our particular focus. We might choose to invest in our passion to lead, in our technical expertise, in relating well – but always looking to strengthen our Christian walk.

Some people prefer to learn on their own, through reading and social media. Others like to learn in groups – small groups, study groups or workshops. 'Plans fail for lack of counsel, but with many advisors they succeed' (Proverbs 15:22). Others are reflectors and improvers, with a lot of learning built into their lives. They might like to spend time with a great mug of coffee on a Saturday reviewing the week and identifying things they could build on and improve. As the disciples learned with Jesus, there was a formal learning process – the reading, prayers, discussion element – but equally valuable is the informal, actively learning from life and how we respond to it.

I have a great friend who is a professor who looked at how people learn. As my job at the time was as a training manager, I asked him the big question, 'How do people learn?'

I sat back, expecting a deep, detailed and learned answer. Instead, he gave me one word three times: 'Practise, practise, practise.'

It is, of course, a profound answer. We practise to find our best approach and the method that best suits us. We practise to review and refine. We practise prayer because we want to get better. We practise getting depth from our Bible study. We practise presenting to a group of colleagues. We review that difficult argument we had at work and look at how we might approach it differently. Each day is a learning opportunity – to practise, review and refine our work, personal and spiritual lives.

One of the great biblical learning tools is testimony, people's stories of God moving. Testimony shows us what God can do – at work, home and elsewhere. You will have noticed that this book carries many diverse testimonies. Again, the wisdom comes through application – how does this fit my situation? The driver, however, is the powerful truth that testimony reveals what God wants to do.

Learning from sport

I have had the privilege of working with some outstanding sports coaches who have taken what they learned and looked at how we can improve performance in the workplace. One was an Olympic gold medallist. One of my most golden moments in life was having a one-to-one dinner with him on the thirtieth anniversary of his victory and I asked him to relive the day. He told of the long waiting, and the determination and focus he had that he would cross the finishing line first. The arrival on the track in the intense summer heat. The refocusing as the athletes prepared – and the race – focused on the line. 'Do you not know that in a race all the runners run, but only one gets the prize? Run in such a way to get the prize' (1 Corinthians 9:24).

The gold medallist taught us that however much we practise, real success comes when we receive feedback and then turn that feedback into action. I believe, 'Feedback is the food of champions'.[46] I heard legendary rower Sir Steve Redgrave talk about the challenge of winning five gold medals.[47] After each gold medal victory, he would return to his coach to be told he had done well, but his winning time this time would not be enough for the next Olympics. For him the target was very tiny: over four years, month by month, they needed to make the marginal differences that would result in a two to three seconds' improvement. The coach kept him going and convinced him it was achievable.

Sports people need truth to help them improve. Bland statements or kind reassurances do not produce champions. We have too many stories of celebrity church leaders and teachers who have fallen from grace and taken large organisations with them. How vulnerable are all of us to slip-ups and sin? Where was the person who loved them enough to look them in the eye and say, 'I am hearing some uncomfortable rumours about you and am picking up that some people are becoming more and more fearful of you. Let's talk about this. Let's be open. Let's look at what needs to change.' 'The discerning heart seeks knowledge, but the mouth of a fool feeds on folly' (Proverbs 15:14).

- How are you with feedback? Do you get any? How well do you apply it?

- How are you at asking for feedback?

---

[46] My version of a quote by Ken Blanchard.

[47] Sir Steve was speaking at a company event in 1998.

The challenge is, there can be a thin line between feedback and criticism, but you need feedback to grow. Who can you ask? Pause for a moment and think of two or three aspects of your job or your character you would like to improve and who you could approach for feedback. It is important that feedback is not primarily about your weaknesses – it is about helping you make the very best use of your strengths and capabilities. It might be a simple question like, 'I want to keep improving how I chair meetings – have you any ideas?'

An England striker is best focused on practising scoring goals, so what he is good at becomes more and more instinctive wherever he is inside or outside the penalty area. A Formula One driver practises driving as fast as he can, seeing the track ahead, anticipating the bends on the many different circuits he tackles. Hone your talents;, refine what is good.

The Babylonian School for Advanced Management

Daniel, Hananiah, Mishael and Azariah were selected for the Babylonian School for Advanced Management course. We are told the selection criteria was 'young men without any physical defect, handsome, showing aptitude for every kind of learning, well informed, quick to understand, and qualified to serve in the king's palace' (Daniel 1:4). While the Babylonians' equal opportunities policies needed updating, their focus on scholars' capacity to learn was notable.

The youths were clearly good learners. We are told they were brought before the formidable King Nebuchadnezzar. 'In every matter of wisdom and understanding about which the king questioned them, he found them ten times better than all the magicians and enchanters in his whole kingdom' (Daniel 1:20). Let us be clear: this was not an easy learning environment; it was a place with an occultic culture, and the four friends were captured aristocracy, Israelites from the royal family and the nobility, from a minor defeated nation (Daniel 1:3). But there are two key lessons from their testimony. First, they worked together. They stood shoulder to shoulder. This was a prayerful, godly group of friends who supported each other in the heart of the world's largest empire. In that most unpromising environment they thrived – because God was with them. Second, they adapted wisely – they did not oppose everything they were made to learn and do in their three-year programme, but they did refuse to eat the king's meat as it had been sacrificed to idols. They became vegetarian.

The other vital lesson from Babylon is that four was enough. Four was enough to challenge the might of the Babylonian Empire. Four was enough people praying to see history changed. Four was enough, even though they were in an incredibly stressful situation. The Babylonian School for Advanced Management shows that when two, or three, or four gather together,[48] God is with them and great things – empire-changing things – happen.

Learning with church

Many Christians in the workplace complain that their church does not understand them. We continually hear the criticism that they want workers for their money, not their gifts. Leaders are told to equip the people of God 'for the work of ministry' (Ephesians 4:12, ESV).

Here is a fundamental question for any leader – where do you think 'the work of ministry' happens? If we follow the command to go – the Great Commission – we should see the Church sending people out like pinpricks of light to minister across their town or city. But some churches confine ministry to the church itself and teach accordingly.

Of course, this is not universally true: many churches have excellent teaching and fantastic, inspiring pastoral support. We mentioned the example of Doxa Deo church in South Africa earlier. It commissions people publicly in its church services, to

---

[48] See Matthew 18:20.

be sent out and blossom in the workplace. It invests in training and development so *every* church member can be someone who brings impact and blessing to the world. Bethel Church, California, has a mandate 'to be a resource centre to impact cities and nations. What we experience in the culture of the local church and the local city, we want to export. We train, empower, and release people to take the kingdom culture to the world'.[49] This equipping and sending-out approach to ministry is vital.

Then the question arises – who equips those sent out, and who supports them? Church ministers may not have experience of the workplace or of the challenges facing people. It will obviously work best if those with the right experience and calling are involved in the equipping. More than that, teaching and testimony go together: some of the teachers must have experienced God moving through them in the workplace context. My local church has done a good job in using testimony interviews to get people's stories, which in turn encourages others in similar situations.

But let's return to the Ekklesia. It takes us beyond the normal church model. Daniel and his friends model the Ekklesia at work. It may be found in our workplaces, with people from a range of churches across our town or city. We should invest time to build unity, like Daniel did with his friends, because together a workplace group has a call and authority to bless and change the workplace.

Jesus gives us a parable about ten virgins waiting for the bridegroom to come. There are five wise virgins and five foolish ones. The foolish ones use up all their oil and are not ready when the bridegroom arrives at midnight. This is a powerful parable with a central focus on being ready for Jesus' return. The foolish ones were selected for the task, but they used up all their oil. The wise ones knew they needed to be ready. They deliberately and carefully looked after their oil and entered the

[49] Bethel Church website, www.bethel.com/church (accessed 20th January 2022).

great feast with the bridegroom (Matthew 25:1-13). Jesus follows this story with the story of three servants given respectively five bags, two bags and one bag of gold. It is essentially the story of the wise and foolish gold investment team. The wise ones use the gold well: 'Well done, good and faithful servant! You have been faithful with a few things; I will put you in charge of many things' (Matthew 25:21).

Wise or foolish? We have looked at how God made us masterpieces, and calls us to the workplace. What do the wise workers do? I would suggest they look after what they have been given (their gifts and abilities) really, really well. To do this, we must understand and value those strengths. We should also look to where we might get the support we need, and wisely build up our support network.

Our personal support network

I have driven many substantive change programmes for a wide range of organisations. One of the foundations for change is the question, have we got the capability – the skills, knowledge, understanding and confidence – to make this happen? I believe God has a fresh call on Christians in the workplace. We need a fresh understanding of our authority alongside an appreciation of who God has made us to be, and how we can still grow if we are to powerfully bless our colleagues, customers and the wider organisation.

To do this, we need to be deliberate about identifying the changes we want to make and have the support in place to make it happen. We often start with good intentions to lose weight, get healthy, spend more time with the family, etc. The vision is clear – but the challenge is to turn those intentions into deliberate and effective actions. That's where having people alongside us helps – the family member or friend who ensures we record our weight weekly and plan our diet, the friend who regularly asks us how our new prayer regime is going. A personal action shared is more likely to be completed than one we keep to ourselves. As we saw with Daniel and his friends, four people, even two or three, can make a huge difference to living out our vision or call.

What deliberate actions can you take? Here are some suggestions:

Find a team of advisors. This can be formal or informal (people may not know you have them on your 'advisory board'!). Find people you know will give you good advice. One of my strengths is thinking strategically and I am really energised by talking to a few people who think in the same way. I learn a lot from them; they bring fresh perspectives to the things I am thinking about and give me the confidence to keep going. Who has similar interests to you? No one will be the same and we do need different perspectives; the goal is the stimulating conversation. In fact, I have different 'teams of advisors' to help me think spiritually about business and about the city.

King David talks about his advisors in Psalm 101:6: 'My eyes will be on the faithful in the land, that they may dwell with me; the one whose way of life is blameless will minister to me.' *The Message* version says, 'I can't stand arrogance. But I have my eye on salt-of-the-earth people – they're the ones I want working with me; Men and women on the straight and narrow – these are the ones I want at my side.' Who do you want at your side?

Find some reflectors. It can be helpful to have conversations that are more reflective in the workplace. There may be non-Christian colleagues who can help us get a better understanding. It could be about recent company or team history and some of the scars that hold them back. We may not be aware that they tried some things before, and it ended badly. We may need to check our understanding of the culture – how things work around here. We might want to understand the people better, not in a gossipy or destructive way. It is countercultural to look at and talk about those people with wisdom, integrity, good networks, fresh thinking. In many organisations we need to work hard at understanding other teams, how they can best support us and where they depend on us, if we are to work effectively.

Find people you look up to, 1. The Bible describes ministries that should create a framework to build the Ekklesia. 'So Christ himself gave the apostles, the prophets, the evangelists, the pastors and teachers, to equip his people for works of service' (Ephesians 4:11-12).

A good way to look at a ministry like apostle, prophet or pastor is on a one-to-ten scale. Some people are just starting out, operating as ones and twos. Others have really significant gifts in these areas and may hit a nine or ten. The gifts operate within an Ekklesia.

The apostles break new ground, thinking strategically, making connections and looking beyond the here and now. We may know people close to us like that or follow well-known authors and speakers with these gifts. Paul was a businessman as well as an apostle – working to make and sell tents and impact the marketplace (Acts 18:1-4). The prophets listen to what the Spirit is saying; they bring hope and challenge the status quo and are often mobilising prayer. Pastors read people well, they spot issues and get alongside; equally, they have a passion to develop and grow people.

These ministries are not just for the Church – with an Ekklesia mindset we can see that they are for the world and the workplace as well.

Find people you look up to, 2. The Ekklesia has elders, people who see the gaps and barriers, they spot talent and mentor people. Elders are mentioned more than 120 times in the Old Testament and more than sixty times in the New Testament. They should be encouragers, generous listeners and enablers, people of integrity and builders of unity. They have a spiritual authority. 'Elders' is not a term in regular use in most churches, and when it is, it often links to governance rather than sharing wisdom. Elders may not be formally recognised or appointed by your church, but I believe you will find some people fit the calling. If you want to be deliberate about your development, seek out some elders with spiritual maturity and relevant experience who will understand your situation.

Find a mentor. Mentors give us advice. They are normally people with more experience who have seen some of the issues and opportunities we face already. People normally pick a mentor to give them specific support – there are many strong mentoring groups for women in the workplace, ethnic groups, or workers with a disability – any group that knows it has to get past more barriers and hurdles to succeed. We may simply look for a mentor who is also a Christian in the workplace. Increasingly, two-way cross-generational mentoring relationships are being put in place – with the older person giving input on organisational issues and the younger person giving input on new technology, how to engage and motivate younger workers, etc.

Find a coach. A coach may be a more formal or even a professional relationship. The best coaches help us to shape our way forward. They help us understand our strengths and our impact on others. Their focus is on getting us to think through the approach that works best for us and our situation. They then encourage us to commit to specific actions. They may work with us on a specific issue where we want a breakthrough, or more generally on issues such as clarifying our priorities, shaping our personal development or preparing for a major project or promotion. Time with a coach should be energising, giving fresh goals and actions.

Keep a journal. Many people journal. It is a deliberate reflection tool. This will take different forms, depending on your personality and interests. Some like to record the details. They can tell you where they were on holiday in 2013, how long it takes them to drive to Bridlington, and what were the fifteen learning points from the project they led last November. This is a significant learning tool for them. Others would like to be more disciplined but find it hard to journal. A deliberate start is to get a good journal and write some key reflections in it – at the end of the week or after a challenging situation. Some people are more systematic and will always put:

1) What went well?
2) What would I do differently next time?
3) A key learning point or action.

Advise and support others. Of course, this is not all one-way traffic. Some people can just be learning sponges: they are at every conference, read in detail, carry considerable knowledge – but accumulating information is not the same as being wise. Wisdom needs to be activated; it gets refined and strengthened when we share wisdom with others. If we look at Daniel and his friends, I imagine them helping each other, asking each other how things were going, and that all-important question, 'How are you feeling about this?' Imagine facing King Nebuchadnezzar, the destroyer of nations: they will have needed each other's wisdom and prayers to prepare. Those who teach, mentor, coach and advise others well are always learning. Indeed, we create a much more mutual learning relationship when we are vulnerable and humble, recognising where we need to improve or rebuild.

Small groups: the engine room

The small group should be the engine room of your spiritual growth. We normally think of it as a church-based group – but I have had experience of small groups from within the workplace and 'project teams' where we are working together on key issues. There is a simple focus – helping each other to flourish in our walk with Jesus.

To do this we need to keep asking the question, why? Often, we lose our purpose and so it is good to ask our small group from time to time, 'Why do we exist?' The good small group is sharply focused on each member's impact in the world, including the workplace. The heart of the small group changes when we see each other with God's eyes. He wants us all to know how deep His love is for us, and to see us released by that love.

That means we invest time in understanding each other's stories and situations. It is praying for Will the anaesthetist at the local hospital – he describes his role as often being the last person someone sees before they go into a serious, often life-threatening, operation. It might be praying for Becky in a very demanding university admissions role, often dealing with an intense workload while juggling family care. It might be Andrew researching causes and cures for cancer. Equally, it might be retiree John helping his sister with dementia to cope with everyday life. Really supportive group members are continually praying and, just as important, encouraging each other, for example, by WhatsApp. They are investing in each other's well-being because they are wonderfully there for each other.

Some good friends lead a 'small group' with twenty-five members (obviously 'small' is a flexible concept!). During Covid-19, the group changed radically and became a 'flourishing group'. They had a Zoom meeting immediately after the church meeting to catch up with each other over a virtual coffee. They changed their meetings to include more worship, prayer and testimony. They set up a women's prayer group and a men's prayer group. They shared their feelings, concerns, worries and hopes in their meetings and over WhatsApp. One morning someone shared that his neighbour had been rushed into hospital with a serious health issue. The group prayed, and soon after the next-door neighbour returned home with doctors saying they could no longer find the source of the problem. The neighbour is telling everyone about the power of prayer. The group, of course, is now praying with even greater commitment and expectation. The members are interdependent, growing closer to God and seeing His favour on them.

Iron sharpening iron

Difficult or disruptive conversations create the sparks that come when 'iron sharpens iron' (Proverbs 27:17). Have you a friend who will look you in the eye and ask, 'Are you doing too much?' Have you a friend who will say, 'Talk me through your walk with God. Are you investing enough time in hearing from Him, in knowing His peace in your life?'

Here are some more challenges – can you find a friend who will discuss these with you?

- How are you doing health wise?

- What does being led 'beside quiet waters' (Psalm 23:2) look like to you and are you doing it enough?

- How is your spiritual development? What type of input really makes you think? Is it a book? Time on your own with God? A challenging sermon from social media or church? Conversations with others? Do you give enough time to this?

- What is hurting you? Frustrating you? Annoying you? Can we pray about this?

- Do you get enough prayer support? Is there someone standing with you weekly? If not, what could you do about it?

- What is God's call on your life at the moment? If you were a boat heading to a port, is anything leading you away from your destination?

- What do you feel are the gifts God has given you? What does it feel like when you are flourishing in those gifts and using them well?

- What are your best gifts to your family? Do you use those gifts enough?

- Who do you want to flourish? What can you do to help them flourish?

- We all have limitations, we all hit difficult patches, we all have times when it feels as though everything is on top of us – what do you do in those times?

- What is your key work focus at the moment? What are your hopes and aspirations? What would cause colleagues to say, 'Wow!'?

Some will ask, 'Who are you accountable to?' Sometimes that can be constraining, but there is the need for people we can have the difficult conversations with. We had a slightly embarrassing but important conversation with my weekly prayer group some years ago when we talked about porn. Being open was liberating. Porn can destroy individuals and their marriages – it can become addictive; bringing it out into the open destroys its hold. You may need a similar discussion about how you manage privilege and power, or the impact of commercialism and the need for 'stuff' in your life. We need the support of 'grown-up' conversations and wisdom around us.

My story

One of the key changes in my life was when a Christian elder in the business community encouraged me to meet with some others in business to talk and pray together. We had many intense and stimulating discussions over a good curry. We found we had a shared aspiration – to see God move in our particular workplace. Twenty years ago, that led to a commitment to reflect on the week ahead and then send a weekly emailed prayer request so we could support each other.

There are so many times when I have been stuck in difficult meetings not knowing what to do next (while keeping my supportive professional face in place!), when I am spurred on by the fact that the guys have been praying. There is a way forward. Over twenty years, all of us have made significant career decisions and faced many moments of great challenge, but the regular pattern of prayer and the ability to contact each other has been like a rock for troubled times. The group started with five of us and is now just three – but three is quorate. Three is enough to bind and loose (Matthew 18:18-20). Equally, there is real comfort in having two guys who are for me, committed to my success and regular encouragers. Richard and Mark, my prayer partners, are an integral part of my story. I am incredibly grateful for them and our simple but powerful weekly prayer cover.

Other groups have also been very important. I used to work with a Christian leadership and change consultancy – it was a privilege to have other Christians around me where we could pray for the business, our clients and our impact.

I am grateful to a church small group that took everybody's commitment to be kingdom people seriously. There was high-calibre prayer support when we stood with fathers and mothers as they prayed for their kids, or for mothers as we prayed for fruitfulness in the school playground, and for us to be able to tell our stories of being a Christian in the workplace. A small group should be a place for kingdom authority; it is one of the key things to learn together, that as we listen together, we sense God's purpose and pray into it. We might have authority to stand against bullying in the school, domestic violence in our streets and team tensions in the workplace. We can pray for wisdom, opportunities to bless and for workplace breakthroughs. Does your small group know enough about your work to give you high-quality support?

Call to action

If we want to be wise, we need each other's wisdom. Others see things I don't see; their approach might be different. 'By wisdom a house is built, and through understanding it is established; through knowledge its rooms are filled with rare and beautiful treasures' (Proverbs 24:3-4). Invest in building a support network.

How much time do you currently invest in your growth – through learning and development? Give some time to think and pray about this. How many minutes or hours do you want to commit each month?

Where do you invest this time in this season? Is it spiritual growth? Professional growth? To grow your confidence in a skill or issue?

Who, given your particular strengths and passions, can help you flourish? In the workplace? Spiritually? Career-wise? In your impact outside work?

If you were feeling vulnerable or felt you were struggling with an issue, who would you look to for pastoral support?

Application

One of the most deliberate things we can do to grow and develop is to get people around us who help us thrive in the workplace. People who help us think, reflect, innovate and change.

Prayer

Lord, You have plans for me. You shape me and call me. I thank You for all the ways You have helped me grow, and the people who have stood with me. Let me value wisdom, let me pursue wisdom, let me speak wisdom. Amen.

Chereta's story

Chereta is a solicitor specialising in banking and finance law. Her story of getting this role shows God's hand in providing wisdom and support. Chereta graduated from university in 2008 and then completed a two-year law conversion course (providing non-law graduates with degree-level training in the key aspects of law). This was not a good time for aspiring lawyers and the job market struggled. She volunteered to work for Birmingham City Mission and felt God would bless her in this. A friend partnered with her in prayer, asking God for a good legal role.

After some months, she discovered that a colleague had links to a local office of a national law firm. This helped her obtain a trainee role. Solicitors' roles were offered annually and Chereta applied, along with thirty other trainees from her firm, plus external applicants. Before the interviews she met with someone from Chaplaincy Plus,[50] a local Christian charity supporting the business community. The person prayed strongly for God's favour on her application, and she secured the one available place.

Chereta is open about her faith and will talk comfortably about her church. She offers to pray with people who are struggling and sees herself as 'representing the body of Christ'.

Being a black woman in the legal profession has not always been easy. She often attends meetings where she is the only black person in the room, and is aware that she clearly stands out and some people may not be on her side. This can be very challenging, and she feels she has not always had the support she would have treasured from within her church. She does not feel able to ask for prayer as she feels the church would not see her workplace challenges as a key prayer priority. She values the ongoing mentoring Chaplaincy Plus gives her. Its City Women group provides an opportunity for women who work in Birmingham to meet together and think about spiritual and practical issues that impact their working lives.

Alongside her job, Chereta still volunteers with Birmingham City Mission and its work with young people. Her vision is that

---

[50] www.chaplaincyplus.org.uk (accessed 23rd October 2021). Chaplaincy Plus is a Birmingham-based support network for people in the business community.

the next generation should be greater than the current (her) generation. 'It's fundamental. They have so much to offer. I listen to them; they have profound things to say. What's to come is really exciting. We are seeing the light switched on in a new generation of torch bearers.'

Chapter Five
The Call to Lead

Why do you want to lead?

The apostle Paul was an interesting leader. A key leadership success factor is followership, and while he had many people who were incredibly loyal, he wrote of how others had abandoned him (2 Timothy 3:8-9), and he famously fell out with his generous mentor Barnabas over taking John Mark with them on a mission trip (Acts 15:39). He talked about people criticising him for being less impressive when he turned up in person than his 'weighty and forceful' letters suggested (2 Corinthians 10:10). But he had a great leader's heart – and we can see Paul's heart in his prayers for the Ekklesia. He was incredibly caring and loving.

There was another side to the intellectual giant and theologian – he led with a deep love.

Paul knew that leadership was hard. People are unpredictable, situations change quickly, and it can be hard to manage your impact. But look at his heart! There are so many remarkable prayers in Paul's letters that show this leader's heart. Here is a famous example – imagine praying this for the people you lead:

> I pray that the eyes of your heart may be enlightened in order that you may know the hope to which he has called you, the riches of his glorious inheritance in his holy people, and his incomparably great power for us who believe.
> (Ephesians 1:18-19)

The words are not normal business language, but it is a simple and powerful prayer for *all* those you work with to come to know Jesus, and for any Christians you work with to have a power encounter with Him. He definitely wants people to flourish! This gives what we will pick up later, a Jesus flavour to the way we lead.

We are called to the workplace, and we want to explore our call to lead. But our starting point is this – Jesus plans to impact the people around us. If we live in the fullness of Christ, we are an amazing asset to our place of work. Listen to this prayer of Paul – he is reflecting God's heart for the people he leads:

> I pray that *you*, being rooted and established in love, may have power, together with all the Lord's holy people, to grasp how wide and long and high and deep is the love of Christ, and to know this love that surpasses knowledge – that you may be filled to the measure of all the fullness of God.
> (Ephesians 3:17-19, italics mine)

We are God's agents for change; every place we go to can be transformed because we are the Ekklesia, with God's authority revealed through His love. Loving is not always easy, which is why Paul makes it a major prayer focus.

The countercultural starting point for Christians in leadership is to follow. We are called to follow Jesus and depend on Him. There is a tendency in Christian circles to get this out of balance and make leadership the great pinnacle of Christian experience. It is not. Followership, a servant heart, humility and seeking God's voice is the pinnacle. The better we get at this, the wiser our leadership becomes.

We do not need to have 'leader' in our job description to have leadership influence. Whatever our job role, we lead when we are the ones who take a risk, encourage someone else, ask for help or raise concerns. Each of us, whatever our role, is called to bless, called to bring God's love and shalom. Each of us can be proactive and set an example. We lead through our impact on those around us. Leadership is watching out for colleagues, and it can include managing upwards when your own leader is struggling, or needs fresh ideas, or asks for feedback.

A leadership role

Of course, for many people, leadership is a full-time role. They may lead teams, projects, departments or entire businesses/ organisations. Leaders find their own particular ways to lead, and some lead significantly more effectively than others. Good leadership impacts commercial success, business innovation, meeting deadlines and staff retention. Good leaders see people giving that extra effort, contributing fresh ideas or ways to improve the current ways of doing things.

One of the most influential leadership thinkers is committed Christian Patrick Lencioni. He asks a fundamental question for all leaders: What motivates you? It links closely with our theme 'The call to lead'. What do you think your call is? He describes two different approaches:

1. **The Reward-centred Call** – They see leadership as a reward for their hard work and contribution, and as a reward it should be pleasant. Reward-centred people tend to stay involved in the areas of the job that interest them, where they feel they can continue to make a good contribution, but they may avoid the aspects of the job they do not like.

2. **The Responsibility Call** – Here, there is a deep sense of responsibility for the people who work for you, to your key stakeholders and customers. It is a call to take responsibility for the performance and morale, to grow capacity and to

ensure people always know what is expected of them. It is a call to see others flourish.[51]

Lencioni is leading a 'moral crusade' for responsible and authentic leadership. He discusses restoring 'the collective attitude that leadership is meant to be a joyfully difficult and selfless responsibility. I am convinced we will see companies become more successful, employees more engaged and fulfilled, and society more optimistic and hopeful.'[52]

I have worked as a leadership coach with many leaders. One of the most fruitful partnerships has been with the deputy CEO of a major hospital. We continually talk about getting the best out of his team; he invests considerable time in their one-to-ones, reviewing their impact and reputation. He puts in place initiatives and support to help them succeed. There is no doubt that he invests in their success. But he is also prepared to have the uncomfortable conversations.

Reward-centred Leaders can go out of their way to avoid difficult and uncomfortable conversations. Responsibility Leaders know the problem won't go away. They are objective about the issues and will give their people opportunities to change, but if the change does not happen, they know the best thing for everyone is to move the individual on. My friend has some very good rescue missions under his belt where he has given people the clear, objective feedback they needed to change their approach. But he also carries the responsibility of removing people who did not lead their own teams well, did not build confidence with their key stakeholders and seemed overwhelmed by the job.

Team meetings are a very good test of leadership. Some see them as a chore and have very low expectations of the meetings they attend or lead. They prepare badly, and this leads to low

---

[51] Patrick Lencioni, *The Motive: Why So Many Leaders Abdicate Their Most Important Responsibilities* (Hoboken, NJ: Jossey-Bass, 2020). This is a paraphrase of key concepts in the book.
[52] Lencioni, *The Motive*, p170.

engagement in the attendees. They struggle to get clear decisions and they do not follow the team meetings up to see if any actions actually happen. Guess what – the actions are not followed through! The key message is 'run great team meetings'! Invest in them, prepare well, follow through and ensure meetings are inspiring and engaging.

Liz Wiseman has written an excellent leadership book called *Multipliers*.[53] She describes the leaders who make their teams think hard – who invest time in new ideas, solving difficult problems and seeing the team meeting as a key engine for progress. These leaders acknowledge that the experience and the ideas of the team are better than the leader alone can bring, they energise and challenge their team in collective and one-to-one meetings. Great team meetings build trust and shared accountability: the whole team flourishes.

A leadership parable

Jesus used parables to stimulate ideas. Here is a workplace parable where we meet Andrea and her husband, Sam, and their mentor/elder, the wise and encouraging Jacob.[54]

Andrea works as a project manager in a housing association. It is an important role to her. Having been brought up by a single mother in social housing, she really appreciates that having their own home changes people's life chances. She knows her customers see having a home as a key step in building their lives, getting work, raising families and becoming part of a local community. She has recently been invited to apply for the job as the company's change and transformation manager. This would be a significant promotion for her, giving her a team of six people to manage, but more than that, it is a leadership role across the organisation, leading a wide range of projects impacting all the key departments.

---

[53] Liz Wiseman, *Multipliers: How the Best Leaders Make Everyone Smarter* (New York, NY: Harper Business, 2017).
[54] All characters are fictional.

Andrea and her husband are both committed Christians and she wants to be sure this leadership role is the right one for her. They have a friend called Jacob, who originally came as a student from Nigeria and now runs a successful civil engineering firm that he started and built up twenty years ago.

Jacob offers to meet Andrea and discuss the future with her. Andrea and Sam see Jacob as an elder/father figure, and a man of deep faith and wisdom.

Andrea opens up the issue she is thinking through with Jacob. 'People say anyone can lead – and to a degree I guess that is probably true. But the challenge for me is, can I lead well enough? Most of this job is about leading people who don't work for me and getting some of the senior people committed to changes that might initially cause extra work.'

Jacob sits back and smiles. 'Andrea, I call it the "kick a cat test". Do I lead people so that they go home feeling depressed, tired out and frustrated? If I do, the poor old cat, and maybe the rest of the family, suffer. If I can inspire them to see that their job is important, but much more that, they are important, and they are adding real value, then the cat can wander about in complete safety.

'My senior managers know that the greatest impact they have is by giving their people clarity. In particular, it's my job to communicate the big picture constantly and repetitively to everyone. My managers must help them apply it locally. An old marketing adage says that when you are driving change, people need to hear the message seven times before they accept and adapt. So I need to ensure my managers understand the *why* message. Why are we doing this? Why is it important to do it well? My firm must compete with much bigger organisations. We win and lose business by our expertise and the quality of our delivery and commitment. For you, Andrea, if you want to drive change programmes, it's on top of their day-to-day work, so they need to be inspired by regular and upbeat *why* messages.'

Andrea looks thoughtful and comments, 'I have led a small team of three people before, but I guess this involves bigger messages, a vision of what we can achieve. But how do I take people with me and, I guess just as important, what happens when people don't actually deliver what I am looking for?'

Jacob leans forward and makes a chopping motion with his hand. 'There are consequences! People's behaviour, what they do, is driven by consequences. If you phone someone and you are dealt with pleasantly and well, you are likely to phone again. But if they are grouchy and this makes you feel as grouchy as they are, you are unlikely to phone again. It's like an action and a response – either positive or negative.

'There is so much you can do as a leader to catch people showing the behaviours you want. It is easy to see the great achievements and it is important to celebrate them. But I've found it's also important to recognise the high level of work and time that went into a big bid that the customer turned down, or the well-designed building that did not hit the delivery deadline because of unexpected weather. I will encourage the person who rarely speaks up when they contribute ideas to a team meeting. Good leaders catch someone doing the right thing and go out of their way to acknowledge it. A key message on praise is – don't be vague. Phrases like 'well done' and 'that was good' are too vague. What was it you specifically appreciated, and you want to see again?'

Jacob smiles as he continues, 'You talk about people letting you down. This is where we get to consequences – part two! When someone makes a mistake or is not performing or contributing at the level I expect, there must be consequences as well. If not, it undermines all those who do make the extra effort. Of course, the problem may lie with me! If I have not properly communicated my standards and timelines it is my fault if they keep missing them! I know some leaders struggle with this, but in my experience, when you really care about what you do, you have to be willing to have uncomfortable conversations. It needs to be done with deep respect – I want to rescue the situation, not undermine my team.

'I find it best to just present the facts – what actually happened ("You said this," "You arrived late," "Melanie was upset by your comments"). Then we talk about what happened as a result (the customer complained, you have a colleague who does not trust you). Then we will look together at what caused the problem (there could be reasons I don't fully understand – perhaps they bumped the car on the way to work). Hopefully the issue becomes an opportunity for learning.'

Andrea and Sam sit thoughtfully for a while, reflecting on what Jacob has said. They appreciate that Jacob has a track record of success and would have learned these lessons as he grew his business. Andrea picks up another theme. 'Jacob, I was reading something the other day that suggests less than 10 per cent of leaders can intuitively see the big picture,[55] and all the different elements that shape the future. What happens if I am not strategic enough?'

Jacob replies, 'To be honest, Andrea, all the discussions you and I have had in church about the food bank work, and collaborating with other churches and linking our food poverty work with Christians Against Poverty[56] tell me you do see the big picture and think strategically. But my advice is two-fold. First, to become more strategic you need a good curiosity about what is happening across your organisation and the challenges and opportunities it faces. A workplace with its workforce, resources and customer base is a complex system, and strategists can see that. It's like looking down from on high at a play and seeing where everyone should go. Strategists see the links; they seek alignment.

'Second,' he continues, 'your work depends on lots of others, so your key challenge is to help your team and colleagues to

---

[55] 'The hidden talent: Ten ways to identify and retain transformational leaders', PwC, 2015, osca.co/pubs/pwc-hidden-talent (accessed 2nd December 2021). This PwC Research suggests only 8 per cent of all leaders in organisations could be classified as strategists.
[56] Christians Against Poverty, www.capuk.org (accessed 2nd November 2021).

think rigorously and creatively, because this builds their commitment. Coming from Nigeria, one of my early challenges was to make sure I was getting the culture right, working with people in a way that got the best out of what was primarily a British workforce. I suppose it made me more curious, not just about engineering, my first love, but about people, and they became a deeper love. I found you need to really invest in your meetings, plan them with care, have tools that open up discussion and encourage input. Keep acknowledging good ideas and contributions and you will increase how much you get. I learned early on, quite painfully, in fact, that I did not have all the answers, and it would have frustrated my team enormously if I pretended I knew it all.

'I know this is business basics, but you need to make it as easy as possible for people to deliver what you want. Don't bog people down in the details. Everyone needs a clear, simple understanding of your vision/outcomes, what the next steps and priorities are and what you expect of them. You need to be deliberate and look at the risks and barriers.

'In my work we needed to keep innovating; customers were very good at giving us difficult problems to solve and we had to develop an approach that made us stand out. You will need to keep enabling people around you to look and ask, "Can we do things differently?" In your field, I guess they need to understand the changing context in the housing market and ask how they can best adopt new approaches.'

They are coming to the end of their discussion and Sam is eager to help his wife as she makes her decision. He asks Jacob a final question: 'Jacob, we really appreciate your wisdom and helping us think this through. I guess the key question is, what do you think? Can Andrea do the job?'

Jacob looks thoughtful. After a meaningful pause, his face lights up as he turns to Andrea and says, 'Well, I wish she was a civil engineer! I would love someone with her personality and integrity working for me. But I can't tell you about this job; you need to pray and ask God if He has opened a door for you. My prayer is for you to really know His wisdom. At times like this I look for His peace, His shalom, His pleasure and ask Him whether He is with me on this.

'But I will give you one last challenge. Will anybody follow you? I suspect you know the answer to that already. When you suggest new approaches, do people listen and follow through? Does it come naturally to you to build others up and encourage them? When you work with others, do you give them feedback to help them improve? A key element to followership is whether they can trust you. This is more than, "Are you a trustworthy person?" I suspect that will be a given for you. It's, "Can they trust you to deliver on your promises? Can they trust you to take on board their ideas and concerns? Can they trust you to communicate well to them?" If the answer to those questions is "yes", then I suggest that helps you to make your decision.'

The encouraging leader

Joseph the Cypriot appears in the book of Acts and gives us a good leadership model. He has developed his leadership credibility with the elders in Jerusalem and they give him a nickname, Barnabas, meaning 'son of encouragement' (Acts 4:36). As nicknames go, it's not a bad one to have! He is described as 'a good man, full of the Holy Spirit and faith, and a great number of people were brought to the Lord' (Acts 11:24).

He is sent on a problem-solving mission to Antioch, 250 miles north of Jerusalem, a vibrant trading centre near the Mediterranean. Barnabas goes to support the growing Antioch church. This is a diverse city, with many Gentile believers, and the Christian faith is being shaped here. They need a revised theology that looks at Scripture through new lenses. Barnabas helps develop a detailed teaching plan. It gives the emerging Ekklesia a new understanding, and it is in Antioch that followers of Jesus are first called Christians (v26). So we see Barnabas, an encourager and teacher. He sees the need for clear leadership –

to enable the growing Ekklesia to come together in this city, and to know what God expects of them. Barnabas spots the skills and passion of Paul and wants to make best use of Paul's gifts. This man was an enemy of the early Church, determined to stop the new faith. He was dramatically converted on the road to Damascus and then spent ten years back in his native Tarsus. Barnabas calls for Paul to come and help him shape what first serves as a theology for Antioch but gradually takes shape as the theological bedrock for the whole Church (vv25-26). They teach for a year. Then they are commissioned to go to Jerusalem to provide funds at a time of famine. This is the start of a series of partnership journeys. They then head to Cyprus and preach the gospel (Acts 13:4). 'Up to this point Saul has been, it seems, the junior partner, himself a protégé of Barnabas.'[57]

This highlights a key, countercultural leadership gift from Barnabas to Paul. Barnabas carries the authority and the experience. But in the Cyprus mission and subsequently, it becomes clear that Paul can preach well and has a spiritual authority as he challenges Elymas the sorcerer (vv9-10). On the next stage of the journey, the writer of Acts, Luke, recognises the leadership reversal and writes, 'From Paphos [the capital of Cyprus], Paul and his companions sailed to Perga in Pamphylia' (v13).

So Barnabas seems to have surrendered the leadership to Paul. We can deduce that this son of encouragement recognises Paul's gifts, and God's hand on his former pupil. More than that, Barnabas is much more focused on Paul achieving all he can achieve than on his own status.

Colleagues of mine have worked with many well-known global Christian organisations. One of the recurring themes has been the reluctance of older people to hand over responsibility. In some ways it is natural that they fear the loss of reputation and authority. But Barnabas shows us a different way – that in releasing the next generation under God's direction,

---

[57] Tom Wright, *Paul: A Biography* (London: SPCK, 2018).

encouraging them to flourish in their call, the wider Church is blessed. It is also countercultural in the workplace. Letting talent emerge, encouraging gifted people to take on more responsibility benefits the wider organisation. It can multiply and spread leadership away from one person to an enthusiastic group of new people.

There is a particular Christian call to release, to spot talent. We want to build a diverse, confident pool of skills and capabilities in the Ekklesia, where everyone is held in honour. We also long to see Christians in the workplace committed to leading teams where every person of talent, whatever their age or background, flourishes.

That added Jesus flavour

In cooking, an added ingredient can make all the difference. Italian cooks know this well and add some fresh basil or oregano to change the taste, smell and appearance. The French might add a delicate sauce which again achieves that impact. We have put some general leadership lessons and good practices in the earlier material – but what happens when we add Jesus?

We came across Terry's story in Chapter One, a well-respected head teacher for what had been a struggling Church of England school. He had helped turn it around and was earning a good reputation for his leadership, so good that the Shadow Secretary of State for Education (from the main opposition party) and other politicians visited the school to see what was different. They picked up two distinctly Jesus characteristics that had impacted the school. One was the belief that all children are made in the image of God (Genesis 5:1) and should be treated with respect and honour. This framed the school's clear vision to serve the children, their families and the local community. The second was forgiveness: they gave the pupils second and third chances. They were clear about what was wrong, but they did not remove pupils; they helped to turn them around, and forgave them for wrongdoing. The visiting politicians were astounded by the impact this had on the school culture.

We are called to bring Jesus into the workplace. His values give a distinct flavour to the way we lead and interact with others.

Distinctive values

We have already looked at six key kingdom values/flavours in Chapter Two. They will inevitably impact our leadership approach.

- **Righteousness.** As righteous leaders flourish and are given opportunity to shape and influence their organisations, their success blesses others.

- **Shalom.** Your peace, your belief that God has His hand on you and your team, your capacity to trust God in the most challenging of situations, has a huge impact.

- **Mercy.** Avoiding the politics and undermining, helping those who struggle.

- **Justice.** Fair decisions, integrity, treating people equally.

- **Compassion.** That gut-wrenching concern for those in need in your team and with other colleagues and customers.

- **Forgiveness.** You give your colleagues another chance, and another, not in a weak way – you want to help them improve – but you are generous.

In addition, leaders will be shaped by:

- **Prayer.** We will look at this in a later chapter, but praying for people gives us a fresh understanding of them.

- **Unity and peacemaking.** Unity is a very Christian concept; Jesus wants us to be one (John 17:11, 22). It is a deep aspiration because we know the Church has struggled to unite. In the workplace, do we actively address the relationship challenges? This is where peacemaking is very different from peacekeeping. Peacekeeping can be like putting a lid on a bubbling pot to hide the turmoil beneath. Peacemakers go deep; they address the hurts, explore misunderstandings, encourage forgiveness and create new ways of working.

- **The gospel.** Again, we will look at this later, and to some extent it is an uncomfortable area because being 'religious' can cause tensions. But you can't help living out the kingdom. Jesus demonstrates the gospel powerfully as He meets with women, children, lepers and tax collectors. Everyone matters – that's good news to the workplace!

Juliet's story

Juliet works for a company that provides a range of support services to the 134,000 RICS[58] members, such as bereavement counselling, stress, mental health, financial support, dealing with family breakdown, etc.

Moving to this organisation was an interesting journey, as Juliet had been working for a parenting charity with refugees, people struggling with poverty and so on, and it seemed a much 'godlier' place to be. But she felt God's call to this professional body giving support to people reluctant to admit they needed support.

Her approach to leading has been to 'find the best in people and polish it'. She will discuss weaknesses and vulnerabilities openly, and help wrong fits find a right fit for them without being destructive. She is committed to development and encouraging people to be their best. She encourages people to share. This commitment to listen, to be vulnerable and to be open is a key element of her job. It helped the team adjust their way of working during Covid-19 as team members juggled their

---

[58] RICS – Royal Institution of Chartered Surveyors.

roles and the challenges of juggling family responsibilities as they worked from home.

She advises leaders in their client companies, helping them manage mental health, stress and other issues more effectively by supporting and rescuing people who would previously have been discarded.

Starting out in her role, she did face some opposition from Christians who felt that motherhood was a sufficient call. Her husband and church have been very supportive, encouraging her to flourish and be who Christ made her to be.

Stepping up to lead

People will read this chapter from many different perspectives. You may lead hundreds of people. You may lead no one. But anyone who has a positive impact on their colleagues or customers is leading in some way. Some may never lead a team, but they lead change through the Jesus flavour they bring in.

On 1st December 1955, one African–American lady, Rosa Parks, in Montgomery, decided to stay seated on her bus when the driver demanded she surrender her seat for some standing white passengers. As a black person in the appallingly divided South, she knew she was breaking a law, but she remained seated for justice. She was arrested. That arrest gave her the determination never to be humiliated again. She became a moral leader although she had no authority, but her character impacted many people's attitudes and behaviour.[59]

One decision, one act of courage, led to a prolonged legal battle, a year-long boycott of the Montgomery buses and the eventual end of segregated travel. It became a catalyst for the civil rights movement.

Many years later, Bryan Stevenson, the author of *Just Mercy*, worked in the same city of Montgomery to release many black people wrongly put on death row and to address many other

---

[59] www.troy.edu (accessed 24th November 2021). Troy houses the Rosa Parks Museum; the website includes her story.

examples of blatant injustice. He tells of meetings with Rosa Parks, and her friend, where she shared her wisdom and mentored Bryan.[60] His determination and courage models hers, as do thousands of others who look to her as a leader because of her moral character and courage.

God moves in our *kairos* moments. He changes our expectations and moves us into action. He gives us boldness and courage for the moment. Paul describes this in 2 Corinthians 12:9-10:

> But he said to me, 'My grace is sufficient for you, for my power is made perfect in weakness.' Therefore I will boast all the more gladly about my weaknesses, so that Christ's power may rest on me. That is why, for Christ's sake, I delight in weaknesses, in insults, in hardships, in persecutions, in difficulties. For when I am weak, then I am strong.

It is that Jesus flavour that enables us to step up into leadership, even when things seem difficult, as the Holy Spirit enables us to do more than we could 'ask or imagine' (Ephesians 3:20).

We can lead by being committed to justice. Ben Lindsay writes about the huge difference between churches being diverse and being inclusive. The same is true for the workplace: are people really honoured and included? Creating inclusive communities, however, where black people feel that they are a valued part of the culture, not just observers, is more complicated. Ben Lindsay, as a person of colour, reflects on church, but again it can be true in the workplace: 'In my experience, black people in leadership or management are seen as a risk.'[61] He describes the leadership in the Antioch church: Barnabas from Cyprus, Simeon (Niger, the Latin for black), Lucius from North Africa, Manaen, raised among royalty, and Paul, a Jew from Asia (see Acts 13:1). This group of five prayed, worshipped and sought God together, releasing Barnabas and

---

[60] Bryan Stevenson, *Just Mercy* (London: Scribe Publications, 2020).
[61] Ben Lindsay, *We Need to Talk About Race* (London: SPCK, 2019), p98.

Paul to their new ministry call. Antioch had a key role in shaping our theology and values – interesting foundations for us!

The elephant in the room

I think we need to identify an elephant in the room. Church leaders and workplace leaders can often be wary of each other. We live in very different cultures; the workplace will normally be faster paced, and directive. The workplace may be a place where we feel more supported and appreciated. Churches' ways of operating and teaching may seem out of touch.

Jesus spoke passionately about the need for unity as He laid the foundations for the Church (John 17:11). It leaves a simple challenge – is there a unity between *all* those with strategic and leadership skills across the Ekklesia? Are the apostolic gifts some workplace leaders have being as well used as they possibly can be? Are we helping church leaders to flourish and handle all the challenges that face them? In these changing times, are there people church leaders can go to for ideas, and new approaches? Is there a big vision that sees God's kingdom impacting all our work spheres and the places where we live? Great leaders help everyone flourish. What can be released as the whole Ekklesia thinks well, listens well and makes good decisions together? Everyone is valued and encouraged.

I know many people who feel stifled in the current church set-up. We need to talk openly about our concerns if we are to build unity. It is time for a reset. The real sign an Ekklesia/church is working well should be how well every member is flourishing in their call and the church's impact on the local community. Are individuals being released and encouraged to change the culture around them and bless their workplace – and are their stories and testimonies used, like Rosa Parks', to inspire many more into action?

Call to action

Having led and worked for a leadership change consultancy, I have shelves full of leadership books. You can follow all sorts of different gurus and theories and models. But for us, the difference must be Jesus. I like the story of sending out seventy-two disciples (see Luke 10) ahead of Him to every town and place where He was to go. It resonates with Jesus sending us to our workplace because that too is where He wants to go. He gives clear instructions. He tells them why they are going – to prepare the harvest field (v2); He tells them how they should act and what they should do (vv3-11). He inspires them to meet the challenge of going to places that may or may not welcome them. In verse 9 He encourages them to heal ill people (a nice challenge for the workplace?). He gives clarity and encouragement. He sends them out.

But I also love what happens next: they learn together. 'How did it go?' He asks, and lets them tell their stories; and He encourages them. He knows He is preparing them for the future, to understand that with 'all things are possible with God' (Mark 10:27). Hear His voice of leadership for you today. He is sending you, to lead like Jesus, and 'all things are possible'.

Application

- We have looked at the characteristics of good leadership – with that added 'Jesus flavour'. What characteristics do you have?

- What impact do you have on people around you? What could you improve?

- Think about three key colleagues. What do you really appreciate about them? What do you value about them? What are your hopes and aspirations for them? How can you best help them flourish?

- How could you really bless your church leader/s? What do they do well that you appreciate? How can you bring fresh ideas in a non-threatening but high-impact way?

Prayer

Help me lead with Your heart, Lord. Let me see people with Your eyes and bless and encourage them with Your wisdom. Amen.

Matt's story

Matt Lambert is a pioneering leader. He is the CEO of a housing charity. Matt has let his Christian faith permeate the organisation and its culture.

Enterprise Homes Group[62] is based in Wolverhampton, formed to look after people transitioning through homelessness and to ensure they are given advice and support. It looks to give people a clear pathway out of homelessness. Through several trading subsidiaries, it now provides a range of building and maintenance services, undertakes house clearances and runs a shop, through which it provides opportunities for training and work experience.

As a young man, Matt was bullied for being different and struggled with social exclusion. It has taken him years to learn that it is not just OK, but actually very good to be him. God has a call on his life, loves who he is and gives him confidence to be who he was called to be.

Flourishing in who God has called him to be, Matt has built and led a different type of working culture. Enterprise is focused on helping its staff and the people it serves to thrive. Matt says, 'Our people are created with a purpose, built for community, and have a place they can claim in the universe. Our role is to help them get there.' They hold weekly staff one-to-one coaching and discipling sessions, inviting staff to talk about

---

[62] www.enterprisehomesgroup.org.uk (accessed 3rd November 2021).

what they want to think through today, encouraging their hopes, dreams and aspirations. The organisation operates like a work-based Ekklesia – believing that God transforms, calls, equips, enables and guides them.

Let us look at some of the key principles that shape the organisation:

- Building vulnerability, accountability and trust. This is a key part of the in-house discipleship programme, helping staff use their skills and build confidence in who God has called them to be.

- Investing time and resources in people and building flourishing relationships. An ongoing question in the organisation is, 'Are you being everything God created you to be? And doing the things He has called you to do?'

- Encouraging every team member to bring their best.

- No advertising for jobs in the past five years. They expect God-appointed people to turn up – and they do.

- Building a culture where people get a clear sense of acceptance and belonging.

- Avoiding the old hierarchical systems to get better thinking. Senior managers are there to enable people to try new things, and find their best approach.

- They like to express joy in the workplace: fun and flourishing go together!

- Forgiveness – if you mess up, managers ask, 'What could we [the organisation] have done better?'

The principles are reflected in Matt's very different CEO job description: 'The CEO is responsible for building and investing in relationships internally and externally, as the primary means of ensuring that the vision and values of the organisation are upheld and promoted and EHG is achieving its social aims and impact. This is achieved through building the right culture, coaching the staff and bringing strategic leadership to the organisation.'

Matt summarises his call to lead this way: 'It is entirely summed up in an expression that is central to our discipleship: "Free people, free people". I believe the call on my life is to lead by walking into a greater measure of personal freedom and taking others on that journey with me so that they can do likewise.' It expresses one of the great differences Christian leadership should have. People should see that added Jesus flavour as we help people around us to flourish.

Collaboration is a key element of the organisation's work. Matt says, 'Our vision is to make homelessness history, but we can only do this in close collaboration and partnership across the city.' As a gifted innovator and pioneer, he is also a keen advocate for Christians and civic authorities coming together to address homelessness nationally.

This is not a 'business as usual' operation. Matt has taken key principles and created a 'kingdom business'. It has that Jesus flavour of putting people first and trusting God to have a day-by-day hand on what it does and achieves.

Chapter Six
That Call to Be a Good Neighbour

Who is my neighbour?

Evangelism teaching can often focus on sharing Jesus with our next-door neighbour, or the people we meet in the supermarket. While this is legitimate, most people in the workplace have much deeper relationships with their colleagues than they do with their next-door neighbour, and considerably more than with those they meet when out shopping. Our work colleagues live life with us day by day. They may have significant financial worries, the stresses of splintering relationships and families, confidence issues, or even bigger problems such as serious illness or other crises. Life is much more in the open in the workplace than behind the closed doors and curtains of our local neighbourhoods. People normally think of their neighbour as someone who lives near them – in their neighbourhood. I suggest we also look on our 'neighbour' as someone we work with.

In Luke 10, Jesus makes our call clear; in verse 27 He picks up the great Jewish prayer, the Shema, 'Hear, O Israel: the LORD our God, the LORD is one. Love the LORD your God with all your heart and with all your soul and with all your strength' (Deuteronomy 6:4-5). This prayer is used twice daily by many Jews. It centres them on God. He is one, love Him with everything you have. They are told to constantly remember the prayer, to talk about it to their children, to bind it to their foreheads and to write it on their doorposts and bind it to themselves (vv7-9). It reminds them that they walk with God.

But Jesus adds a second commandment to the great Shema – quoting Leviticus 19:18 – to love our neighbours as we love ourselves (Luke 10:27). He links this central call to love God with the call to love our neighbour. When Jesus is asked, 'Who is my neighbour?' (v29) he describes the man who is beaten and left for dead but is helped by a Samaritan. This story stretches our understanding. Here the neighbour is not someone we have met before, nor someone who lives near us. He is from another ethnic group, but the good Samaritan is simply moved to help another human being. 'Love your neighbour' (v27). Three words that resonate through history. But we need to put them in context – our greatest command is to love God with all our heart, and that drives the call to love our neighbour.

Much of Jesus' ministry is in the marketplace. We do not know who Jesus lived near, but we do know He was open and approachable; we know He listened well and gave considered advice. We know He mixed with centurions, fishermen, synagogue rulers, widows, children, five-times married Samaritan women and many more.

Being a good neighbour in the workplace

'Oh, you've got to watch out for people like that, they're mood suckers!' I came across this memorable phrase while running a training session. Everybody nodded wisely, you have got to watch out for mood suckers. It demonstrates a powerful workplace lesson: our behaviour and attitude affects the people around us, and the impact can be positive or negative. The mood suckers moan a lot, they get stuck into the detail, they cut across others and will focus on why something can't or won't happen. They create a miserable, what-is-the-point mood and all joy heads for the exit signs!

Lots of things can suck the life out of a team or even an organisation. The atmosphere can be toxic, poisoned by office politics or lack of trust, where people undermine each other and try to create division. The team, or some elements of it, can be disengaged, they do not produce any ideas or improvements (they believe that's management's job!), they do not respond quickly and there are very low levels of participation in team meetings. This can then lead to peer pressure where keenness and hard work are criticised or frowned on by colleagues. Many cultures suffer from overt aggressive, get-it-done-now type bullying – or it can be the more drip drip drip of criticisms and undermining, where no idea, achievement or contribution is ever good enough.

Can a place like this be turned around or rebuilt? 'Live such good lives among the pagans that, though they accuse you of doing wrong, they may see your good deeds and glorify God on the day he visits us' (1 Peter 2:12). Good deeds can include acts of kindness, and they clearly have a high impact. These are the actions of people alert and aware of the needs and concerns of their neighbours. We can build a 'good neighbour mentality' in our workplace by asking God to keep our eyes and ears open.

As we have seen, 'Barnabas' was a nickname, and it means 'son of encouragement'. Can you imagine the impact on our workplaces if God were to release a one-million Barnabas task force, to infiltrate work and make it a place where people felt supported and blessed? Can a toxic or demoralised culture turn around? This could have more impact than the biggest football stadium evangelistic campaign. But let's step back – God in His wisdom has already put His million-strong change force in place! If we began to think more like Barnabas and saw our call to encourage and bless, we would be a huge counterculture force across our society.

Of course, so much of this links to our mindset. How do we view our fellow workers? Many talk about creating a culture of honour – can this be done in the workplace? What does honour actually mean?

Honour is about how we see people. It is about valuing who God made them to be. We normally see and value people by their history, by our previous experiences with them, by their mistakes and their attitudes. When we honour someone, we see beyond this. It is like meeting someone who has an honorary title or office: we value the office as much as we value the person. So we honour fellow believers as children of God (Romans 8:14-17). We honour those we work with as people Jesus wants to have a relationship with, because Jesus wants 'all people to be saved and come to a knowledge of the truth' (1 Timothy 2:4).

This is such a key call for the Church. We impact our community – including our workplace community – through relationships. But relationships post-Covid are being strained. There are many workplaces where the norm is working from home or going to the office occasionally. Work used to be a place of friendships, conversations and support. We celebrated our football team's results, the concert we went to, our achievements, with our colleagues. We had important discussions about what would happen next in trending TV programmes. We are trying to balance that reduction in human interactions with the challenges of protecting people from mental health issues – loneliness, anxiety, depression. Now we need to find new ways to invest in workplace relationships. We need to create time for the 'How are you doing?' conversations.

An encouraging parable

Back to our fictional story. Andrea, now confirmed as change and transformation manager at the housing association, has gone for coffee in her church after the Sunday service with her husband, Sam. He works as a manager in the kitchen department at his local department store. They bump into Jacob and sit together. Jacob opens the conversation, 'Well, that was a challenging sermon about Barnabas – he was quite a character. I look forward to talking to him when we get to heaven!'

Sam responds enthusiastically, 'I love all the stuff about being an encourager. They keep telling us managers at work that the secret to good customer sales and good customer service is to work at encouraging our teams. It just seems so natural if we want to create the right environment.'

'I couldn't agree more,' says Jacob. 'It was really important when I was building the company up and seems even more important now. I want my workplace to be a happy environment to work, the sort of place where people give that extra effort because they really want to. As the owner I want to build an 'encouragement culture' where my senior and middle managers keep building their people skills. I also need to give a lead to that – how do I handle disagreements? Do I treat everyone the same – do I honour the cleaning team and the receptionists?'

Andrea sips her coffee and realises this is another opportunity to learn from her 'mentor', Jacob. 'I have just started out in my new job, and I really need to encourage people who don't work for me to give me great ideas and make sure they do their piece of the project plan. My previous boss was good with the thank-you cards, and he filled them with meaningful phrases like, "I really appreciate all the hard work you have put in to get the project over the line. I was proud to have you representing our team." What encouragements work for your team, Jacob?'

Jacob leans forward and says, 'I think of my team as a family. Encouragement needs to be credible – they need to know that if I tell them it is good, it really is good. I get that credibility by being honest and telling them when it is bad as well! As family, I need to go beyond talking about the task and results – important though that is – and encourage them as the unique people they are. I make it a habit to know about my teams, their families, where they live, what their interests are, and I do the same with key customers. Actually, my PA helps me. We make little cards with people's details, because it's important to me. I must admit I have not always been good on this. I can be very tasky, and when we first started the business all I would talk to people about was how we were doing against our targets and finance figures. But I have realised that treating everyone with respect is a key bottom-line issue as well.'

Sam pipes up, 'At work we have a weekly hero award. It all seems a bit silly but actually people like the recognition. We once opened a major extension to the store with some new facilities and a whole new range of goods. It took us a lot of extra hours to prepare and then run a series of opening events. The management put a flip chart in the canteen area and asked us to suggest some rewards. Jagwant, the facilities manager, suggested the prize should be, "The team goes to Jagwant's house to decorate his lounge." That did not get many votes, but we all went out for a paintballing evening.'

Andrea decides to keep pumping Jacob for ideas! 'What is it like for you when you want to reward or encourage someone who isn't in your top team?'

Jacob laughs. 'Well, I have made some mistakes there, as well. To encourage innovation and improvements we had an idea of the quarter scheme. People submitted ideas on a card and the top three answers got to have dinner with the board. When we saw a drop-off in the ideas, we realised that staff saw dinner with the board as more of a punishment than a treat and felt really uncomfortable! I find now it is worth talking to their manager about whether they would like something done in public or more quietly, and I get them to tell me their story. So I encourage them by listening to their story to understand more of what they have done.'

Andrea takes another sip of coffee and gives Sam her best disapproving look as he eats another biscuit. 'I guess as Christians we can use this to show our love to the people we work with. As you said, Jacob, our appreciation and encouragement need to be credible, because we want people to hit high standards. Being daily encouragers, like our friend Barnabas, really does help people to flourish. People want to be appreciated, and that appreciation is much more powerful if you tell people specifically what it is you appreciate them doing. Then they know what they can do again.' She laughs and says,

'So we can start the Barnabas system of everlasting appreciation and encouragement! Heaven at work.'

'Wow!' says Sam. 'That's deep, I think it deserves another biscuit!'

Like sheep without a shepherd

Matthew, in his Gospel, tells us that Jesus went through the 'towns and villages', teaching and healing and bringing good news (Matthew 9:35). He looked at the crowds and 'had compassion on them, because they were harassed and helpless, like sheep without a shepherd' (Matthew 9:36). Jesus was deeply moved by what He was. Do we stand with Jesus' eyes to look at the teams we work with?

Jesus asked His disciples to pray for 'the Lord of the harvest ... to send out workers into his harvest field' (v38). It mirrors the Great Commission; we are sent out to make disciples and to teach them (Matthew 28:19-20).

So Jesus and the disciples find places to interact. Paul talks to Lydia, a dealer in purple cloth, just outside the gates of Philippi by the river (Acts 16:13-14). Paul and Silas use the opportunity of being in prison (Acts 16:31)! Jesus talks to a woman at a Samarian well in John 4.

Here is another challenge to us. Can we change our mindset so we see ourselves as shepherds in the workplace, with our neighbours? In doing so we align ourselves with Jesus who sees His call to be the good shepherd. 'He calls his own sheep by name and leads them out. When he has brought out all his own, he goes on ahead of them, and his sheep follow him because they know his voice' (John 10:3-4).

The Message gives us this insight:

We're all like sheep who've wandered off and gotten lost.
We've all done our own thing, gone our own way.
And GOD has piled all our sins,
everything we've done wrong,
on him.

(Isaiah 53:6)

There are many times in the workplace when the harassed sheep need a shepherd – or at least, the local under-shepherd. It might be a time of bereavement; it might be a time of stress or uncertainty. People have deep needs; they might be financial, emotional, relational or spiritual. It happens in most workplaces.

Mental health. One in four people suffers from mental health issues[63] – anxiety, trauma, depression, stress and many other issues. They link with issues like loneliness, physical health issues, confidence, work pressure, divorce and separation. As a shepherd, you will want to accept those around you who are struggling, and understand what you can do to help – and where you can signpost for help. I recommend the resources and wisdom of Kintsugi Hope.[64]

Bereavement. Different cultures cope with bereavement in a variety of ways. But the impact of losing someone close and adjusting to the changes can take many months and sometimes a lifetime. Bereaved people often say their work colleagues handled them badly, often ignoring their struggle. Care for the Family has a range of teaching materials for a variety of situations. 'For decades death and grief have been a private matter, but our society is beginning to realise the huge impact that bereavement can have – also the potential for unprocessed loss to lead to mental health issues and other negative outcomes.'[65]

---

[63] 'Mental Health: New understanding, new hope', World Health Organization, 28th September 2001,
who.int/whr/2001/en/whr01_en.pdf (accessed 20th January 2022).
[64] www.kintsugihope.com (accessed 14th October 2021). This a great source of godly wisdom and encouragement – including training materials.
[65] www.lossandhope.org (accessed 22nd November 2021), a great source of resources and wisdom and materials for a bereavement course.

Stress. Stress happens when things feel out of your control. Out of control means different things to different people – some may be prone to an immediate panic, while others feel the situation can be handled and can react too late. Some jobs are more stressful than others; this may relate to the scope of the job and the time demands, whereas other jobs are just unpredictable and you need to be adaptable enough to handle them. For many, their stress is outside the workplace, but it inevitably impacts their behaviour and confidence. So stress hits us all differently.

These and many other challenges and issues hit our colleagues at work. It may be our whole team gets hit by an issue. It could be that we observe a change in a colleague's behaviour. They look more tired, they may be less punctual, they appear distracted, they may flare up or become more risk averse. The normal, 'How are you feeling?' or, 'You look tired, anything I can do?' may be met with, 'No, I'm OK.' Often people do not want to open the window on to what they are going through. We may need to be stronger: 'My friend, you don't seem to be your normal self. I would really appreciate a conversation to see if I can help you. Can we find some time today?'

Back to being a shepherd. Watch the sheep. You may not be an expert in mental health, or stress, or extreme tiredness, but you can listen, reach out, show them they are valued when they are feeling low. Given you may have no expertise in the area, you may have no solutions or ideas, but giving people your time and showing you value them can be so important. With deep issues, time and attention really make a big difference. You can listen, you can talk together about how they feel and what the options might be for them, you can offer to pray a blessing for them. I remember when a close friend of mine died at work unexpectedly. Another friend from church just sat me down and listened for an hour as he encouraged me to talk about Mike, what had made him special, what I would miss about him and how I was feeling. That hour was such a gift.

Talking by listening

Good shepherds have great conversations. The secret is in listening well. We live in a time when people are much more polarised on many issues. That means we don't listen well. We can find it easy to take offence or quickly dismiss other people as idiots, or arrogant, or uninteresting – and the conversation goes down from that point. Equally, we are more easily distracted by our phones, by the noise around us and by social media pulling us into the world of sound bites. Neighbours talk. *Good neighbours learn how to listen well.*

Conversations are key to life but are seldom something we practise or look to improve. Do you ever have that situation where you are forced to talk to others, and it all seems really strained with all the signs that it is heading for boring? Or you are with a person who talks with great enthusiasm but goes on and on and on? It's all about them and their story. You just have to look awake and make the occasional encouraging remark. But conversations are more than that. They are about listening, too. A good listener encourages, picking up key things the speaker is saying. A good listener honours the person talking and builds their confidence.

So here are some key tips on going deeper, and I am using them with an illustration. Let's imagine you are talking about someone's holiday plans.

- **Ask open questions.** 'Who, Why, What, When, How, Where?' Such questions get fuller answers. Why are you going there? What do you want to do when you are there? Why is that important to you? What will a really great day look like to you?

- **Avoid closed questions:** 'Did you?' Can you?' Will you?' These get short – often yes or no – answers.

- **Listen out for 'ping' words** that can take the subject deeper – especially words that show feelings. For example, 'You said you were worried. Why was that?' Or, 'You said it was great to spend time with the family – what other things do you do as family?'

- **Listen well, giving people your full attention.** Encourage them to talk. Be fully present – it's a gift you give the other person/people.

- **Go with the flow.** If they are really into the conversation about going to the theatre, let it flow. Don't cut across it; for example, 'That reminds me of a story of my dog...'

- **Don't play conversation tennis,** where we keep hitting the conversation ball back and forth. For example, 'We are going to Wales on holiday.' 'Oh, we're going to Suffolk.' 'Our kids will get to do lots of swimming.' 'Ours like birdwatching.' Conversation tennis creates brief and shallow discussions.

- **Don't pontificate.** It makes it very difficult to get a conversation going.

- **Be open.** If you don't know, or don't understand, vulnerability builds contact.

- **Summarise** what you have heard; that makes them know you have been listening and gives them the opportunity to add anything you might have missed.

- **Feelings matter.** You are going deeper with a person when you ask questions like, 'How did you feel about that? What do you feel should change? Why is that important to you?'

- **Encourage.** Be prepared to let the other people in the conversation feel they are the most interesting people in the room! Keep finding out more about them.

Yes, from time to time you will meet the person who just talks and talks and never breathes as they move effortlessly to a completely different subject. They don't want you to contribute. It's another God-given opportunity to practise patience and grace!

Alongside listening to conversations, there is the need to listen to God. He gives a shepherd's wisdom, and knowledge. He may point you to something in the conversation that you need to follow through. He may inspire you as you respond. We can keep practising that 'double listening' to God's voice and the other person's voice.

We know many people have a sense of worthlessness. They need others who are prepared to reach out and encourage them. They may drop hints that show they want encouragement (talking themselves down). We can help people emerge. One of the key foundations for relationship building is telling our story/our history. Good listening conversations, encouraging people to tell their history, thanking them for doing so, tells our neighbours we value and respect them. It is part of our call to the workplace.

Marie's story

Marie Reavey is a police inspector based in Norfolk. She is the national lead for the project Faith and Police Together and the chair of the Christian Police Association. She joined the Police in 2004 and became a Christian five years later. She describes herself as someone with a love of adventure (she took a three-year career break to travel the world) and she has a passion to see people freed from addiction, justice outworked and God's kingdom come. She wants to progress her career and is excited by the challenges and opportunities her national roles give her.

She says:

A great day always starts with quality time with Jesus. It would usually include being busy, connecting with people and seeing God's kingdom break into situations and conversations. That could be by encouraging someone, showing compassion and knowing that has made a difference. Seeing justice being done. Sharing a story of hope or implementing a process or system that makes the lives of everyone a little easier, or the supernatural breaking in. It would be through a bold and obvious kingdom impact from praying for someone or sharing testimony or the gospel.

It is inspiring to see how God has been preparing Marie for what was to come and using her passion and experience.

Since 2014 I have known God was calling me to call the Church to step up and help to tackle addiction. I suspected this was on a national level but had no idea how. I would pray that God would make a way and show me what He wanted me to do. Then in 2018 Faith and Police Together was launched. Amazingly, I was released to lead the project for two years. It was decided that one of the key priorities I would look at is how faith communities can help to tackle addiction. As a result of this work, I have produced the *Faith Communities Guide* to engaging with police, which has a section on addiction. I had to pinch myself many times throughout 2019 as I was doing my work which clearly felt God-ordained.

Marie brings a range of values to her role – compassion, integrity, respect, justice and fairness. She describes herself as 'honoured and blessed to be in a job where I live out my values'. She has a key role with the Christian Police Association, established in 1883 and still a strong source of support for Christians in the Force at all levels.

Marie has a special understanding of the links between church and people in the workplace.

Churches need to equip Christians to see their workplace as their primary mission field. All too often we talk about mission as purely a church-based activity. Churches need to recognise that the workplace is where we are called to be salt and light and to encourage their congregations to think differently about their workplaces. Churches need to equip their members to be bolder in the workplace. I dare say even encourage them to invest extra time in their colleagues and workplace with the sole mission of seeing the kingdom of God advance. That may be at the expense of serving in a church ministry. Imagine the impact if every person within the church prayed for their workplace and went to work knowing they were sent there by God on mission to bring the kingdom of God to that workplace. We are all missionaries, we are all in the ministry; we need to change our language to stop talking about church ministry/mission in a way that makes that seem more spiritually superior.

Churches should encourage their members to pray for their sector. For example, all teachers should be encouraged to come together to pray for their schools and the education system and to seek God for how they can make a difference within their educational establishment or more widely. By connecting with other Christians in the same sector of work, it will also encourage them in how they could be bolder witnesses for Jesus.

Call to action

In Matthew 20:26-28, Jesus challenges us with a clearly countercultural statement: 'whoever wants to become great among you must be your servant, and whoever wants to be first must be your slave – just as the Son of Man did not come to be served, but to serve, and to give his life as a ransom for many.' At the Last Supper He abandoned His status and risked His reputation by washing His disciples' feet (John 13:1-17). It was a practical help to friends who had walked the dirty and dusty roads; it was close-up and personal. What have we done in the past week to serve friends in the workplace?

Application

- Can you think of some role models whom you work with, or have worked with, who have been good neighbours to you? What did they do that impressed you?

- Are there people in your workplace that you could encourage or honour more? What can you do differently?

- The secret to having better conversations is to practise! Who could you have a deeper conversation with? It may be task/work-related, to better understand their hopes and aspirations or the things they have learned. It may be about them, their family or history, to help you know them better.

Prayer

Equip me, Lord, to be a wise and loving neighbour, to see things with Your eyes and serve people with Your heart. Amen.

Steve's story

Steve is the design manager for a new and important station – the prestigious Curzon Street landmark where HS2 meets Birmingham. It is a large job leading the multi-disciplinary teams as they turn the architect's dreams into long-lasting reality. A civil engineer, Steve has led many projects and is a highly experienced engineering director. He took a similar role in the building of New Street Station in the heart of Birmingham. It is a pressurised role, twelve hours a day, five and a half days a week.

We are exploring our call in this book, and Steve's story illustrates this really well. He and his wife, Jane, used to work in the same organisation, but about fifteen years ago Jane felt she had a call to teaching. So she gave up her project manager role and trained to teach. She is now a school's deputy head. Steve was challenged by Jane's call and started to ask what his was. He realised that many people came to talk to him about their personal and work issues. He listened, often prayed for them and gave wise counsel. He recognised that his call was to be a pastor in the workplace. He is that good neighbour!

Steve pursued this call, reflected on it, got advice, and realised that God gave him wisdom and discernment that was beyond his natural ability. He felt God's hand of encouragement. People in crisis would come to him and say, 'You're the only Christian I know that I can talk to.' His values underpin his call – he believes that people who work for him (and he has managed teams of 400 people) want to be safe, want to be able to care for their families and want to flourish at work. His call is to help them.

Some years ago, when colleagues died in an accident in the Middle East, Steve ensured there was a qualified Christian pastor to comfort families and friends. He was able to do this because he has credibility as a pastor, as a leader and as a programme manager. He delivers the goods! He has good antennae, he spots the person who is tired, distracted, tense, subdued – he works with his eyes open. For Steve, the task is important but he believes it is best achieved when you care for the people who deliver the task. Some have said he isn't 'hard enough', but his different culture produces results. Inevitably there have been times of pressure, times when he has been treated badly, times when things seemed uncertain. Steve's response is, 'I still get on and do when I am treated badly, because I feel called.'

In the middle of Covid-19, with no direct contact with people, he was being acclaimed as a hero to the organisation because of the change he has made to the culture. He is open with his teams. He recently talked about the pressure they were under and the challenges he faced, which encouraged others to open up about what was tough and demanding for them. This created a changed atmosphere, more freedom and a more relaxed and fun approach to meetings.

We have a call to our workplace, but we may also have a call to our city. Steve illustrates this well. He was looking for a fresh challenge and saw the Curzon Street role advertised. His wife encouraged him, saying, 'If you are pushing against the right door, it will open' – and it did.

The challenge for Steve was to help build something that would bless his city. HS2 will bring many jobs to Birmingham and re-energise the local economy. The station is part of a larger transport hub opening up the city and linking the Birmingham suburbs with London and elsewhere. It is regenerating a rundown part of the city and will bring new shops, accommodation, plazas and squares. Spiritually, the Bible talks about watching and praying over the gateways (Isaiah 62:6-10) – with his work on New Street and Curzon Street, Steve has been right at the centre of opening new and attractive gateways into the city. Steve says he is 'energised by the opportunity to be part of the team delivering to my city'.

Finally, I asked Steve for some pointers on being a good neighbour – or pastor – in the workplace. As you read through them, ask whether this is your call too.

- **Help people to think wisely.** Ask good questions, encourage their response; this in turn builds their confidence and contribution.

- **Stay humble.** Most jobs give us the opportunity for pride – but as Christians we need to acknowledge that wisdom, discernment and understanding come from God.

- **Prayer is 24/7.** An activity that involves listening to God's wisdom for others.

- **Let people know** you are interested in them as individuals, not just their contribution. 'How are you?' is a simple question but we often choose not to ask it.

- **Invest in your pastoring role.** Talk to others, get ideas, improve (Steve has a good friend who coaches him).

- **It's a mindset issue.** Steve genuinely loves his colleagues and the opportunity he has to work with them. Take your love to work – and keep refining it!

- **Understand people.** What motivates them? What's their family situation? When they seem difficult to work with, what is driving that? Can you keep appreciating them?

- **Value people** and the challenges they face. They want to succeed. A pastor enables others to look good.

- **Surrender** your time and conversations to God. He can give you an awareness that there is an issue and the wisdom you need to help people through it.

Steve says, 'I've not got all my theology sorted. I often have questions about things, but I make myself available to God and love the people I work with.'

Chapter Seven
The Call to Dream

Dreams shape us

Andrew Lloyd Webber's first hit musical was based on the story of Joseph from the Old Testament. It changed Joseph's image – from the man who was pharaoh's deputy, he became known as Joseph, the fashion icon, with his 'technicolor dreamcoat'![66] But it also reminds us that Joseph had a remarkable job; he rescued Egypt from famine and strengthened Egypt's regional power. He became the redeemer/saviour for the twelve tribes of Israel. His story, however, starts with his dreams (and how to upset your brothers – see Genesis 37!).

Joel 2 speaks of a great spiritual turnaround: if people will turn to God, He will bless them with grain and oil and fruitfulness. But it starts with a warning that an army of locusts will destroy their nation. There's a call for the people to repent, cry, fast and pray for turnaround. Sometimes we look at our city, neighbourhood or workplace in depth and see its pain. We begin to frame a dream that things must change. Alan Platt from Doxa Deo church tells of going around the streets on a Friday night, seeing hundreds of people homeless, and it broke his

---

[66] Andrew Lloyd Webber, Tim Rice, *Joseph and the Amazing Technicolor Dreamcoat*, 1968.

heart.[67] Les Isaacs, founder of Street Pastors,[68] tells us that people on our streets at one o clock in the morning go looking to get drunk, to party, to build relationships, but they often find emptiness. His dream was that they could meet street pastors who would give them time and compassion. We like to sweep the pain, hurt and brokenness of our cities under the carpet, but that does not make anything go away. Many dreams are born of compassion.

God gives us big, disruptive visions. In the book of Jonah, we read that He sees that the huge and mighty city of Nineveh could be made to repent. The prophet Jonah is not so keen. But God makes His vision come to fruition and the city does indeed change remarkably. God stirs another dream in His people through His prophets. It is a vision that they meditate on – that the children of Israel and Judah will return from exile and Jerusalem will be rebuilt. This becomes a dream for Nehemiah, as we read in the book of his name. As in the story of Joel, Nehemiah weeps and prays. This is his prayer 'LORD, the God of heaven, the great and awesome God, who keeps his covenant of love with those who love him and keep his commandments' (Nehemiah 1:5).' We could pray this prayer for our workplace or business dreams. God is awesome, He keeps His covenant with us. Nehemiah continues, 'let your ear be attentive and your eyes open to hear the prayer your servant is praying before you day and night for your servants, the people of Israel' (v6). As he spends time with God, Nehemiah's dream aligns with God's vision.

---

[67] Alan Platt, Movement Day South Africa, 22nd April 2015. Details on Movement Days events gathering cities together to build unity and raise impact can be found at www.movementday.com (accessed 25th November 2021).

[68] www.streetpastors.org (accessed 14th October 2021). My organisation worked closely with Les Isaacs to produce the training manual for Street Pastors.

How big is your dream?

One of the huge impediments to God moving in us is our limited expectations. We are in danger of losing sight of the miracles and focusing on the do-ables. A friend of mine reports on a range of church growth courses he ran where it became more and more apparent that the churches he was working with expected the vicar to do all the evangelism or growth. The strategy for this was through a fast-diminishing number of baptisms and marriages. It was a dream of decline.

The truth is, many of us do not put much time into dreaming. We probably don't dream for our workplace, our church or our city. This in turns sucks the faith and expectation out of our prayers. We go through the 'bring peace to the entire world, bless all the children and let us all know Your love' prayers. As many a businessperson knows, none of those counts as a measurable, time-bounded or achievable goal.

The Bible is full of courageous dreams and courageous dreamers. It takes us back to another time much dreamed about by the children of Israel – the dream to enter the Promised Land. God gives a leader, Moses, and He gives that leader a voice through Aaron, and credibility through signs and wonders. It is clear Moses' leadership comes from his time in the presence of God. He longs for God's presence; he spends much time in consultation and listening. He hears God's heart. God gives him incredibly clear and specific instructions on how to build a tabernacle (Exodus 25:8ff). A cloud settled over the tabernacle as a visual sign of the Lord's presence in their midst (Exodus 40:34). The ongoing story is of guidance from the Lord as Moses spent time in His presence. Moses' courageous dreams were birthed in that time.

Songwriter Kari Jobe tells the story of how the remarkable worship song, 'The Blessing' was born. On 3rd March 2020 a group of church leaders, songwriters and worship leaders came together to spend time in God's presence and write some new worship material. As they waited, God took them to the blessing prayer in Numbers 6:24-26; the words captivated them. In this intimate moment with God, the words and music of 'The Blessing' emerged. Spending time in God's presence brought a remarkable heaven-to-earth gift. It was premiered on 6th March 2020 and went viral globally at astonishing speed. At the same time, church after church was going into lockdown as Covid-19 spread. God wanted to say something very important – His heart is to bless us, and in the midst of great pain and the solitariness of lockdown, He wanted us to know that 'He is for us'.[69]

Then we saw this phenomenon go global; cities like Pittsburg in the USA adopted it and brought people together to pray blessing on their city; then whole nations did it, with the UK being a global pioneer. It was followed by Canada, Australia, Nigeria, South Africa, New Zealand, Israel and many others. Because our global God wanted to bring unity and blessing, He wanted us to release blessing across the generations; He wanted us to know He is with us. Time in God's presence turns our dreams (in this case it was 'we wanted to write something') into God's dreams (He wanted to say something powerful). Our dreams turn from black and white grainy versions into the full HD colour picture when we spend time in His presence.

Now here is another mindset test. Do we believe that we have a right to talk to God about where we work? Do we believe we can spend time in His presence – on our own or with others – to ask what His heart is? We can bring key issues to Him, such as what does integrity in the business look like? Are we treating people justly? Are we helping those around us in church, family and the workplace to flourish? How do we bless our city? Spending time in His presence can be as simple and wonderful as just having a conversation with God, to ask for His take on things. Then you ask for His best, for His dream, His purpose.

---

[69] https://youtu.be/Zp6aygmvzM4 (accessed 25th November 2021) for the background story.

Peter has a dream in Acts 10 of a sheet being 'let down' from heaven (v11), containing all sorts of creatures. All were forbidden for an orthodox Jew to eat, but He hears a voice saying, 'Get up, Peter. Kill and eat' (v13). Peter argues with God, but he hears God say, 'Do not call anything impure that God has made clean' (v15). God is changing Peter's inbuilt prejudice against the Gentiles, and the dream is followed immediately by an invitation to visit a Roman centurion, Cornelius, something no Jew would do. One of the key New Testament themes is the coming together of Jews and Gentiles against fierce opposition, but Peter can now cry, 'I have a dream!'

Alan Platt talks of going through different stages with his concern about homelessness in Pretoria. He was shaken when he saw hundreds sleeping on the city's streets, and the church started to take people into their homes, and then created places where people could stay. After a while he and God had more conversations. He realised that what they were doing was helping but not rescuing. They had a dream for an employment centre teaching a range of skills, from hotel food preparation to handbag making, from nursery helpers to vegetable farming. Called the People Upliftment Programme (POPUP), it now serves 1,000 people a year. They give people time, love and support to rebuild their lives and grow confidence. The personal and skills development training gives people a route to employment and getting a place to live. Along the way, thousands on this scheme[70] have become Christians as they have found a depth of hope in the work of Doxa Deo church.

I was one of four directors of a Christian-owned and -led leadership and change consultancy. There was a lot of dreaming in God's presence. How could we bless our clients? How could we find a Jesus-inspired leadership approach? How could we

---

[70] Alan Platt, presentation 23rd May 2015 in Pretoria. I had the privilege of visiting this centre with Movement Day colleagues from across the world, and hearing this presentation. It was filled with the joy, hope and laughter of turned-around lives.

help people understand who God had made them to be? God put many tools in our hands and opened up many doors. We had the privilege of praying for and serving many individual leaders and a wide range of organisations. We understood their dreams and were inspired by those dreams to help them succeed.

The generous dreamer

Some people have a generosity dream. They dream how they can best use their business to generate the finances to build and release others. It might be in their local community. It might be a bigger dream to invest in kingdom-building organisations with a significant impact. I have worked as a consultant with the team of a Christian entrepreneur who put millions on one side from a range of businesses and created a separate Christian-run organisation. This man is a great dreamer; he turns thoughts and issues into ideas and vision. He wanted people to come to Christ and established a global Christian radio presence. As technology moved on, this has become a social media presence with a range of very well-produced testimonies. He invested in academy schools, building Christian values into the culture of the schools, giving thousands of young people great opportunities in well-designed and well-resourced facilities.[71]

I have another friend who is self-employed but he wanted to be a generous giver. As a self-employed person, this needed to shape his business plans and ambitions for the year. God has prompted him to give to a range of works and has blessed his business. He does not do this in a superstitious way – the more I give, the more I get. No, the dream is generosity and God loves his heart so gives him more to give away.

Generosity, of course, is not all about money. One of the most valuable things we can give is our time – and again, dreaming about our time and offering it to God gives us a

---

[71] www.cvglobal.co (accessed 4th November 2021).

different perspective than just making ourselves busy out of a strong sense of responsibility. God sees you as a kingdom asset. Your story may be a significant blessing to a specific person; your wisdom and advice may bring breakthrough for someone. Dreamers make themselves available.

The entrepreneur

Entrepreneurs turn ideas into a business; they see opportunities and look to exploit them.

One of the inevitable challenges in being an entrepreneur is that many set out wearing the entrepreneur badge but soon after they exchange the badge for a hat with 'business failure' on it. Enthusiasm meets reality and reality wins. There are many high-calibre resources and tools for entrepreneurs. So enthusiasm needs to be tempered by determination and wisdom. It is a determination to keep refining and learning. It's a determination to do the market research. It's a determination to keep searching for investment past your tenth rejection.

Many Christians have a passion for social entrepreneurship. It might be a scheme to help people find work, or a food bank, or a local coffee shop. Cinnamon Network[72] provides advice, training and grants for organisations wishing to branch out in this field, and has a rich mix of success stories. It also has a good track record in linking churches and social entrepreneurs in areas like child food poverty, supporting families with newborn babies, mental health support, employment opportunities and a range of other schemes.

- Do you look in the mirror and see an entrepreneur?

- Do you think big? Is your dream one that will engage others?

---

[72] www.cinnamonnetwork.co.uk (accessed 14th October 2021).

- Why? Why are you doing your current role? Why is it important?

- Do you have faith? Not 'faith' that does not think things through, or believes God will bless everything, but faith that comes from taking your dream into God's presence. Faith is strengthened by prayer and waiting for God's plan.

- Do you think vision before resources? The vision drives, resources support: both need to be aligned.

- Don't wait for a consensus from friends: people process things at different paces. You only need a few early adopters to champion what you are doing, and they will bring others on board for you.

- Have a great team of advisors: don't get a room full of encouragers who simply agree with everything you do; you need people who can help you keep improving the idea.

- Seek wisdom and understanding.

- Risk management needs to support this, not drive it. But there are risks and you need to be objective about them and find ways to handle them well.

The innovator

Innovators come in many forms. They might be science or new technology pioneers or the very practical person who finds a new process or improves the way an old machine is working. Innovators may be creative, like a Beethoven with a new approach to writing symphonies, or a C S Lewis with all the wonders of Narnia. There are those who are naturally better at initiating things, or creating new ideas, or sharpening up a process.

But I know we can be encouraged to think outside our own particular box. Let's imagine your church has gathered a group to look at supporting people being made redundant or worried about their jobs – let's do some creative thinking. These topics, positive and negative, are to help people think broadly.

- Imagine these people were a group of famous film stars visiting our church – how would we welcome them, honour them and make this a really memorable occasion?

- Imagine running a scheme where we don't actually want them in our church! What can we do that will make them want to leave the church? (This helps us think about the mistakes we don't want to make.)

- Imagine we have to get something ready for two days' time. What would we do? (Creating urgency can help our creativity.)

- If the scheme were really successful and the local TV came around to film us in two years' time, what would we want the news story to be? What would we want the cameras to see?

- In a year's time, what would success look like?

Jesus was skilled at getting His disciples to think and to look outside the box. This enables us to be innovative in the workplace, in the community and in church.

Wisdom

Solomon has the hard task of following Israel's most famous and influential king and knows that he is called to build a temple that would be a wonder of the world, meeting God's high expectations and plans. He meets with God in a dream in 1 Kings 3. God says, 'Ask for whatever you want me to give you' (v5). God makes no stipulations; this is the opportunity for Solomon to speak what is on his heart.

'Now, LORD my God, you have made your servant king in place of my father David. But I am only a little child and do not know how to carry out my duties. Your servant is here among the people you have chosen, a great people, too numerous to count or number. So give your servant a discerning heart to govern your people and to distinguish between right and wrong. For who is able to govern this great people of yours?'

The Lord was pleased that Solomon had asked for this. (1 Kings 3:7-10)

Dreams and wisdom, wisdom and action. So much comes out of spending time with God. How do we know that it is God's wisdom? James gives us some good pointers: 'But the wisdom that comes from heaven is first of all pure; then peace-loving, considerate, submissive, full of mercy and good fruit, impartial and sincere' (James 3:17). With God's wisdom, you feel at peace with God's purpose. 'The Spirit of the LORD will rest on him – the Spirit of wisdom and of understanding, the Spirit of counsel and of might, the Spirit of the knowledge and fear of the LORD' (Isaiah 11:2). The fear of the Lord is a recurring theme; it is mentioned more than 300 times in Scripture:[73] 'The fear of the LORD is the beginning of wisdom' (Proverbs 9:10). This is the fear of not being in God's will, not understanding His ways; it is a humble heart focused on wisdom and aware of God's awesome holiness.

This is not a call to blind faith – far from it. God will give us wisdom; and it does not mean that every situation we face will be successful. All of us spend time in the storms, and sometimes we might feel our boat has sunk altogether. But God is with us. He gives us wisdom and fresh ideas for the difficult times, for the great challenges. Sometimes it is the wisdom of waiting and trusting when we want action and results. Sometimes it is the wisdom of self-examination as we look to improve. Sometimes God is drawing us back to Him, to listen, to be quiet and to

---

[73] www.partnershipministries.com (accessed 25th November 2021). Alistair Petrie has studied and written about the fear of the Lord and these stats are taken from a series of presentations in the UK in 2017 when I accompanied Alastair for four weeks.

dream afresh. Sometimes it is the wisdom of failure, and the changes we make as a result. As Solomon's story reminds us, God looks at our hearts, and wants us to be aligned with His purpose, whether it is a time to be on the mountaintop or in the valley.

Roger's dream

Here is my friend Roger Sutton's dream from his book, *A Gathering Momentum*. This has come from a long commitment to justice, prayer and discussion with God. Let it stir your heart, and you will dream of different things. What are they? Can you articulate them like this?

> I dream about a day when the gap between the very richest and poorest is reduced, a day when a poorer resident in a socially deprived area is able to live as long as the richer resident down the road and not die eleven years earlier, as now.
>
> I dream of a day when the five food banks in Trafford close down because people are being paid a living wage, and those out of work are supported to find employment quickly.
>
> I dream about a day when those most in need would be better served and cared for, the very poor, the sick, the depressed, the isolated, those with disabilities, those living in fear in their homes and in the streets.
>
> A day when churches are so immersed in their communities that they are at the forefront of community life, partnering with authorities and other churches to provide and serve the place God has called them to bless.[74]

Call to action

We all have dreams. But do we have dreams with that added Jesus factor? Let us marinate our dreams in Him, let them be

---

[74] Sutton, *A Gathering Momentum*, pp29-30.

shaped and flavoured by Him and let us ask Him for more. We can serve our colleagues, family and neighbourhood more effectively when God gives us dreams.

Application

- Have you ever taken your dream/s to Jesus? Imagine being sat together on a park bench. What would you talk to Jesus about? Might it be how you want to behave differently at work? How could you respond better to that colleague who irritates you? Or bigger dreams that turn into prayer about what a new level of peace/shalom would look like in your workplace?

- Your career – what is He calling you to do in the future? Can you 'book' quality time with God to have a 'dream' conversation?

- Your city – God loves your city, your town or village. What would it look like if God were to visit it? What would be removed? What would be blessed? This may be a dream fuelled by prayer walking. Let Jesus shape your heart to His.

Prayer

Lord, give me a dream of all You want to do in my workplace and in my life. Let me walk with You in Your plan and purpose. Give me a dream of what it means to see Your kingdom come and Your will be done. Thank You that You have put me where I am so that I can see You at work. Amen.

Martyn and Jim's stories

Martyn and Jim have a passion for God moving in the workplace. That passion has led to them developing a network for Christians in the workplace in Aberdeen and Edinburgh and a national conference and conversation across Scotland.[75] Their starting point is relationship. They recognise that many Christians in the workplace need to share ideas, concerns and hopes but have often felt isolated and lacking in confidence. Their dream is now to encourage, empower and equip believers right across Scotland.

The work started in Aberdeen as the city experienced a wave of challenges following the 2008 recession and the knock-on impact on oil prices – oil being a major local employer. It started simply with fortnightly informal breakfasts where people could come and discuss their work and, for some, the challenges of being unemployed. People of faith and no faith found it a haven, and numbers grew. This led to a WhatsApp group giving accessible prayer support.

Martyn and Jim recognise that Christians get very different support depending on which church they attend, with some churches really encouraging people to be aware of who God has called and equipped them to be. In other situations, there is little or no support and people don't feel valued – hence the need for cross-city networks and a national conference.

Martyn works as chief strategic officer for a global organisation shaping energy transition and climate change, where he has been at the heart of driving transformational change in a fast-moving market. He has set up a Christian network in his firm linking with seventy-two colleagues.

Jim is the founder of P3 Business Care CIC, providing support to employees in the corporate business environment. He has experience in business development, general management and director roles within the UK oil and gas sector, operations management, coaching and mentoring. Jim stepped out of full-time work to establish P3 Business Care CIC as a social enterprise to support people in the workplace. His story is that 'when you step out in obedience, God moves. Blessing follows obedience.'

---

[75] www.thrivescotland.org (accessed 11th November 2021).

The partnership between the two has been critical to their dream. God has paired two people with a strategic understanding and given them a vision to see Christians in the workplace mobilised. Up to this point they feel the workforce has been God's frozen people, but Martyn and Jim have a passion for Christians to know and be confident in their call and for God to move powerfully in the workplace. Their bigger message to Scotland is 'work with us and we can transform our workplaces'. They have been called to see Scotland's business community become a powerful, confident and transformational arm of God's kingdom.

Chapter Eight
The Call to Pray

Our extraordinary God

A colleague told us that his wife was unwell and he was worried about her. That evening she was taken into hospital. A few days later we got the message that she had been moved to intensive care. At about three o'clock on that Wednesday afternoon, I felt a strong compulsion to pray for her. We had two more strong Christians in our team, and we went into an office to pray. We cried out to God for mercy and prayed intensely for her health. At just after 3.30pm we felt we had done what we were called to do and went back to our desks.

My colleague did not return to work till the following week. He told us his wife was recovering slowly and was expected to be in hospital for quite some time. Then he told us that at three o'clock on the Wednesday afternoon the consultants had told him to go and sit by his wife's bedside because she only had half an hour to live. It was an awful time for him, but she pulled through, to the doctors' delight and surprise.

This lady did not die because God called us to pray in the workplace at exactly the right time. We simply answered that call. He had his hand on her life, and it establishes a clear principle for me – God is at work miraculously!

Standing in His presence

In the last chapter, we looked at being in His presence to shape our dreams and vision for the future. But we also stand in His presence for each day, for the one-to-one meeting with the boss, the challenging presentation to a client, the finance review, whatever it may be. Is God interested in these details of life?

Brother Lawrence's conversations and letters were gathered together in the seventeenth-century book, *The Practice of the Presence of God*.[76] It remains a popular book today. The book is not the thoughts of a classically trained theologian or scholar. It contains the reflections of a simple man who had served as a foot soldier and valet before joining a Carmelite monastery as a lay brother and cook. He practised the presence of God with joy and gentleness in his workplace. For many years this was the kitchen, until gout forced him to a seated job repairing shoes. He simply took each day and each hour as a new beginning and a fresh commitment to love God with all his heart. It was a pure example of shalom – finding peace from being aligned with God's love and purpose.

In many ways, this is another thing for us to 'practise, practise, practise'. The truth for many of us is we often spend vast chunks of time in our workplace with little thought of God, let alone acknowledging that His presence is with us. We inevitably get caught up in the urgent and immediate. But He is there every hour, partnering with us. Jesus is with us in every meeting and situation. Our challenge is to be much more aware of His continuous presence with us, to guide us, give us wisdom and to shape our behaviour.

C H Spurgeon said this:

> When a person really prays, it is not a question whether God will hear them or not, he must hear them; not because there is any compulsion in the prayer, but there is a sweet and blessed compulsion in the promise. Since he is the most high and true God, he cannot deny himself.'[77]

---

[76] Brother Lawrence, *The Practice of the Presence of God* (Eastford, CT: Martino Fine Books, 2016).

[77] C H Spurgeon, 'True Prayer – True Power!' sermon, 12th August 1860, www.hopefaithprayer.com/prayernew/true-prayer-true-power-spurgeon (accessed 25th November 2021).

The heart of prayer's driving force is relationship. We have the privilege of access. We need to ask ourselves, how close can we get to God? I sometimes think I am standing at the edge of a large crowd with my prayers trying to get God's attention. But the reality is our amazing access into the throne room. When we come into God's presence in prayer, we are touched (and changed) by His deep love for us.

Jesus taught us to pray, 'Our Father in heaven, hallowed be your name' (Matthew 6:9-13). This prayer starts with us accessing the throne room, standing with our Father. It starts with our relationship with God. We sometimes need to get ourselves in the right frame of mind. There are times, especially during the working day, when we are lobbing prayers at God. They may be the short 'Help me, Lord' or 'I don't know what to do next – I need some wisdom here' prayers. Father hears. But it's a shallow relationship that is shaped with lots of requests all going one way. I can do those 'emergency' prayers with more conviction and faith if I have also invested good, quality time with my Father.

It is important to have places where you can give all your focus to Jesus. Where you can sit quietly and come into His presence. Scripture tells us, 'Come near to God and he will come near to you. Wash your hands, you sinners, and purify your hearts, you double-minded' (James 4:8).

Who may ascend the mountain of the LORD?
Who may stand in his holy place?
The one who has clean hands and a pure heart,
who does not trust in an idol
or swear by a false god.
They will receive blessing from the LORD.
(Psalm 24:3-5)

We are coming with reverence to a holy God. Numbers 20:6 describes how Moses and Aaron fell face down at the tent of meeting. This displays reverence honouring God's power and presence. 'Reverence' is an underutilised word now, but it describes deep respect and should be a key feature in our relationship.

The workplace gives us dirty hands: it can be a place of arguments, frustrations, despair, guilt, anxiety, lies and anger. When we come in prayer, we may need to do some 'cleansing' first so we can really draw near to Jesus.

In coming into His presence, of course, we are creating a heaven-to-earth situation. We learn about this when Moses is given very precise instructions in Exodus 25–40 of how to construct and fill the tent of meeting. He is working to a very clear and precise heavenly blueprint because he is replicating the tent of meeting found in heaven.

> It was necessary, then, for the copies of the heavenly things to be purified with these sacrifices, but the heavenly things themselves with better sacrifices than these. For Christ did not enter a sanctuary made with human hands that was only a copy of the true one; he entered heaven itself, now to appear for us in God's presence.
> (Hebrews 9:23-24)

God can give us a heavenly blueprint as we spend time with him.

Being the tasky person I am, I can fall into the trap of just bringing a list to Jesus. But Jesus wants relationship. He gave me a vivid picture where Jesus and I were comfortably sitting on a rock in the middle of a fast-flowing river, and we were fishing. We were relaxing in companionable silence. In truth, I don't fish, but the thought of spending that time just 'chilling with Jesus' delights me. It's a reminder that sometimes God just wants us to 'hang out'. There are special moments when we stop the noise. We quieten ourselves and our souls. We ask our Father, is there anything we need to talk about? Being quiet with Jesus may be enough to restore my soul (see Psalm 23:3, ESV). We want to be different before we do anything different, so we wait for God.

Let us just reflect on what a close relationship looks like to us. We don't sit down for a meal with our family and close friends and bring our list of requests. We are prepared to sit in a special companionable silence. We might reflect on some things together, dream together and plan together. Intimacy brings a different and special relationship.

Scripture plays a key element in hearing from God. Psalm 119 tells us it is a 'lamp for [our] feet' (v105). Time spent with Jesus reading the Scriptures should bring aspects of the Word alive, so we hear God speaking and shaping our prayer. We need to get past reading Scripture as a duty or reading it only occasionally. God speaks through His Word; we need to be expectant, we need to be ready for a verse to jump up at us. It is a simple rule: if we want to hear God speaking into our lives and situations, we need to come into His presence, ask Him to speak and expect His Word to inspire us.

Back to Psalm 24. Who may come into the presence of God? Anyone who belongs to Jesus – this is where hierarchy, roles and position break down. Every one of us, from the newest or youngest to the most mature, from the poorest person out on the streets, from the works' toilet attendant to the CEO, can come to Jesus.

As we come into His presence, we see him as King, Judge and Warrior. He works to restore *tsedaqah* (righteousness) and shalom (wholeness and peace). David frequently comes to the Lord to seek His direction, permission and guidance (1 Samuel 30:8) and so does King Jehoshaphat (2 Chronicles 20:3); both govern under God's hand. Daniel sits in God's council: 'As I looked, "thrones were set in place, and the Ancient of Days took his seat … The court was seated, and the books were opened' (Daniel 7:9-10). This is why people seek God with all their hearts, so that they can hear from Him and then pray with authority.

Of course, your finance figures, whether or not to invest in some new machinery or who to recruit are not history-making events. The further up an organisation someone is, the more reluctant we are to contact them, and we certainly don't want to waste their time. But this is different – you and I might not get to see a president or even the CEO, but the King's son or daughter always has access to heaven and a warm welcome, whatever the issue.

The prayer of government

I was so blessed to visit the Bible college of Wales[78] and to spend time alone in Rees Howells' prayer meeting place. It was effectively a large front room in the house at the heart of the college. Rees Howells, the founder of the college, was a man of deep prayer. He had been impacted by the Welsh revival, and he had high expectations of his God. The building itself was a miracle answer to prayer, as were the students who flocked there in the 1920s and 1930s. But the key prayer call he is remembered for was in the Second World War. Day after day, week after week, as the terrible war and the dark threat of Nazi Germany shook the nations, Howells and his colleagues prayed.

The key thing for me in that prayer room was the message that Rees Howells would pray nothing unless God told him to. I guess there were many periods of silence as they waited on God. God gave Howells and others scriptures that came alive and resonated with the daily news and war reports. As they waited and meditated on Scripture, God gave them authority to have spiritual governance over major battles. They saw Nazi advances halted, they prayed for seas to calm and snows to fall. God gave them an understanding of the situation that only became fully apparent many years later when historians reviewed each event. They stood on the principle that 'the battle is the LORD's' (1 Samuel 17:47). It drove them to seek God's strategy, plan and timing.

---

78 The Bible College of Wales, Swansea.

We pray as members of the Ekklesia. Let us revisit the Great Commission. Jesus is sending the disciples out to serve His kingdom and declares:

> All authority in heaven and on earth has been given to me. Therefore go and make disciples of all nations, baptising them in the name of the Father and of the Son and of the Holy Spirit, and teaching them to obey everything I have commanded you. And surely I am with you always, to the very end of the age.
>
> (Matthew 28:18-20)

Let's let this sink in. Jesus is commissioning, sending out His Ekklesia. Jesus tells them that He has all authority. Not just a little bit; He has *all* authority. More than that, He is with us forever. That's why our being a Christian is the main thing we bring to our workplace. We are there to make an extraordinary contribution.

He is with us when we face that problem meeting with a colleague, or need to create a complex project plan, or do some financial work that we normally struggle with. More than that, He has given us authority. He is with us when we feel stressed and overwhelmed, to give us shalom which comes when we trust Him in the midst of the storm. We can sometimes pray with apologetic 'If You don't mind me asking again, Jesus' types of prayers. Prayer is the way the Ekklesia legislates for change. Prayer hands the situation over to God.

Heaven to earth is very important in this. God wants heaven's plan to be enacted on earth and He gives us authority to make this happen. He tells us to pray for things 'on earth as it is in heaven' (Matthew 6:10). One of my first introductions to prayer for the workplace was in my first professional job working in the now vanished car maker, Austin Rover. It was the early 1980s and this giant manufacturer had been through many years of struggle between management and the unions. The then Thatcher government wanted to restore industrial relations across the country, and Rover was in its sights. It appointed a new CEO, Sir Michael Edwardes, a tough South African, with a brief to beat the unions. Things came to a head when Edwardes introduced new ways of working and said if they were not accepted by the unions he would close the business down, losing 38,000 jobs directly (including mine!) and another 180,000 through the knock-on impact on suppliers. One weekend, those of us in HR were told to take great piles of paperwork and contracts home with us. If the negotiations, scheduled for that weekend, did not achieve breakthrough, we would be working from home and making everyone redundant. These were serious times. These were times for prayer.

In hindsight, one of my observations is that when God has called us into serious prayer like this, He has also prepared the way. So five close friends with experience of praying together, including two Rover staff, were meeting for a meal on the Saturday evening, as the union/company negotiations reached the critical stage. More than that, we had a critical insight, because of our HR/personnel links, that this was deadly serious. That evening we prayed, we cried out to God for mercy, not just for us but for the hundreds of thousands who would be impacted by a Rover closure. We prayed to God for a clear settlement. At about 9.30pm we felt we did not have to pray any more and a great peace came on us. Later we learned that was when the breakthrough happened.

In some ways, this is a story consigned to history, an era of different fashions and hairstyles, of deep divisions and threats. But there is a key prayer truth here: this is our God. This is the God who can use five of us to bring a breakthrough from heaven. This is our God who gives us authority – spiritual governance. We were all in our twenties, and there is another truth here: you do not have to be grey-haired and wrinkly to see God move powerfully in prayer!

I share these stories of answered prayer because they are our testimonies of God working in the workplace and encouragements for us to say, 'Do it again, Lord.'

Binding and loosing

When Jesus announces the Ekklesia, He goes on to say, 'I will give you the keys of the kingdom of heaven; whatever you bind on earth will be bound in heaven, and whatever you loose on earth will be loosed in heaven' (Matthew 16:19). It is another powerful picture: we are given the keys of the kingdom. He elaborates on this a little later in Matthew's Gospel:

> Truly I tell you, whatever you bind on earth will be bound in heaven, and whatever you loose on earth will be loosed in heaven.
>
> Again, truly I tell you that if two of you on earth agree about anything they ask for, it will be done for them by my Father in heaven. For where two or three gather in my name, there am I with them.
> (Matthew 18:18-20)

Here is yet another important mindset challenge.

- Do we believe God gives us authority when we pray? Do we exercise that authority?

- Do we believe that we can bind and loose? This is a heaven-to-earth prayer; we are hearing heaven's plans and purposes and praying for them to happen here on earth.

- Do we believe that just two or three of us can move mountains?

  Much of what passes for binding and loosing is the result of presumption and silliness rather than genuine prophetic authority. The translation is misleading – it should be, 'Whatever you forbid on earth must be already forbidden in heaven, whatever you permit on earth must be already permitted in heaven.'[79]

---

[79] Briggs, *Ekklesia Rising*, p165.

This reinforces the authority that comes from being in the presence of God when we pray. Bad practice, declaring chains broken after five minutes of worship or releasing blessings across the whole world after two minutes of prayer must not stop us from seeking the genuine article. As Rees Howells found when he waited for God to tell him what to pray, God's plans and purposes are targeted and wise and create lasting change.

So groups of two or three have Ekklesia authority. As we saw earlier, Daniel prayed with his three friends and sought God's will and purpose. Just four of them took on the might of the greatest empire in the world with all its occultic practices – but God had positioned them in their strategic roles and used them to shape history. You may find your Ekklesia in the workplace, or have others you pray with weekly with that divine insight and authority.

Co-missioning

Thirty-nine out of forty miracles in Acts were in the marketplace. Jesus wanted to be where *everyone* could see what He was doing. We in turn are the prayer watchers or protectors of our chosen work stream – education, health, business, politics, the arts, etc. We are on a mission from God!

One of the main themes in Scripture is of God cleaning a place and then restoring and rebuilding it. Manchester, Kentucky, a small community in the Appalachians, was seen as one of the worst places to live in the US in 2004. Drugs were rife, reinforced by wide-scale corruption. Eventually, when all else failed, the Ekklesia took action and church leaders and others started to work together. They prayer walked, they united, they repented, they cried out to God. A momentum built and eventually a prayer rally was held with 3,500 people from sixty-three churches.

The pastors asked God to forgive them for their spirit of independence and their focus on narrow agendas instead of responding to the pain of the city. As they repented, God moved powerfully on the meeting. Many people were weeping, others reported they could hardly breathe because the presence of God was so tangible. This was a city admitting to powerlessness and asking God to give breakthrough.

Change came, and 600 fraudsters, including the mayor and chief of police, were convicted. The biggest drug dealer came to Christ and became an evangelist; previously dead land became fertile. Within days of prayer events, drug dealers were arrested and gangs broken up. Ordinary people stepped into their spiritual authority and prayed the prayers that led to a rebuilding and restoration.[80]

This partnership is replicated in cities and places across the world. What does it teach us for our workplaces?

Do we need to turn and repent? It may be needed if there is past sin in the business. There may be corruption, disunity, rivalry, immorality, fraud, bullying, racism, people injured or even killed at work. There may have been negative words spoken over some parts of the business or individuals. Lots can poison an atmosphere. We can ask God to forgive us. It is countercultural for a business to repent and be humble, but God calls even nations to do it.

When Solomon dedicates the new temple to God, he asks God if He will be with them in all the situations they might face as a people (2 Chronicles 6:14-40). The power of God's presence falls on the building and brings the huge assembly to their knees. God answers Solomon's enquiry:

> When I shut up the heavens so that there is no rain, or command locusts to devour the land or send a plague among my people, if my people, who are called by my name, will humble themselves and pray and seek my face and turn from their wicked ways, then I will hear from heaven, and I will forgive their sin and will heal their land.
> (2 Chronicles 7:13-14)

---

[80] www.sentinelgroup.org (accessed 10th February 2022); their resources include a DVD about this event.

These verses lie at the heart of effective prayer. If we humble ourselves, if we seek His face (come into His presence), if we confess our sins – then God will hear us and heal our land.

'Healing the land' is a powerful phrase. There are frequent references to the land in Scripture. God is passionate about our stewardship of the land. In the Old Testament there were issues of the land given over to idol worship and prostitution (linked with the worship of Baal), there was bloodshed on the land, including child sacrifice, there was exploitation of those who worked or owned the land. There were plagues and infections and locusts. We need to look for the equivalents today. We may see it in anxiety, tension, greed, a lack of trust or integrity, disruptive cliques or a poor reputation with customers.

The workplace can be shaped by corruption, injustice, greed, lies, abuse and bullying. Who is going to repent and ask God to move? Not as a technique or methodology – but because we want to see the mercy and forgiveness of God setting people free.

A visiting preacher was travelling around a large city centre. He saw a pyramid-shaped building in a prominent position towering over the police headquarters, the law courts, the cathedral and the commercial centre. He knew this design was a sign of Masonic influence over the city centre. He said, 'We need to pray for Christians to go into that building.' A month later I found myself appointed as the company's training manager. There were a handful of Christians, but we found it so hard to pray in there that we often had to leave the building to do so. We discovered the foundation stone had been laid by a senior Freemason. It was a place of intense spiritual struggles. In hindsight, I would have invested more time repenting of the Masonic links and asking God to cleanse the land where the building stood.[81]

---

[81] Ian Gordon, *The Craft and the Cross* (Northampton, MA: Branch Press, 1996) gives a comprehensive overview of Freemasonry.

Prayers for justice

A clear example of this consecration before we can move forward has happened for many places and businesses addressing racial justice challenges. In recent times, people have become more aware of the often appalling injustices suffered by our black brothers and sisters (and other people of colour) and the need for repentance, turning and bringing in a new way of working. This is not a quick throwaway prayer. It needs conversations and research. Are there any slavery links in the business? How were black people treated in the 1960s and 1970s? Is it still the case that it is harder to succeed in the business as a person of colour, or as a female? There is a healing to take place that addresses the roots of the issue because we have listened and understood previous hurts.

We may be repenting of previous issues and challenges, but we balance that with praying for blessing and mercy. Often this will be standing on a word of Scripture: 'Let justice roll on like a river, righteousness like a never-failing stream' (Amos 5:24); 'LORD, I have heard of your fame; I stand in awe of your deeds, LORD. Repeat them in our day, in our time make them known; in wrath remember mercy' (Habakkuk 3:2).

The Old Testament has a recurring prayer and action focus for 'the widow or the fatherless, the foreigner or the poor' (Zechariah 7:10). They can be found in our workplaces. They may be in our street or neighbourhood as we travel to work. God has a heart to bless, to protect them. Our impact in prayer is directly related to our values – our desire for mercy and justice; our attitude of righteousness and compassion. Our prayer must align with our behaviour; again, we may be the countercultural people who break down barriers and are inclusive and welcoming.

Bryan Stevenson is a remarkable campaigner for racial justice. Speaking at a Christian gathering in 2016, he said:

We can redefine what success looks like. I don't have much money, but I am incredibly rich. Why do we make accumulation of wealth our success criteria? How engaged are we? How faithful are we? How much do we feel grace and mercy? How much do we feel God's love pouring through us?[82]

Prayer rhythms and goals

We all pray in different ways. Some people will be incredibly disciplined and structured, putting time aside every day. They may have a regular Bible-reading time, or pattern, to help them prepare for prayer. They may have a list of people and issues to pray for regularly. John Wesley created a very strict systematic religious practice; hence his followers were called Methodists. Others would just not be able to pray that way. They will adapt their approach daily to match their circumstances, praying when they can, or on the move, or throughout the day.

But there are some basic principles to ensuring we pray regularly, and with the authority God has given us.

- **Prayer goals.** Many people pray regularly for five friends to come to Christ. It is a clear and measurable goal. Other goals may include targets for change.

- **Person-marking prayers** for key individuals in the church, city, family or workplace.

- **Jump on the Scripture springboard!** Let God speak as you read the Scriptures. I know how hard it can be to do this daily, but I have to say it is a key investment into our day because it allows God to speak to us and guide us.

- **The toughest prayer** can simply be, 'I trust You, God.' Everything seems to be awful, yet I declare my trust in

---

[82] Bryan Stevenson – Grace, Mercy and Justice event at Redeemer Presbyterian Church, Manhattan, with Tim Keller, 3rd June 2013. The film *Just Mercy* tells the inspiring story of Stevenson rescuing wrongly convicted people from the death sentence or lengthy prison terms. Distributed by Warner Bros Pictures.

Him. 'But I trust in you, LORD; I say, "'You are my God."
My times are in your hands' (Psalm 31:14-15).

- **The powerful prayer from Matthew 6:10**, 'your kingdom
  come', is a prayer for heaven to break through, for the
  kingdom to replace the prevailing culture.

- **Prayer with others.** I pray weekly (via email) with my two
  good friends Richard and Mark. We review the past week
  and recognise times when God has moved, and we identify
  our key prayer needs in the coming week in a few
  sentences. We all have a workplace background, we
  understand each other's challenges, and we also meet face
  to face to share updates. All the major events in my work
  life in the past twenty years have been shared with this
  group and it has made so much difference. Our desire is to
  see one another flourish in God's call.

- **Dreams and prayers.** We have looked at dreams already
  in this book. If you and God have talked about your career,
  keep praying, because you want to fulfil God's call on your
  life. God may give you three to five key areas to pray for in
  your business. They might be for new customers and sales,
  for product innovation, for your boss or the senior team,
  for a culture of peace and integrity. A simple list gives us
  focus.

- **Consecration.** We want to consecrate ourselves to be in
  God's presence and we want to be in God's presence all
  day. You know where you need 'clean hands' (Psalm 24:4):
  the meetings that wind you up, the problems that seem
  intractable, the customers who are unreasonable.
  Consecrate yourself – remind yourself that God is holy, and
  that you can stand in His shalom and hear His voice.

- **Persistence.** The Ekklesia gather to pray for Peter. They
  pray that 'ridiculous' prayer that he will be released from
  prison (see Acts 12:5). Despite being guarded by 'four

squads of four soldiers' (v4) behind locked doors, Peter walks out. It's reassuring that, having asked this big and audacious prayer, they find it hard to comprehend when Peter actually appears before them (vv15-16)!

- **Persistence and faith** are key drivers. God is teaching us to pray with authority, to seek Him, to spend time with Him. He wants us to see prison doors open after earnest prayer, and workplace cultures transformed because we have kept to the task.

- **Declarations.** Sometimes we may feel God has given us a scripture or more for our workplace. We need to keep returning to it. We may turn this or other words into declarations. This might be something simple (after we've waited on God for the words!) like, 'We declare God's hand on this business to bless and bring peace, to show Your favour.'

    So our prayer for our work is not only that we might do it well, that it might serve other people, but also that God be praised. We pray as we make our way there. Ask God to give you a nudge if there's anyone in particular He wants you to talk to, and allow a bit of extra time for chance encounters.[83]

Prayers and parables

I know many Christians who find it hard to pray for themselves. Sometimes it is because they are focused on other people; sometimes they do not value themselves and God's call on them enough. Let's take another look at our work parables about Andrea and Sam.

At their church, Sam goes forward for prayer and ministry and finds that Jacob has come to stand with him. Jacob puts his

---

[83] Greene, *Fruitfulness on the* Frontline, p92.

arm around Sam's shoulders. 'Well, Sam, it's a pleasure to pray for you and with you this morning. What's on your mind?'

Sam is a little hesitant to share but realises that Jacob is a man who would be generous and supportive, and he really does want to see things change. 'It may seem like a silly thing, Jacob, but I know I don't pray for myself enough, and I think it's a mindset matter. I don't value myself enough and I don't expect God to move through me as much.'

'That does not sound like a silly thing, Sam, it seems like a very big thing, because you are putting up barriers to God moving through you. It seems a good starting point is to pray for you to have wisdom and understanding about this.'

'Well, I can always do with more of that – what type of wisdom and understanding?'

'It's the understanding that you, I and many others are people on a mission. You work in the retail business, at the department store. You need a deep wisdom and understanding as to why that is. Why does God want you there? It's such an important question. Then you can take more responsibility for praying for yourself.' Jacob then starts to pray for Sam, for God's insight and guidance. As he is praying, Jacob pauses and says, 'Sam, I think there is a barrier here and I keep thinking about praise and thanksgiving. Does that mean anything to you?'

'Yes, it does. I know I need to do more just thanking God for where He has put me, praising Him for my colleagues and customers and for my wonderful family as well.'

'I can see that; praise is acknowledging that God is in control. Then we see Him in more situations. What would you praise God for from your last week?'

'Well, two things spring to mind. I sold an expensive kitchen rebuild to a couple on Wednesday after a bit of a tortuous process, but they were really pleased by the time we got their signatures on the contract. The other thing was asking God for peace when Mrs Robertson came in – she's a regular customer but incredibly indecisive and time-consuming. I know that if I am dealing with her, I can lose another four or five potential customers who get fed up waiting. I normally throw up a quick, "Help me, Lord!" when she arrives and a "Give me peace!" but this time I did a quick, "Help me to see what You see. Help me to love this lady like You do." It changed the time I had with her. I was actually more in control and said, "Mrs Robertson, you like to have a good look at all the options. What are you hoping for today? How can I give you my very best advice?" It changed my approach; it all flowed swimmingly from there.'

'There's an important principle here, Sam: the more you recognise God at work in others, as well as yourself, the more you expect God to move. Now, let me ask you a question. If you are not praying enough for yourself – letting God into your work situation – are you praying enough for your family?'

'Oh, that's a challenging question. I guess I would have to ask, "Am I praying with enough wisdom and care for my family?" I am quite good at the "bless Andrea" prayers and "bless both the children" prayers. I probably don't spend enough time with God, asking Him, "How do You want to bless Andrea?" What would her flourishing in her workplace look like? What would the kids, filled with Jesus, look like, and do I pray at that level of detail?'

'Good observation. Well, I would like to stand with you in prayer. This is something I love to do. I want you to step into your patriarch's role. You have spiritual authority as the father in your family. I would like to stand with you as *you* pray a blessing on your family. Just let God give you wisdom as you pray.' Jacob puts his hand on Sam's shoulder and Sam begins to pray…

Strategic prayer

Sometimes we pray strategically for our business and workplace; it might be for a financial breakthrough, for God's wisdom as we produce a strategic plan, or for a time of change or challenge. But God also wants us to pray for our cities. Businesspeople can bring a broad perspective to city prayer; they understand the importance of generating jobs, attracting new investment and the need for effective working in other sectors of the city.

My friend Dave King can tell you about prayer for his beloved Salford. Salford was a major cotton, silk and weaving city. Based on the Manchester Ship Canal, Salford Docks became one of the world's leading port authorities. In the twentieth century, however, it entered a long period of decline, with the dock's business dropping sharply from the 1930s and the town shrinking in size. In the 1980s and 1990s, crime grew rapidly, and some neighbourhoods became gang controlled.

Dave and his dad served the city for many years and would regularly walk its streets praying for God to rebuild, restore and renew their beloved home. It seemed blighted with house prices falling, low employment and little hope. Aligned with this, church attendance had dropped from really high levels to a point where the biggest church had twenty-five members. Dave and his dad knew that determination was key, and they had a dream of a different city.

Once, when walking down the desolate area around the docks, now closed, with its broken buildings and filthy canal, God spoke His dream to them – that the world would come to Salford and Salford would go out to the world. They held on to this dream and prayed into it for many years. In the twenty-first century, the city attracted considerable investment, including many new houses and the arrival of the BBC's Media City, which brought a rebirth to the docks. Media City brought the world to Salford and Salford to the world, and the once dead docks became a beautiful, landscaped area with clean water, fishing and canal-side activities. So economic regeneration was prayed into place, but alongside that was significant spiritual regeneration, with a range of fast-growing medium and large churches and some powerful moves of God.

Suffice to say there are hundreds of stories of remarkable change in cities – from dramatic reductions in crime to collaboration against food poverty, from large city gatherings repenting of the slave trade to collaboration to rescue children from modern slavery and help them rebuild their lives. God's Church is on the move! Ordinary people from the workplace and elsewhere are being used by God.

The Old Testament encourages us to pray at the gates, to act as watchers for the city (Isaiah 62:6-7). We can all do this. We can scan the local paper for what is happening locally where we need the mercy of God. There is crime, exploitation, corruption, etc, in your town or city. When we stand at the gates (sometimes literally, often just in prayer), we have Ekklesia authority to declare what we want to see leave our town or city and what we want to see bless it. As in Salford, this may take years of prayer, but our God is in the transformation business.

The prayer of blessing

In the book *The Grace Outpouring,* Roy Godwin describes moving job to run a small Christian conference centre in rural Wales.[84] He had been used to evangelising and wanted to continue with it – but he and his wife did not see any non-Christians! They asked God to help them, and suddenly people felt compelled to come up the long drive to their house, not knowing why they were there. Roy started showing them round, and at the end of the visit he would say, 'It is a tradition to pray a blessing on each visitor.' They started to have a remarkable impact, and Roy and his wife, Daphne, discovered the power of the blessing prayer. They encouraged people to pray in their villages, towns and workplaces. People found it a wonderful formula for prayer.

Many of you will be familiar with the blessing, or Aaron's prayer, from the book of Numbers, which we mentioned earlier:

The LORD bless you
and keep you;
the LORD make his face shine on you

---

[84] Roy Godwin, *The Grace Outpouring* (Eastbourne: David C Cook, 2012), p45.

and be gracious to you;
the LORD turn his face towards you
and give you peace.
(Numbers 6:24-26)

I find it such a key prayer to keep handy. If you are heading into a new situation, or a challenging meeting, perhaps with someone you don't find easy, use the prayer. It changes your expectations and attitude. Here you are in a meeting you have asked God to bless – and you might be the answer to your own prayer. You know best what will work for you and your situation, but a prayer blessing is a lovely gift.

We are a people of blessing. Jesus sent His seventy-two out to simply bless by saying, 'Peace to this house' (Luke 10:5). How about peace to this meeting? Peace to this lunch? Peace to this Zoom call? We are praying for God's shalom: it is a peace that changes lives.

Many routes to peace are offered. You can join classes and groups, often in the workplace. But God's peace is deeper, more substantial and unique. Shalom is a key theme in Scripture; it comes not just from reduced stress but when we know we are aligned with God's purpose and plan, when we know His favour. Shalom is an essential part of our spiritual toolkit. It acknowledges that God is with us, even in the most trying circumstances. It comes because we trust Him. We get to take that shalom into our workplace, it impacts our relationships, it changes the spiritual atmosphere.

Do not be anxious about anything, but in every situation, by prayer and petition, with thanksgiving, present your requests to God. And the [shalom] of God, which transcends all understanding, will guard your hearts and your minds in Christ Jesus.
(Philippians 4:6-7)

Call to action

When I spoke to my team at work, I had authority because of my job title. When I spoke to my colleagues, I had authority because of my expertise. It is vital that Christians learn to pray with more authority. The enemy wants to take our authority away; he does not want the Ekklesia to stand in the power it truly has.

- We have authority because God has called us.

- We have authority to ask God for His plans and purpose for our workplace.

- We have authority to pray for those purposes to happen.

We need to learn to use the authority God has given us, and spend time listening – and 'practise, practise, practise' hearing so we raise our prayer impact.

Application

- Create a list of five workplace things to pray about regularly.

- Both my prayer partners understand the stresses, challenges and joys of being called to the workplace. We pray weekly. Others meet every Saturday for coffee or have a regular weekend away. Whatever works for you, these prayer 'stakes in the ground' build our focus and commitment to God moving in the workplace. Who could you stand with in prayer?

- Let us keep thanking God for answered prayer; the more we do, the more aware we become of His moving in our lives.

Prayer

May the Lord bless my workplace, may the Lord bless my colleagues. May He bring His shalom, may He give us wisdom and integrity and may He use me to serve His kingdom in the places where He has put me. Amen.

Jeremiah's story

Jeremiah Lanphier was born in 1809. Through his story we see what amazing city-changing things God can do through people in the business community. He trained as a tailor and became a cloth merchant in New York's Lower Manhattan district. At the age of forty-eight he answered the call of his local church to become a lay missionary. Within a few weeks he realised his passion was for prayer, and this passion could drive his missionary efforts. He felt he could mobilise other businesspeople to join him in their lunch hour. He used his business skills to promote a prayer meeting to be held on 23rd September 1857. At noon, the room was empty apart from Jeremiah himself. By 12.30 one person had joined him, and by 1.00pm there were another four people. It was a start, and Jeremiah felt it was right to continue with the weekly meeting.

On 30th September, twenty men came (the workforce being predominantly male). On 7th October, forty people came. On 10th October, the stock market collapsed, and the district was filled with distraught and nervous workers. The crisis accelerated the prayer; many more businesspeople wanted to cry out to God for mercy and wisdom. By mid-March 1858, Lanphier decided to book the huge Burton's Theatre, which was filled with 3,000 prayers. Still the numbers grew, and by early April every church and public hall in Manhattan was filled to capacity as an astounding 10,000 people gathered to pray daily. The call to pray spread to many other cities in the US, with similar results, and then overseas.

What came first – the revival or the prayer? Many commentators say the two ran together. God was stirring a revival and it started with this extraordinary prayer movement. Indeed, many came to Christ in the prayer meetings. This was a workers' revival. It was birthed not through large-scale campaigns or through church leaders. It was born on the heart of one businessman who inspired many others that this was their moment to see God move. It was a diverse movement: denominations were unimportant. People joined the movement as clerks, draymen, lawyers, financiers, lawyers and mechanics. There was a great cry across the meetings, naming the loved ones and friends people wanted to come to know Christ.

That deep cry echoed God's heart; He knew that America would be ripped apart by civil war in a few short years.

The revival fire flared up in New York and spread. The local newspaper in New Haven, Connecticut, wrote how the town's biggest church was packed twice daily for prayer; another paper reported businesses shutting down for an hour each day so all the staff could pray. Over two years, around 1 million Americans came to Christ and the move spread to places like Ireland (the 1859 'Ulster revival').

Former cloth merchant Jeremiah Lanphier died in 1898 after following his heart and leading 11,000 prayer meetings.

God has shown He can do remarkable things through the business community. My prayer is that we would see God do it again, stirring a fresh call to pray in the workplace with many, many lives changed.

Chapter Nine
The Call to Make Disciples

On a mission

All of us meet people who do not know Jesus. Yet in our actions, words and lifestyle they see our representation of Jesus. 'God has chosen to make known among the Gentiles the glorious riches of this mystery, which is Christ in you, the hope of glory' (Colossians 1:27).

But there's a reality check here: many of us feel uncomfortable about sharing our faith, in the workplace or elsewhere. Many of us also feel 'unskilled'; we may have not received help or training and there is a fear that if we did do so it might end badly, and we will become 'Billy no mates'.

I was in a study group looking at a series of videos on telling our story. It led to an interesting discussion on evangelism in the workplace. Most of us were very nervous about the reaction we would get even from admitting we were Christians. It became clear we were also nervous about getting into a theological debate with our work colleagues. As we reflected further, we agreed that, in reality, having a theological debate at work was very unlikely. We live in a culture where discussion about politics and religion is frowned on, but also a culture that says, 'Whatever you believe is fine, as long as you don't impose your views on me.' We felt our fear of theological discussion came about because any training we had had on evangelism had focused on the theological debate issue, even though it was unlikely to happen.

Indeed, much of what we had been taught about evangelism made it feel as though it was a specialist calling and not one that involved us. Let us get behind this. There is a difference between evangelism and mission. Evangelism is more focused; it is the process of trying to raise someone's awareness of Christianity. Some people are gifted evangelists, most of us are not, but we all have Christ in us (Colossians 1:27). Mission is about being sent out, to reflect Christ in our lifestyles and values. It's back to the Great Commission – mission involves us all.

Of course, we live in a world in conflict, and one of the key areas of conflict is around secularism. It goes beyond, 'My truth is a good as your truth'; some aspects of the media will represent secularism as truth and faith as a distortion of the truth. In the public sector, I have been in meetings with political leaders telling Christian organisations not to proselytise. When we discuss it they are not clear what it means, but they are concerned about coercion and intimidation. In practice, this fear of criticism constrains Christians from sharing their values and beliefs. We get wary and paralysed – and fail in our call to mission.

Those videos our study group used simply focused on telling our story.[85] This breaks through the constraints: everyone has a story to tell. Three Christians in the series talked about their interests/hobbies; they could just as easily talk about their holidays, their families or their upbringing. This is normal, everyday conversation. Storytelling is a bridge on which we build relationships.

Material in this section is based on work I produced with Phil Knox from the Evangelical Alliance on praying for our non-Christian friends to come to Jesus. It is based on the simple assumption that everybody tells stories. We speak very matter-of-factly about why we like to holiday in Skegness, why Aston

---

[85] 'Faith Shared' (churcharmy.org/resources/faith–shared) (accessed 11th November 2021) resources for small groups.

Villa will have a better season this year than last year, and why our children are impressing us by the way they look after their guinea pigs. As we share our stories, the conversation goes deeper as we share our values – we might say, for example, 'Family is really important to me,' and relationships strengthen.

Make disciples

The Great Commission tells us to 'go' and make disciples – read Matthew 28:18-20.

You might feel like arguing at this point. 'I'm just an ordinary Christian! Leaders do discipleship-making.' Or even, 'We have a good course in our church for making disciples.' But each of us has been called or commissioned to do the work. We are salt, light and servants. Could it just be that Jesus made a mistake, that heaven needs better troops and workers than the likes of us? The Ekklesia emphasis on the Great Commission does not allow us that get-out clause. We are called to work together, support each other and go into our workplaces, into our neighbourhoods and into our families to make disciples. It is part of a great divine plan to change nations, and we get to do our bit. We are stuck with the misconception that this all happens in a church setting, because that's where teaching happens, that's where people are baptised. But the real focus is discipling, and that happens through relationships in people's homes and workplaces.

Before we get too carried away, let me put in a note of caution. We work for an employer; they hired us for our organising skills, or our selling or numeracy or engineering or a whole host of other things. We have a duty to serve that employer. More than that, we will be pretty poor at our mission if everyone thinks we are rubbish at our jobs. Mission is being an excellent employee and colleague and leader because Jesus makes a difference in our lives. We take a Jesus 'aroma' into the workplace (2 Corinthians 2:15). The more time we spend with Jesus, the more He naturally shines through.

Discipling can be an off-putting word. You might think of it as a process a trained person would do with someone who has become a Christian. You may have come across formal discipling programmes. We may think that discipling has no role in the workplace. But we have been sent out by Jesus to create disciples; it is not a 'specialists-only sport'. The starting point for discipling isn't a process; its love. It's inputting into someone's life and wanting them to succeed.

So mission or discipling in the workplace is not announcing to the office that we are inviting them to our sixteen-week series in the canteen on the book of Romans. We create disciples because we demonstrate Jesus' teaching. It changes the values around us. It may be when we forgive the colleague who stole our ideas and claimed them as their own, when we are brain-stretchingly tired but find time to ask a stressed colleague how they are doing, and whether we can help them. We create disciples in the team meeting when everyone is annoyed at the latest rules from the finance team and we say, 'You know, I believe we need to think of finance as our customers; we want to help them succeed in keeping us all afloat.' We start to change the culture, and influence what others believe about their workplace. 'Live such good lives among the pagans that, though they accuse you of doing wrong, they may see your good deeds and glorify God on the day he visits us' (1 Peter 2:12).

In some ways, the mission perspective is about giving some workplace time to God. He won't abuse it. But finding that extra ten minutes to listen to a struggling colleague or going out of our way to carry out an act of kindness is opening the door to Jesus working through us.

We have talked before about having that Jesus flavour, that added Jesus element that breaks through and stops us being ordinary. Jesus, of course, called this 'salt' in Matthew 5:13. Salt preserves what is good and brings out what is good; it breaks up the frozen ground.

Fear can hold us back. We may feel intimidated about sharing our faith. But look at this from Barna, a US Christian research and teaching company, analysing 'Perceptions of Jesus, Christians and Evangelism in the UK', and you will see much of our fear is in our minds rather than in the real world:[86]

- Two-thirds of non-Christians surveyed said they know a practising Christian – of these, 58% say they have had a conversation about Jesus.

- 60% of non-Christians enjoy being with their Christian friends/family.

- 65% see Christians as friendly, 51% caring and 46% good humoured.

- We are often concerned they see us negatively – these figures are far smaller – 13% see us as narrow minded, 10% as hypocritical and 7% as homophobic.

- When engaged in conversation about Jesus, 18% wanted to know more, 20% were open to an encounter with Jesus and 22% felt more positive towards Jesus Christ.

- 72% are comfortable about sharing their faith but 32% are concerned about not causing offence when talking to non-Christians.

So keep praying – with expectation! The more we pray for our friends, the more we hear God's love for them, and the more we realise that we can be the answer – not through a complicated evangelism process but because we are their friends and want the best for them. Why not simply pray for five people to come to Christ? Spend time with God praying about who your five should be, and put their names on a small card to remind you to pray regularly. This is a great way of making our call to mission a deliberate daily action.

---

[86] www.barna.com/research/perceptions-of-jesus-christians-evangelism-in-the-uk (accessed 22nd November 2021) report published 2nd October 2016.

Strengthening relationships

One of the key drivers of success in the workplace is relationship-building. For most of us, our job outcomes are normally dependent on other people. One of my early lessons was driving a large change project by simply sending people weekly planning charts. This avoided conversations, but meant I failed to help them understand what we wanted them to do, or hear their concerns, so failed to get commitment to action.

We all have different levels of comfort with relationship-building. Some love to do it; others find it harder. This links in with where we stand on the introvert/extrovert scale. Many are energised by regular contact with others; they love to be bubbly and friendly. More introverted people, however, work well on their own; they concentrate well but find relationship-building demanding. Others, introvert or extrovert, are more focused on putting their time and energy into the task and prefer to only use relationships to get the job done.

The truth is, we all need to build relationships – some will be deep and long lasting, others may be shallow and not last past coffee time, but we are interdependent. Good neighbours get to know each other; they take an interest in each other.

But what happens when they ask, 'I see you heading out every Sunday morning. Do you go swimming or something?' Or, 'I noticed you felt uncomfortable when the boss was ranting and swearing – what was the problem?' Or, 'They had that Christian politician on the news last night. He seems to hate everyone and everything. I don't know how anyone can believe such rubbish. What do you think?'

This is one of those pivotal moments where we have to decide, do I admit I am a Christian? But we need to bear in mind that if we don't admit to it, this constrains future conversations. Paul said, 'I am not ashamed of the gospel, because it is the power of God that brings salvation to everyone who believes: first to the Jew, then to the Gentile' (Romans 1:16).

I am a Christian

If we are to build deep relationships, this is not something we can hide from our friends and colleagues. The goal is that people know but feel this is not closing conversations down. Remember the Barna research? One in five people is open to conversations about their friends' faith. We need to know where they stand – are they are sceptical or cynical? Hold other beliefs?

To be a Christian is to be distinctive. We believe things many others don't, and this shapes our behaviour and values. In today's work environment, being different or distinctive is OK. What people look for is authenticity. That means being comfortable with being different. For many of us that is a big challenge because we want to 'fit in'. There's a helpful management textbook called *Fit In, Stand Out*.[87] It argues that we need to do both to be successful in the workplace. We need to 'demonstrate we are aligned with the organisation's goals'; we relate and listen well, but we stand out by contributing our difference. It might be our insight, experience or wisdom; it might just be because we bring a calm into the room. It's described as our ability to both integrate and transform. God has made us to be people who both fit in and stand out – like salt! We just need to embrace the idea that we can do both.

Are we prepared for this 'I am a Christian' conversation (and is this the right time)? We make a choice here. Do we give them the 'I believe' speech, or do we simply say something like, 'My faith is really important to me as it shapes who I am – but I don't want it to be uncomfortable for you. What would suit you?'

The problem with 'I believe' is it can put people on the defensive and maybe create some anguish, which means it is unlikely they will hear what we say. They will jump to

---

[87] Blythe McGarvie, *Fit In, Stand Out* (New York, NY: McGraw-Hill 2005).

conclusions. We want to build a conversation bridge that enables us to keep talking. The route is often storytelling.

A good example is telling stories about our church. A lot of people find that hard: again, we need to practise! So when people ask, 'How was your weekend?' are you able to say, 'We had a great time at church'? Have a think about the positives that you can add into your story:

- I love the worship. We sing lots of up-to-date songs, and it's probably one of the few places people do that. I just find it really uplifting.

- I love the stillness of church. I can go in on my own and get a deep sense of peace, and then soak up the beautiful singing. I always find the liturgy moving and the sermon thought-provoking.

- I was talking to some people who give money advice, in our church. They have worked with this guy, he's not a church member, but he was in debt and really distraught, but they have helped him turn his life around.

- The talk was on the story of the prodigal son.[88] I just found it really moving because the guy in the story went off and did his own thing and abandoned his father, but his father never abandoned him. As a parent myself, it moved me that he could keep loving his son even though the boy had thrown all his money away and ruined his life.

Are we prepared? What story could we tell next Monday?

Are we sitting comfortably?

We all tell stories. It is a key communication tool. We all like to listen to stories. Told well, they transport us to somewhere else and they give us a memorable picture. 1 Peter 3:15 tells us: 'Always be prepared to give an answer to everyone who asks

---

[88] See Luke 15:11-32.

you to give the reason for the hope that you have. But do this with gentleness and respect.'

I wholeheartedly believe that if we as Christians were prepared and intentional about sharing our faith, in the everyday of our lives, we might see unprecedented numbers of people coming to know Jesus.[89]

Telling our story is one of the most precious gifts we have, and we want to be well prepared. There is no substitute for practice. Try out your story in your small group (if you have one), or with family or friends, and keep honing it. Here are three fundamental questions we might get asked: let us not stumble over our answers but be prepared. Perhaps our small groups could give time to help us practise conversations like the three below. It would be interesting to see what different people's answers are.

- Why do you go to church?

- Are you a Christian?

- You're religious, aren't you?

God's story

Can we tell God's story? Here are some key elements. How comfortable are we sharing these stories? Do we need more practice? How do we put this in our own words, so it flows naturally? Thousands of books have been written about our faith, yet the core message is simple and powerful. Jesus changes lives fundamentally. Let us understand the clear gospel message.

- God created us and loves us personally. He is not distant; He is very close. God wants a personal relationship with us.

---

[89] Phil Knox, Story Bearer, Great Commission resources, www.eauk.org/great-commission/resources/story-bearer-small-group-sessions (accessed 21st January 2022).

- We have messed up and separated ourselves from God.

- Jesus died and rose again. He did it for us to bridge the gap between us and heaven.

- When we come to Him and surrender, give our lives to Him, He forgives us, reaches out to us and starts us on a new journey with Him.

The Gospel writers told stories about Jesus; they captivated and intrigued people.

Writing our story

> Experience is the best teacher. A compelling story is a close second.[90]

We all tell stories. We learned the art as children; we recognised that it captured people's attention. Writing and then telling our own spiritual story is so important, and yet many of us have never done it. I recommend you give it a go! Get the story written and then share it with your small group, if you have one – or with someone who will give you honest feedback, if you don't. This is such a key moment in your history. Everyone who values and loves you should know about this.

Think about when you became a Christian. Let's gather the basic facts first.

1. What was the situation; *what was happening*?

2. How would you describe yourself at that time?

3. What were the *key steps/events* that changed you?

4. What actually happened to move you to faith in Jesus?

5. What was the *result*?

---

[90] Paul Smith, *Lead With a Story* (New York, NY: American Management Association, 2012), p2.

Now add a wider narrative – who did what? How did you feel? What words best describe the situation? What made this event interesting/exciting/unique?

Find somewhere to write your story. Aim for 300-500 words.

What's the headline of this story? Imagine telling your story – how would you start it? For example, 'I want to tell you about what I see as the key day in my life.' Or, 'I want to tell you about my gradual experience of coming to faith and why it changed me.'

How prepared are you for this opportunity?

Many Christians do not envisage leading someone to Christ, and yet testimony after testimony tells of how it is the most important moment in changing many people's lives.

Let us be honest with God. He calls us to be and to bring good news. Are we up for this? If not, we need to ask God to equip us. We need to turn from our reluctance or fear. It boils down to a simple prayer: 'Use me, Lord.'

Offering to pray for someone

Another step is to offer to pray for someone. It could be for a colleague at work, or a friend who is really struggling with illness, bereavement, family, stress, etc. You might feel you want to pray for peace, or wisdom, or a breakthrough. Ask if it is OK to talk about how prayer can help. Explain how you find praying can be very powerful. You can simply pray the blessing prayer from Numbers 6:24-26.

My colleague Don[91] was very close to his father, who died unexpectedly. Don struggled with grief for quite some time afterwards and this left him tired and lacking in energy. I offered to pray for him. This needed to be done sensitively, giving him permission to turn down the offer. But so many people respond positively when another offers to pray for them. In Don's case,

---

[91] Not his real name.

I wanted to be specific and pray for him to know God's peace and wisdom for the way forward. A few months later, Don started going to church and gave his life to Christ.

A friend goes to local shops and says, 'I am from the local church, and we are prayer walking today, going around local shops asking if we can pray for them and bless them. Is there anything we can pray for you?' The response is usually positive. It is a simple offer: 'I would love to pray a blessing on your baby, on your family, on your work – is there anything in particular you would like prayer for?' Of course, we may get a 'Go away and don't bother me' response that we must respect. But we can always go away and pray for them silently.

Some find when praying for friends or colleagues that God gives them words of knowledge,[92] or a sense of, perhaps, deep sorrow or grief. Sensitivity is called for, but if God has given us this, it is for a purpose. We will become more confident and proficient in our prayer for others when this flows naturally from praying for church friends first. It does not have to come across as weird: 'I was thinking about you and I just felt you have a deep sorrow over something. I may be wrong, but if there were something, I would like to see how I can help.'

Even the discipline of praying for your colleagues every day you enter the office (yes, even if you work from home), for God to bless them and open doors for you, may see things change.

To Yan's story

To Yan (Tina) is the owner/leader of an education centre in Macau, China. She sees her call as teaching and training her students and staff and providing good-quality education to build student confidence.

Her 'discipleship' flows naturally. She cares about her team and talks to her staff about their lives. Parents will ask for advice and support. She guides her students with open questions about

---

[92] See 1 Corinthians 12:8. A word of knowledge might be around health, life circumstances and so on.

God. 'Whenever there was a chance, I would share the way I live and how I spent my days among church, work, family. Also, our centre was a bridge to let the students join some of the children and youth activities. Some of them become our church members later on in their life. I praised God for letting us have the opportunities as the bridge.'

Leading someone to Christ

My friend Phil Knox has written a great book about storytelling.[93] One of his challenges is that most of us would freeze up if someone were to say, 'I want to become a Christian.' Phil believes we should all be able to lead someone to Christ. It seems to me that this is a key skill for every Christian in the workplace. Phil is an evangelist; he does naturally what others find intimidating. He tells us there are some clear and simple steps:

He will have a REVIEW conversation with them:

- What have you found helpful in our previous conversations about Jesus?

- Are you ready for a conversation about giving your life to Jesus?

He will have a SURRENDER conversation with them:

- Are you ready to turn away from your old life?

- Are you ready to say sorry for the things you have done wrong in your life?

- Do you want to choose a new way? Do you surrender your life to Jesus?

He will then have a FIRST STEPS conversation:

---

[93] Phil Knox, *Story Bearer: How to Share Your Faith With Your Friends* (Nottingham: IVP, 2020).

- One of the great things about being a Christian is prayer; the more we talk to Jesus the closer He comes to us, and the better we are at listening to Him.

- It would be good to start with a thank you prayer – that Jesus has changed you.

- Pray that change will continue, that you will become more and more like him.[94]

Disciples

Discipling starts before someone comes to Christ. After someone we work with comes to Christ, we will want to help them find Christians near them with whom they can join in and learn from. We might volunteer to go with them to a local church, but they are also part of our Ekklesia – the Church in the workplace. We will want to help them to grow in their faith. Each person will be different, and our advice needs to be 'made to measure' – not everyone will want to read something, others will look for a social media solution, or prefer time with us.

Here are some tips:

Give them three simple prayer steps to get going: Give your life to Jesus throughout each day. You could start with, 'I give this day to You (or this meeting, or this journey, etc). Please give me Your peace and wisdom. Your will be done.'

- Ask God to bless a) your family, b) you, c) friends, d) where you live, work, study or spend leisure time.

- Bring your worries and concerns to Jesus – ask for His peace and wisdom

---

[94] Steve Botham, *Praying for our Friends to come to Christ – Life changers* (EA, CV and WPC). Awaiting publication.

Bible study: We want our friend to enjoy the Word of God, but it can be hard to get started. Recommend they read a Gospel but start easily with around six verses at a time, circling things they what to discuss, and underlining verses they find inspiring.

Testimony: Many people have made this journey and found that faith in Jesus has turned their life around. Some examples can be found on the CV Global website.[95]

Friendship

Our friend needs friends. It could be us, but we may not be able to give the regular support needed. This faith journey is full of new discoveries and challenges. They need to ask questions. It would be good to study the Bible together and to pray for them and their situation, inviting them to pray for us too. We need to help them think through joining a church and how that transition will work.

Keep going

Praying for our friends to come to Christ and telling our story is a lifetime commitment. It is central to our walk with Jesus – the Spirit of God is always working through us to carry good news.

If we belong to a small group/Bible study/life group, can we set aside some time regularly to discuss how well we are telling our stories? What have we learned? How can we pray? Where do we need a breakthrough? Is our small group willing to be a practice area to keep telling our stories of God working in our lives? Or can we find some others as part of our 'advisory group' to work with us?

---

[95] www.cvglobal.co/impact/stories/ (accessed 17th November 2021).

Call to action

We need to get our head around people in the workplace coming to Christ. It is God's plan and we have often been reluctant to do it. Most of Jesus' work and ministry was in the open. It did not rely on meetings or buildings. It relied on people experiencing Him.

Jesus is like a spring within us. He constantly bubbles up and releases joy, compassion and unusual insight. We need to get better at telling our story. Let's not hide Jesus away. Let's take the steps we need to take to let Jesus' light shine.

Application

The call to disciple, to be on mission, is part of the Great Commission. It is for those of us in the workplace. How do you feel about that?

- What is our story of coming to faith? Could we write it down?

- Can the members of our small group (if we have one) practise telling their story to each other? Can we get to a point where we are fully comfortable in telling our story in accessible language?

- If someone were to ask you about your faith, how do you feel you would respond? They are asking because they are interested; how can you build on that interest?

- Who at work needs prayer? What would be the best way to offer prayer to this person in a way that would feel natural and encouraging?

Prayer

Lord, help me to tell your story, graciously and sensitively. Help my story to be attractive. I pray for my colleagues, that You will use me to show You in my actions and my words. Amen.

Charlotte's story

Charlotte works for an investment and financial planning firm that has been established for more than 250 years and is one of the UK's leading wealth managers. She started her working life with YWAM[96] and then the Alpha course[97] and then felt a call to get into a role where she could interact with lots of non-Christians. She felt the best way to witness was in a team where they saw her, where she was real and where she could make deeper connections. She is clear: 'God wants me in the workplace being a witness, demonstrating integrity and doing a good job.'

She hit a crunch point when she wondered whether she should leave her current employer. She went on a Christian women's weekend and quietly asked God to speak to her. In the Saturday morning session she had an overwhelming feeling that she should stay. A little later, someone else on the conference took a big step of faith and shared what she felt God was saying to Charlotte. The message was that God knew it was hard but He would loosen things and make it better. This gave Charlotte the faith to carry on, and in the intervening period her job has changed substantially, giving her much more of a customer relationship role, which she loves, and has seen her become the best performer. 'Business has flown in,' she says.

For some years, Charlotte was the only Christian in her firm, but more recently another Christian has joined her, and they are able to pray together. Two colleagues have recently completed the Alpha course. She was given permission to email the entire office with details of another Alpha course and two more colleagues have joined this online programme.

Her approach to being a witness is very clear – be real. Tell people you had a good Sunday and went to church. 'Be real, be me.' She has been working with Street Pastors into the early

---

[96] Youth With A Mission, ywam.org (accessed 14th October 2021).
[97] alpha.org.uk (accessed 14th October 2021).

mornings at the weekend and will talk about her experiences helping people who need love, help and someone to listen to after the buzz and excitement of a night out falls away. She loves relationship-building, it's a key strength and comes naturally. She will be honest and open about her mistakes, she is available for clients, and she builds trust – which, of course, is essential when dealing with colleagues and with her clients' financial futures. She is often carried by the peace of God, which keeps her calm when others are feeling pressurised, and helps her make wise decisions.

Chapter Ten
The Call to Community

Where is my community?

From heaven's perspective, people matter and place matters. It is not happenstance that plants us on a particular road or street. We are called to communities to make a difference, to have an impact. The workplace is one community – it is a place where we can serve. The call is to be there for our colleagues.

Alongside the workplace, we all inhabit a range of communities – where we live, worship, learn, where we spend our leisure time, and there may be other communities that we participate in. Our contributions to and what we want from our different communities will vary. The challenge we raise here is: what might we be called to do outside the workplace?

All communities depend on relationships. As we look at relationship-building within our particular communities, there is a challenge for us. When we think of 'us' – the community we feel comfortable with, gravitate to and are refreshed by – is our 'us' too narrow? Who (let's be honest here) would we put in the 'them' category: people we avoid or feel uncomfortable with? So in our thinking about our 'us' and 'them', do we need to broaden our outlook and community?

The Spirit of the Lord is on us

Isaiah 61:1 is a pivotal verse, linking God's promises in the Old Testament to His promises in the New. Jesus reads from it when He speaks in the synagogue in Nazareth. He says, 'Today this scripture is fulfilled in your hearing' (Luke 4:21). You can imagine the awe and wonder in the congregation: 'What did He just say?'; 'Did He really mean today?'; 'What does He mean — "fulfilled"?'

Let us look at it in more detail.

The Spirit of the Sovereign LORD is on me,
because the LORD has anointed me
to proclaim good news to the poor.
He has sent me to bind up the broken-hearted,
to proclaim freedom for the captives
and release from darkness for the prisoners,
to proclaim the year of the LORD's favour
and the day of vengeance of our God,
to comfort all who mourn,
and provide for those who grieve in Zion —
to bestow on them a crown of beauty
instead of ashes,
the oil of joy
instead of mourning,
and a garment of praise
instead of a spirit of despair.
They will be called oaks of righteousness,
a planting of the LORD
for the display of his splendour.
They will rebuild the ancient ruins
and restore the places long devastated;
they will renew the ruined cities
that have been devastated for generations.
(Isaiah 61:1-4)

These four verses are some of the most powerful in Scripture. Jesus uses them to announce the coming of His kingdom. This is what 'your kingdom come' (Matthew 6:10) looks like on earth. It is an anointing from God; as kings were anointed, so we have been anointed: there is a call on our lives. There is no day, situation or place where the Lord does not go with us. He has anointed us for some key reasons:

- To bring good news to the poor;

- To bind up the broken-hearted;

- To release prisoners from darkness;

- To proclaim God's favour;

- To comfort those who mourn and grieve.

How do we make these familiar words come alive in our own experience?

During the Covid-19 crisis we became more aware of the proximity of death. In traumatic times, grief goes deep and lasts long. One wise lady, gifted in this area, is promoting the concept of the 'Bereavement Friendly Church'.[98] It reminds us that we used to be the place of refuge for many communities enduring loss and grief. We need the skills – and the compassion – to be the people others come to when they are in need.

The Isaiah 61 challenge is, do we know this call of God in our lives? How does it shape how we see ourselves and others?

Isaiah 61:3 gives us yet another profound truth: 'They will be called oaks of righteousness, a planting of the LORD for the display of his splendour.' So who are 'they'? It's the broken-hearted, the grieving, the prisoners – their changed lives have a profound impact on everyone around them. It's the homeless, the addict, the abused, and it's our stressed and struggling work colleague who can be changed to display God's splendour. They will show the great story that Christ really does set us free and revolutionise our lives.

Church has no impact if it is invisible. A church that exists just for its membership is a club, not an Ekklesia working out how it can shape, bless and transform its locality. We are called

---

[98] www.ataloss.org (accessed 17th November 2021). The wonderful work of AtaLoss.org is shaped by Yvonne Richmond Tulloch – its aim is that nobody in the UK suffering a significant loss should be left floundering or alone.

to display the splendour of the Lord; His splendour is seen in His good news changing the lives of people around us.

Increasingly we live at a time when God is sending His people out; we are serving in a way that engages and challenges the surrounding community. I suggest many of us need to ask, 'What are You calling me to do, Lord?' It does not need a quick or hurried response. There is no guilt trip here. All of us need to spend time listening to God's heart for our community. What does He love? What distresses Him? What can change? Let us not be afraid. Earlier, we looked at how God created a masterpiece when He created us. 'For we are God's masterpiece. He has created us anew in Christ Jesus, so we can do the good things he planned for us long ago' (Ephesians 2:10, NLT).

Listen to God's call: He has prepared work for His masterpiece to do – it will bless us and bless others. He will also guide us on how involved we should be.

Starting at home

God's starting point for community life is in the home. Whatever our status – single, separated, married, with or without children – how we live life in our home impacts who we are and how we impact our community. If we are parents, our children go to the local schools (generally) and learn to be good neighbours. We meet in the school playground and build links; we stand in the cold and wet with other parents to watch our children play sport. In Deuteronomy 6:5 Moses says, 'Love the LORD your God with all your heart and with all your soul and with all your strength.' He goes on, 'These commandments that I give you today are to be on your hearts. Impress them on your children. Talk about them when you sit at home and when you walk along the road, when you lie down and when you get up' (vv6-7).

As parents, we shape how our children see their community. Care for the Family and others have comprehensive research that shows that the time people are most likely to come to Christ is under the age of eleven. Increasingly, there is a high loss of faith during teenage years. Care for the Family shows that in the teenage years peer pressure becomes a more influential voice than the parents' voice and teens lose their faith.[99] The message in Deuteronomy is work at it, tell the stories, but also show by your actions what matters to you. Do your children know your stories of God moving in your life, and how you serve and behave in your different communities? Do they know the many ways God has blessed you and moved you?

How can I serve my community?

This is the bit where some of you go, 'You're joking. I'm far too busy.' Of course, that is legitimate. Let me suggest that we can all do something. How much will depend on our circumstances, passion and gifting. We may be called to an activity that deals directly with the broken-hearted and grieving, but it is equally legitimate to do something that helps change people's life chances or self-worth – like sports coaching or mentoring. For many, the call may be to concentrate on our workplace. There are different levels of engagement across your many communities. The simple challenge is, Lord, am I answering Your call on my life at this time?

Levels of community engagement

1. **Blessing.** I commit to pray for where I live and where I work. It may be as simple as regularly using the blessing prayer from Numbers 6:24-26 'The LORD bless you and keep you …' I pray for God's kingdom to come, not as a throwaway prayer but believing this is God's heart.

2. **Awareness.** I find out what the local issues and concerns are. I create a prayer discipline; maybe praying when I travel

---

[99] www.careforthefamily.org.uk (accessed 17th November 2021). Care for the Family has a wide range of well-researched teaching resources.

or, say, every Thursday. I get to know the neighbours. My small group sends thank-you cards to the police and the library; we pray for local schools and our councillors.

3. **Engagement.** This may be at a number of levels.

    Prayer: where I live, we have a monthly prayer meeting and we pray about local issues – car thefts and muggings, domestic violence, local businesses and the local church. This is a gathering from a range of churches, and we keep up to date through WhatsApp.

    Give time: Throughout my time as a school governor, the school kept achieving better results, raising the life chances for our pupils. That long-term commitment helped address school improvement, financial challenges, talent management and other issues with eyes on the horizon. But there also came a time when it was right to step down, when I was becoming too 'samey' and less innovative.

    Give wisdom. We develop skills and wisdom in the world of work. Local people and organisations can benefit from this. We can be encouragers when so many people snipe and complain.

4. **Commitment.** You may find yourself in a key role within the community. See the end of the chapter for the story about David. He is a key catalyst in our community with a clear and powerful call from God.

Having run many workshops and team and planning events, I found that communities wanted my skills in facilitating and leading meetings. I led many meetings with nationally known politicians. One that stood out was for 200 members of the local Somali community wanting to discuss the issue of khat, a narcotic from Somalia then sold openly in local shops. The men in the community would spend up to four days a week in khat dens, smoking, leaving the women to bring in income, raise the family and deal with the men's throat cancer, mental health and other consequences of their addiction. This was a special occasion to finally allow open discussion about a deep wound in their community. It was a privilege to do it, because God wants us to be people of peace and mercy.

Where can I serve?

Many of us will already be doing this, so I have included a brief list of options below. A comprehensive report by the Cinnamon Faith Action Audit in 2015 showed that the UK Church and faith groups gave time and service to their communities each year worth an impressive £3 billion. 'There were over 200,000 church and faith group led social action initiatives involving 1.8 million volunteers.'[100] Its website provides short films on a wide range of initiatives that serve the poor and hungry, give family assistance, money advice, mental health support, work with young people and newly released prisoners and help the unemployed and homeless. Many of these initiatives have started small with Cinnamon funding but have grown rapidly as other communities take up the schemes. Christians are finding a wide range of ways to serve their community through:

- **Volunteers/feet on the ground.** Many organisations just need people's time. Volunteers play a key role, from tidying streets to distributing food to linking with the elderly. It is all vital.

- **Thanksgiving.** It is important we don't just have a deficit model about our communities, focusing on what is wrong or broken. A friend working in a difficult inner-city area tells of how they set out to spot the good – the local flowerbeds in the park, the helpful neighbours, the welcoming coffee shop. These then become foundations for future development.

---

[100] www.cinnamonnetwork.co.uk/wp-content/uploads/2019/10/26081-National-Report-CFAAR-20pp-2016-AW_hr.pdf (accessed 28th January 2022). The Cinnamon Network supports a wide range of community-based projects with start-up funding and advice.

- **Prayer.** See below.

- **Advice.** Community groups, school governors, charities, etc, need advice – it might be legal, financial, HR, people issues, technology, marketing, engineering, environmental, civic engagement, commercial. Your workplace wisdom can serve the community.

- **Initiatives.** You may be creative and pioneering, and see how a new initiative or an idea from elsewhere can be used in your community. Young people in particular can be encouraged and released to bring in the new.

- **A catalyst.** Communities need people who make things happen; they gather groups together and look at challenges and say, 'What can we do differently?'

- **Networking.** Networkers are invaluable: who do you know, who can you link us to?

- **Governance.** Most organisations need help with governance. As a school governors' board, we were constantly asked to demonstrate that we had the skills to review the budget, the curriculum, conduct recruitment, etc.

- **Mentoring.** We need young community leaders, people in their twenties with energy and drive and the passion to drive change. They need mentors and encouragers – people to get them started. Equally, older people need mentors to help them understand how to relate and engage with the younger generation and keep up to date with technology. Fruitful mentoring can be two way.

- **Bridge building.** Many communities are diverse and need bridge builders, people who listen to other groups, to ensure those other groups are included and understood. Bridge builders identify the marginalised and constantly ask, 'Is everyone included here?'

A question you will probably ask is, 'Is this in the church or elsewhere?' Many churches have wonderful, often stunning programmes that need support. But remember the power of working with non-Christians, of sharing your enthusiasm and compassion with them. Jesus was constantly in public places, and when challenged by the Pharisees He made this powerful comment: 'Even though you do not believe me, believe the works, that you may know and understand that the Father is in me, and I in the Father' (John 10:38).

High hopes

Isaiah 61 is also a prophetic call, made before Judah went into captivity, to the subsequent generations who found themselves living in Babylon. God has a remarkable plan; He is going to restore Jerusalem after many years of devastation and shame. Years later, as we have seen, Nehemiah weeps when he has an update on the state of the city (Nehemiah 1:4). This is God's own dwelling place in ruins. But Isaiah issues a promise to those in exile in verse 4: 'They will rebuild the ancient ruins and restore the places long devastated; they will renew the ruined cities that have been devastated for generations.' It is a specific promise for Nehemiah's generation, where God's Spirit is on them. But many communities and cities throughout history also feel these verses speaking to them, prompted by the Holy Spirit to rebuild, restore and renew.

Let us do a spiritual audit. Here are some questions to bring before God and reflect on. You may have no clue as to the answers, so how can you find out? Who can you talk to?

- **What needs rebuilding?** Is there enough housing? Are there places for young people to meet? Are there places for the elderly, or the lonely? What about the local parks and open spaces – are you proud of them?

- **What needs renewing?** We live separate lives, but many communities are trying to build new connections, to work across ethnic and racial lines, to build support and hear each other's stories. I worked with a community that had a 'telly buddies' scheme, linking elderly and housebound people together weekly to talk and check on their welfare – a simple but powerful way to renew lives.[101]

- **What needs restoring?** This gets us to principles – restore generosity, friendliness, a shared approach to each other's welfare. This is not about going back to the good old days, but it might be about reframing the good old days – for instance, in the past the community shared and worked well as a monocultural group and now we want to restore that across a range of ethnicities and backgrounds. In some ways this is about the question, how will we live and work as community? How does this engage those with mental health issues? The disabled? The single parents?

Sometimes the community needs to rebuild, restore or renew quickly. It needs to respond to a crisis. This tests and hopefully strengthens community. Has it got the good will and capacity to respond? Covid-19 flagged many issues around food poverty, mental health, bereavement and grief, job loss and dented aspirations, economic instability, family breakdown. No one church, no one organisation can respond to these challenges. In response, the rebuilders, like Nehemiah, pull teams together and work hard to repair their section of the wall alongside others (Nehemiah 3). The whole people of God can do what individual churches and groups can never achieve.

Isaiah 61 is partly fulfilled in Nehemiah. Jerusalem is restored as a safe place to live, and as a place that gives glory to God after just fifty-two days (Nehemiah 6:15) of rebuilding. When God initiates rebuild, renew, restore, remarkable things can happen. So pray for God's heart for your community, and work with others. Successful community rebuilding looks to the long term – what could this community look like in ten years' time? This

---

[101] www.pioneergroup.org.uk (accessed 22nd November 2021).

takes us past all the barriers that currently exist and helps us dream an attractive vision.

Acts: communities transformed by Jesus

I love the verse in Acts 2 about the first Christians who were 'enjoying the favour of all the people' (v47). That credibility was shaped by their lifestyle. 'They devoted themselves to the apostles' teaching and to fellowship, to the breaking of bread and to prayer' (Acts 2:42). Everything they did flowed from that devotion – a passionate commitment to learning, friendship and fellowship, and sharing communion. This put their roots deep in Jesus, and we see the remarkable fruit from it.

The Ekklesia 'movement' is equipped and birthed at Pentecost; they learn together how an Ekklesia blesses its community in Jerusalem. The Ekklesia is then sent out to impact towns and cities throughout the Middle East and beyond. Acts shows we are a gift to our communities.

In Acts 8 we learn, 'Those who had been scattered preached the word wherever they went. Phillip went down to a city in Samaria and proclaimed the Messiah there' (Acts 8:4-5). As God's servants, we might get a new job and must move locations. God is in the real estate business, often surprising us as He moves us to a new community and calling.

Alan Scott in his outstanding book, *Scattered Servants*, speaks as a pastor. 'It's not difficult to reach the community. It's just really hard to change the church.' He recognises that church can be making all the demands on our spare time and energy. But he says this is all wrong; the Ekklesia is called 'to make disciples who change cities', 'the call is to release unstoppable, impassioned scattered servants'.[102] Hear the release in this. Church finds its Ekklesia identity and is measured by its impact on the community, not by its gathered meetings. It is time for our communities to pulse with the love and dynamism that

---

[102] Scott, *Scattered Servants*, p18.

God's people bring. It's time for our young people to release their pent-up energy and passion and values into their community.

Jesus impacted His community enormously. He was visible; He was present. Crowds followed Him as He walked into a town and through its streets. He responded to people. We have talked about the kingdom call to compassion. It drove Jesus. 'When he saw the crowds, he had compassion on them' (Matthew 9:36). He saw two blind men on the outskirts of Jericho. 'Jesus had compassion on them and touched their eyes. Immediately they received their sight and followed him' (Matthew 20:34).

He had a large crowd (4,000 men) with Him who had not eaten for three days: 'Jesus called his disciples to him and said, "I have compassion for these people"' (Matthew 15:32). So He fed them miraculously. A man with leprosy came to Him and begged Him, 'If you are willing, you can make me clean.' Filled with compassion,[103] Jesus 'reached out His hand and touched the man. "I am willing," he said. "Be clean!"' (Mark 1:40-41).

Jesus was very aware of what was happening around Him, and He allowed it to touch His heart.

Serving your community in prayer

Let prayer shape our call for our community. It helps us see it through God's eyes – we recognise His concerns but also the ways in which He can bless our community. We have looked at prayer elsewhere, and there are some key principles that apply equally to praying for our community.

- **Pray with thanksgiving**. Jesus loves this community. His eyes are on our neighbours, our shops, our schools; thank God for what is good in our community.

---

[103] NIV footnote for Mark 1:41 reads: 'Many manuscripts *Jesus was filled with compassion*'.

- **Praise.** We praise Him as Lord of our community, as its redeemer, healer, restorer.

- **Listen, listen, listen.** What is God saying? We want His prompts – sometimes they come through Scripture; sometimes He will bring a situation or group of people to mind.

There are also aspects of prayer that are important when we pray for a place.

- **Dream with God.** I don't want to shape God's agenda for my community; He already has one. The more I spend time in His presence the more I can dream what a move of God will look like. We ask Him to give us vision and understanding so we can pray wisely about how He might bless the children, bless the widows, orphans and aliens, bless the different churches and schools, bless community leaders. We pray for God to shine His face on our community – and show His love and favour.

- **Watch the gates.** We guard the gates. There are physical entry and exit points for our community – road junctions, railway points. They are good places to pray. There are also strategic places of influence – schools, the shopping centre, community areas. What do we believe God wants to release into our community? Care for the broken-hearted? The gospel to go forward? Healing and peace in struggling families? What do we stand against? Domestic violence, theft, sexual abuse, racism, etc?

- **Understand our local history and context.** God has moved in the past, churches have grown, people have been saved. History tells us of God's love, what He has done in the past – and can do again. There are also historical things that may hold you back now, for example, significant disunity, sin, violence. Sometimes you learn from knowing your community's reputation – good and bad. There may be particular areas in the community that are darker than others. Police records of local crime may show areas that are especially vulnerable.[104] Can you pray for them? There will be times when God calls you to repent for your community, and you need knowledge of what has gone on and is going on to ask for forgiveness with confidence.

- **What is bound in heaven?** We need to know the things that heaven is against – death, sickness, corruption, poverty, gambling, addiction, child abuse, suicide, trafficking, drugs, violence, pornography: they are forbidden in heaven. What is God saying to you about here on earth?

- **Church is the people of God placed in every sphere.** 'Every sphere is influenced to act in a Godly way that genuinely enhances goodness and acts as a catalyst for the presence of God.'[105]

- **Pray for unity in the body of Christ**, within and between churches, within and throughout Christians serving your community. Unity is not just a few meetings; it is honour and love, it is prayer for each other, it is standing shoulder to shoulder to see God's will done. It is a deep passion to see others flourish. Unity releases blessing.

- **Pray for our children.** This needs to be a constant focus. A few churches commission parents and pray for them in their role annually, I would love more to do it; this role of parent is so important. Small groups should also have a continual focus on children, not just their own but also

---

[104] www.ourwatch.org.uk (accessed 17th November 2021) – the Neighbourhood Watch website will enable you to enter your postcode and gather information on crime issues in your community.

[105] Martin Scott, *Impacting the City* (Tonbridge: Sovereign World International 2004), p32; the spheres are the key areas of a community or city, eg education and families, business and employment, media and the arts, health and well-being, politics, communities and religion.

those in the local community. I love it when we let the parents take the lead and pray a blessing on their children with the authority and understanding they have, while we stand around them and pray for that parental role. But for many, the family experience is a broken or painful one and we pray for all parents, single, married and separated from their kids. Under eleven years old is the key age when people come to Christ, and the teen years are the key stage when people lose their faith – keep praying for families!

I love local prayer gatherings and praying for the neighbourhood. Even better is when we do prayer walking: we get out and let the local area speak to us. We listen to each other's perspectives. This is a great encouragement for young people – let them go out and pray and bless their area. Let them listen to God and share pictures or words they have. God speaks through children; encourage them to pray and hear from God. Even better is prayer across the generations, hearing from each other, because we will see and be moved by different things. Pray for key places – the doctor's surgery, the schools, the commerce, the police – and share God's promptings. We were prayer walking near the local cemetery and were suddenly very aware of the grief in the place and people's need for prayer and practical support. Listen to the promptings!

The Balsall Heath story

Let me take you to a community I have served but don't live in. It is about a mile away from me – the neighbourhood of Balsall Heath. This was once seen as a blighted community. It has a history as a housing dumping ground. Initially it was home to large part of the cities' Irish community, then a gradual transition took place when it became a place for Muslim families primarily from Mirpur in Pakistan. Housing was cheap; it was a place for first-time buyers and evolved into a community with large families and new businesses. It is the home of the Balti, a

Pakistani dish originally made and served in a metal Balti bowl. New restaurants were built, supported by new shops, and the Mirpur community started to make Balsall Heath home.

But there was another business that shaped the character of Balsall Heath: prostitution. It was Birmingham's red light area, and this created a darkness and despair, attracting drug dealers, a host of kerb crawlers and pimps who brought fear to the community. The community felt abandoned by the police, the council and everyone else they felt should help them. So they acted for themselves. They sent patrols out onto the streets, monitoring the kerb crawling. They monitored the criminals and gradually took back the streets.

They moved from despair to a 'can do' attitude. The sense of an emerging Balsall Heath community grew; people gathered to discuss the other issues they were concerned about – the rats, the rubbish, the dangerous driving, the schooling opportunities, funding from the council. They began to strengthen links with the police and the council. The flowers started to appear, a community pride developed, the festivals happened. They became the first neighbourhood in the country to have a referendum on a neighbourhood plan. They moved from seeming hopelessness to a transformed and flourishing neighbourhood. Gradually, people came from across the nation to hear their story, and there were regular visits from eminent politicians, TV crews, royalty and others. A government initiative, the Big Society, was heavily influenced by what happened here.[106]

What's my point? Every community can change and flourish; it can be helped by the police and the council, but primarily it takes people. Christians were part of the story, working with the majority Muslim population to serve and support. Our church sent teams of sixteen- to nineteen-year-olds to help tidy up overgrown areas; others supported the generous distribution of

---

[106] www.balsallheathforum.org.uk (accessed 17th November 2021). This gives a flavour of the Balsall Heath transformation.

food and supplies to the poor and vulnerable at Christmas and other times. The local Muslim leaders asked the schools to make sure they covered the Christmas story properly and set up evenings when they could sing Christmas carols because they did not want to miss out! Relationships were and are strong and deep and generous. Jesus is at work. Christians did not lead the change; they supported it and blessed it.

Called to shape our communities

Jesus' call to build His Ekklesia has a strong community feel to it. Some describe the Ekklesia as 'God's local council'. A New Testament Ekklesia would meet, review local events and agree how they would focus their prayer and action. Today, Christians can have the same authority to 'spiritually oversee' their local community. They may ask, what are the key concerns of people who live here? What are their concerns for children and families? For local safety? What is holding this neighbourhood back? Our churches need this strong local community focus, investing time in understanding and collaborating to bless where God has placed us.

We need to discover our spiritual authority. Instead of our own plans or strategy being put in place, we look for God's authority. We have looked at the transforming power of God's kingdom values in the workplace. This is equally true for our community – reflecting on the values of righteousness, shalom, mercy, justice, compassion and forgiveness helps us see what God can change in the community. When two or three or more of us pray for kingdom transformation, He gives us authority.

We carry lots of labels: Anglican, Methodist, Baptist, charismatics, evangelicals, liberals. I want to make the radical suggestion that they should not be how we define ourselves. How about, 'I'm a Christian in Moseley, or Westhoughton, or Worcester Park,' or wherever you live. As we identify with our community, we identify with our call rather than our 'tribe'. We identify with the pain in our community. The broken families bother us; the hungry children distress us; the young people with limited aspirations, gang disputes and violence, sex trafficking, drugs and addiction all become drivers for prayer. Sometimes it's the failing school or the rise in crime. There may be deeper issues like a general sense of hopelessness or despair. Many congregations have the skills and talents to make a real impact and can do even more when they work in collaboration – recognising that the Ekklesia are all God's people who care for and have an authority over the geographical area.

The Great Commission calls us to make disciples. For this to happen in our local community, we need to demonstrate God's kingdom, and relevance, in the midst of our communities – as Jesus did. Jesus' compassion drove Him to engage with people suffering illness, poverty and mental ill-health; people with complex relationships; those caught up in prostitution and collecting taxes for the Romans. His gospel spoke to individuals in their homes and streets and engaged them emotionally. The positives of the kingdom rebuild and renew.

The Ekklesia finds people of peace and builds with them – like the Balsall Heath story. The Ekklesia has the calling to build local unity (because there is only one Ekklesia), to collaborate, to listen to each other and to agree in prayer. The story of Acts starts with the Ekklesia waiting together, as one. They wait on God who prepares them and dramatically sends them out into the streets. So it is with us: don't neglect the waiting, be prepared to move, and have high expectations.

A community parable

Andrea and Jacob have arranged a Zoom catch-up. They have been asked to represent their church at the community hub planning meeting and want to talk about their approach.

'Andrea,' Jacob says. 'How are you? Isn't this an interesting initiative?'

'Hi, Jacob. I'm good, thanks. Yes, it really is, quite a radical way of working. I am really looking forward to seeing how this comes together. Are you well?'

'I'm fine, thanks. As you know, our church has been talking to other churches in the Boroughtown Constituency in our city and they have agreed to set up this community hub. I am so delighted and surprised they asked you and me to represent the church. But it's really part of this move over the past twelve months to be a "kingdom-changing church", where the whole church is being mobilised to serve. As you know, the church leaders are going through this time of asking, "What has God already put in our hands?", looking at the talent and expertise in their midst. It's been great to get so many testimonies of people being used in their workplaces, communities and schools. I've loved the stories from schools about our youth learning about shalom, justice and compassion – it seems to have really fired them up.'

'Yes, things are changing fast. It is so good to have the church leaders come to us saying, "We recognise you both have great strategy and organising skills, so we want to get you to help shape the community hub." It's a really interesting concept, for us to work together as fifteen churches and ask, how can we best stand as one to serve our community?'

'Getting the foundations right seems really important to me,' continues Jacob. 'In some ways this is like a campaign. A key issue is, "What are we going to focus on?" What can we do well? How do we mobilise people? I've been talking to our local councillor about what he feels is the pain in our community. He was concerned about our young people – we have a high number of under twenty-ones and they seem to be struggling with who they are. Our schools try hard, but the city is unable to cope with the rising levels of mental health problems and the high levels of hopelessness.'

'He's right, Jacob. I was talking to Siobhan who works in children's social services, and she is really worried about a significant growth in parents at their wits' end, not least because many are seeing their kids caught up in gangs and they become kids who live at home but are not home. When they are at home, they spend all the time in their rooms and hardly communicate and they keep turning up with new trainers and phones and other stuff. My colleagues in the housing association are particularly concerned about the Clocktown area which seems top of the league for rising crime, poor school attainment and homelessness.'

'I am looking forward to hearing from others. You and I will have a particular perspective; others will see different issues. We can be like watchers on the walls, looking at our town and sharing our understanding of the pain of the town, but also what we can do as a united group of Christians. You and I know from our work experience it's really important to have a shared commitment to act, which comes when we talk things through together.'

'Yes, and I know from my organisation's work on social housing with community groups how vital it is to have a clear focus and clear next steps, so people know what is changing. Jacob, I also know that real change means we have to engage with others – yes, we are talking to the civic authorities, but again they have a particular perspective. It will be good to talk to some of the neighbourhood forums, and schools and local charities.'

Jacob reflects for a moment and says, 'Yes, you are right, and to be humble enough to say sometimes the answer is not the Church. There may be excellent work going on locally and we can get behind it.'

'Very good,' Andrea responds.' One of the things you and I can do as well is not just come up with all the answers. We want to work together, and people in this group will have different levels of understanding on the situations facing us and how we can practically do something. We really need buy-in and trust if we are to succeed. One of the key things is to help us get clarity on what we believe we should be achieving.'

'Yes, you're right, Andrea. I find with my team at work it's important to differentiate between the short term (things we can do now, low-hanging fruit, and obvious opportunities) and the longer term. We can make an amazing difference if we agree to look at what we want to see changed in five years' time, and beyond that.'

'I know the council is desperately strapped for cash. It's very nervous that every approach from the churches or community groups is a request for money. How refreshing to have a "How can we serve?" and "What are the key needs of our town?" conversation. The councillors have an expertise that can really help us focus on some big impact issues. More than that, I want the whole church to be seen as a gift to our town.'

'I agree,' says Jacob. 'I pray we can get the balance right between enabling prayer, well-delivered actions and the opportunities for Jesus to be seen as good news. As we build new relationships, alliances start to form and we can start to see God's kingdom impacting every part of our community. It is an incredibly exciting opportunity.'

'You are absolutely right, Jacob! I have to say I have never been so excited at being part of the body of Christ. It's like we've been empowered and released. If we do this well, it will change us all – and definitely for the better!'

Call to action

We have looked before at the sending out of the seventy-two, in Luke 10. They simply went in twos to a village and were open to what God wanted them to do there. They hoped to bless that place. We can bless through our prayers, support and actions. What community could we get more engaged in? If already engaged, how can we be a greater blessing?

Application

- What would you say are the three main concerns in your local community?

- What more can your small group do to understand, embrace, support and pray for your local community?

- What change can a fully invested, empowered, united Ekklesia make in your community?

- If you are part of a family, how can your family share a concern for your community?

Prayer

Lord, I thank You for every touch of God on my community. I pray You will guide me to my call in this community. It may be to pray, it may be to encourage, it may be to serve, it may be to build something new. But I pray You will bless my community, that we will see Your kingdom come and many lives changed. Amen.

David's story

David and Linda have lived in Moseley, Birmingham, for forty years. There are (at least) two Moseleys – the middle-class neighbourhood with leafy trees and gardens populated by many professional, academic and 'arty' people; then there are the poorer neighbourhoods with multi-occupancy flats, first-time buyers, hostels and low-level crime. David spent many years as a geography teacher who 'did his bit' to serve the community by being on the Moseley Council of Churches. This gave him an increased understanding and passion for the place.

We can see God's hand on David's job choice. The geography specialism gave him a good awareness of local planning and the teaching gave him confidence to speak and take a lead in public. He got involved with others to consider Moseley's economic future, and it did not look good. Birmingham city centre was very accessible and investing in new shopping experiences and nearby Kings Heath was growing as well. Moseley's retail and hospitality centre could die. In response, David took a lead to establish Moseley Farmers' Market.

Twenty years on, David still pours immense amounts of time and enthusiasm into it. It worked both economically and socially, becoming a key gathering point for the people of Moseley. David put spiritual principles into the DNA of the market: it would be generous and welcoming and create a sense of belonging. In the twenty years, it has won three national awards,[107] been profiled in the national press and even *The New York Times* and has raised Moseley's reputation.

David has spent time dreaming with God about this community, referred to affectionately by locals as 'the Village'. He has used his interest in shared space and planning to bring national experts into Moseley to look at ways to renew its retail centre. He made a detailed input to the commissioners when council ward and parliamentary constituency boundaries were being redrawn to ensure they really reflected the community. He chairs election debates and other local forums.

The West Midlands Combined Authority (seven key West Midlands boroughs and cities) announced plans to open a new train track. Included in the plans was a rebuilt Moseley Village Station and we were treated to our elected mayor interviewing David on social media to thank him for the way he and others had reshaped the original plans to better suit the community.[108] Put simply, he is Mr Moseley. Retired from teaching for some years, he describes his community call as driven by his belief that 'God can and will do more'. Strongly supported by his wife, Linda, he is passionate about his impact as a Christian reaching out, and therefore his need to really understand and network well in his community. He joins others regularly in prayer for Moseley to protect and bless the 'village'. Spiritually, he has an unrivalled overview of the community and a deep heart for God to move.

---

[107] Moseley was the FARMA 'Best Farmers' Market in the UK' in 2009, 2012 and 2016 – the only market to have won it three times.

[108] See www.andystreet.org.uk, for Moseley Station video, 1st October 2020 (accessed 10th February 2022) for video interview between Andy Street and David Isgrove.

Chapter Eleven
The Call to the City

Why the city matters

Most of us live in cities and towns. Each city, and each part of the city, has a different character based on its history, its economic wealth, its social capital and community feel and its 'spiritual temperature'. Jesus loved the city of Jerusalem, not least because at its centre was the temple, the place of God's presence. One of the exciting new things God is doing globally is a fresh, three-pronged call:

- To the whole Church to stand as one to change their town/city;

- To individual churches to become town/city-changing churches with a vision to send out people to serve the whole city;

- To individuals to simply ask, 'What are You calling me to, Lord?' To know God's heart for our town/city.

The historian Tristram Hunt wrote an informative book about nineteenth-century British cities, called *Building Jerusalem: The Rise and Fall of the Victorian City*.[109] He describes the great social change that came because people were in such awful conditions that, for many, living in the city was a death sentence. It was the poverty and destitution that inspired writers like Charles

---

[109] Tristram Hunt, *Building Jerusalem: The Rise and Fall of the Victorian City* (London: Penguin 2019).

Dickens and politicians like Lord Shaftesbury. There was a transformed thinking where a new generation of leaders started to question the inevitability of widespread death through disease, malnutrition and poor care. He tells how cities across the country discovered a civic pride and a new sense of responsibility for their citizens' health, education and income. Cities became places of high aspiration, culture, the arts, architecture and commerce. Queen Victoria's long reign was a time of global transformation, not least in the British city, and much of it was led by Christians. In my own city of Birmingham, people opened their eyes to unhealthy and appalling housing, where overcrowding led to significant health issues including cholera, malnourishment and many avoidable deaths. Citizens began to ask the question, 'Do we accept this?' The status quo needed challenging.

I love the legacy of these pioneers who questioned the deep-set way things were done and asked, 'Can't we do this better?' Birmingham became the home of the civic gospel. Politicians, businesspeople and church leaders worked together as a holy coalition to bless the city. Business played a key role as leaders like George Cadbury gave the churches a broader strategic vision. This joined-up approach had so much more impact than the smaller pieces of good works that had characterised the city before, and it was this collaboration that enabled the substantial change needed. George Dawson led the Church of the Saviour, and had a significant impact on the civic gospel. His church alone provided seventeen councillors, including six Birmingham mayors. Businesspeople supported both the church and councils across the country to literally rebuild the city. Elements of Isaiah 61, rebuilding Jerusalem, were enacted in Victorian Britain.

Transforming the city

I know lots of people who absolutely love their cities (and their towns and their villages). Their eyes light up when they talk about them. This is not a blind, mindless perspective: they are more aware than most of the pain and needs of their city. They have a big overview of their city, but they see it with Jesus' eyes. Sometimes they weep for their city, but often they bring the dreams that have come from their time with Jesus and ask, 'Why not more?'

As there is an Ekklesia for the workplace and the neighbourhood, there is one for the city (or town, village or locality). This takes us back into Old Testament times and the famous Ekklesia of Athens, where male citizens more than eighteen years of age gathered regularly to shape policy and hear appeals from the courts. Freedom of speech was central; decisions needed to be informed.[110] Interestingly, this 'called out assembly' is seen as key to democracy in Greece, and to see Jesus' call for this democratic, open assembly gives us insights into what He wanted His Church/Ekklesia to be like. The Ekklesia model of governance was replicated across many cities and towns and would have been well known to Jesus. He was calling for a Christian alternative.

This is another angle on racial unity: the Ekklesia cannot just represent part of the city; that will make it ineffective. The Ekklesia operates in every neighbourhood and must combine every ethnic group. 'Knife crime in London disproportionately impacts black people and is on the rise, yet the response from the UK Church has been slow to non-existent.'[111] We must recognise that this is unacceptable. A broken Ekklesia is a failure; we are one body, and when the arm hurts the rest of the body hurts. Ben Lindsay gives us a really valid challenge: 'Why must it be only the responsibility of black majority churches to deal with "black community" issues?'[112]

---

[110] N S Gill, 'Ecclesia the Greek Assembly', 24th August 2018, www.thoughtco.com/ecclesia-assembly-of-athens-118833 (accessed 18th November 2021).

[111] Lindsay, *We Need to Talk About Race*, p127.

[112] Lindsay, *We Need to Talk About Race*, p128.

Many are discovering this ancient Ekklesia model. Take the Black Country (Wolverhampton, Dudley, Walsall and Sandwell). It is full of neighbourhoods and towns with a history of graft and hard work, and chapels and prayers. Leaders from business, churches and the third sector have been praying together for many years, within each of the four boroughs. Across the wider Black Country region, they laid down strong prayer foundations with large-scale gatherings. They realised that this politically and economically neglected part of the UK was not forgotten by Jesus. A core group of leaders now meet regularly and wait on the Lord for direction. Lots of wonderful initiatives and collaborative working has grown out of this. We will look at this later with the story of Tim Fellows, a businessman called to lead this unity movement.

The Gather Movement works with city and town unity movements across the UK.[113] It consistently finds a remarkable unity and clarity comes when it shares its widely diverse input on the issues in the city, but reduces the discussion on its ideas and solutions and increases the waiting and listening.

This is reshaping the role of pastors. If they commit to a city agenda, they find a call to serve the wider congregation. They commit to investing in unity, and from that they invest in collaboration. Collaboration builds fellowship and support and joint prayer. Of course, initially it is easier to do it yourself, but if you really want to make a long-term impact on food poverty, or in sharing the gospel, or praying for a neighbourhood, it is going to bear much more fruit when others are engaged. Jesus calls us to be one. It's simple, it's clear, and it is so that the Father may be glorified.

The other change of emphasis for many pastors is that the call to 'equip [God's] people for works of service' (Ephesians 4:12) is getting more complex, because God wants to release *all* his people into their calling. Pastors are discovering the fathers,

---

[113] www.gathermovement.org (accessed 18th November 2021). The website contains a wide range of city-changing resources.

mothers, elders, apostles and teachers who are all around them. They are finding they have vastly underutilised wisdom sitting before them. The Ekklesia is not a one-man or one-woman band; it is an orchestra of talent, where the music comes from many maestros placed all over the city.

As we have discovered, the Ekklesia operates as a decision-making body for the kingdom of God. It has an authority to pray, to decree and to act for the city. But Paul gives us a fuller picture when he tells us the body is made up of not one part but many. It is eyes and lungs and ears and bones and skin – its diversity and unity are remarkable.

This helps us to see the Church/Ekklesia in our city in a different light. It is accountants and security guards; it is councillors and road sweepers; it is teachers and pupils; it is stay-at-home mums and walk-the-street police officers. It is you, it is me, not just being part of the city but contributing to it.

> But God has put the body together, giving greater honour to the parts that lacked it, so that there should be no division in the body, but that its parts should have equal concern for each other. If one part suffers, every part suffers with it; if one part is honoured, every part rejoices with it.
> (1 Corinthians 12:24-26)

City unity honours every part, and stands with the parts that are suffering (whether it is local businesses or traumatised families). The call to bless and steward the city needs us all.

A passion for my city

Roger Sutton has a passion for transforming cities. He has worked with city leaders across the UK and globally. He knows their stories and he speaks prophetically, reflecting God's heart to move in our cities and large towns.

> I believe with the gathering momentum of unity for the transformation of the city arising all over the world, we will begin to see another reshaping of the church. Surely the

vision we have for our church members must be larger than the needs of the local congregation?[114]

He tells the story of his daughter, Naomi, but it could be your story, or your friend's story. Let his father heart passion challenge you, because you want the kingdom's best for your family and friends as well.

> I want Naomi to be the very best teacher she can be, serving some of the most disadvantaged and damaged kids in the country. I want [her builder husband] Scott to be a very good businessman, providing employment, setting high standards of workmanship and making people's homes more beautiful. They will, of course, serve their church, but it is not the main place they will find their callings, it is not the main area of impact they will have in life.[115]

He gives another challenge for all of us in business. For many this will be outside our experience, but it shouldn't be. This is God's call, His heart: we should expect things to change, and perhaps we might be a catalyst for that change.

> If a Christian business owner began to feel supported and validated in his role by his local church, if he joined in prayer with other Christian business owners across town, if they began to connect intentionally with the local business forums and started to develop with them a vision for business across the town, could they begin to see some kingdom transformation producing more employment and more investment?[116]

As mentioned earlier, thirty-nine out of forty miracles in Acts happened in the marketplace. The marketplace was the great hub for community engagement, where the mood and confidence of the city was shaped. The business environment is where our community meets to use their skills. It is where we

---

[114] Sutton, *A Gathering Momentum*, pp183-184.

[115] Sutton, *A Gathering Momentum*, pp 192-193.

[116] Sutton, *A Gathering Momentum*, p226.

learn and develop together; it can be a place of dreams and aspirations. Equally, it is where life is real, the targets need to be met, the budgets achieved and the sales dispatched, but Jenny's dad died last week, and Sonia's relationship is crumbling, Shabhana has money worries, and Kirk is in a job he doesn't really like. Everybody has a name. All those names interact with the city, the schools that support our children, the hospitals that treat our parents and babies, the police struggling to deal with the rising levels of drugs. We are interdependent.

The Ekklesia are placed in every sphere, and every sphere is 'influenced to act in a godly way that genuinely enhances goodness and acts as a catalyst for the presence of God to come'.[117]

The Gather story

There is a powerful, global, movement of God in our cities. It sprang up in places like York, as leaders gathered regularly to pray for their city. Unbeknown to them, it was also happening in Bristol. It continued springing forth as people in Liverpool, Reading, Teesside and Stoke and the Black Country and countless other places gathered to pray for their place, their hometown or city. The prayer then led to a 'What if…?' discussion as people began to explore God's heart for the city and the call He was putting on His Church. Initially it was often church leaders who drove this, but increasingly others became involved, including many business leaders who saw how their skills and expertise could enhance what was happening.

England's experience was replicated elsewhere in India, Australia, South Africa, Brazil, the USA, Germany, Sweden and countless other nations. In New York, a group of pastors looked at their city with its low percentage of Christians and a host of needs and started to work together. They brought people together to pray, build support networks and raise their

---

[117] Scott, *Impacting the City*, p32.

expectations for their city. It led to a gathering and organisation called Movement Day, which started working within the States and then went global when they realised that hundreds of cities were doing similar things. God is on the move!

In England, the Gather Movement, led by Roger Sutton, started when national leaders observed the growth in city unity and said, 'Can we support and bless this, and encourage it?' A key Bible verse for this move is Jeremiah 29:7: 'Seek the peace and prosperity of the city to which I have carried you into exile. Pray to the LORD for it, because if it prospers, you too will prosper.' We are called in the Old Testament to seek peace.

In the New Testament, Jesus brings shalom/peace: 'Jesus himself stood among them and said to them, "Peace be with you"' (Luke 24:36). He also sends out the seventy-two to be bringers of peace: 'When you enter a house, first say, "Peace to this house"' (Luke 10:5). As we have seen in the workplace, Jesus calls us to bring kingdom values, and our communities and the houses within them need peace/shalom.

Stoke responded to an Experian report in 2001[118] which named the city the worst place to live in England and Wales. Christian leaders came together to declare, 'Not on our watch,' and set prayer targets to see improvement in the city. They strengthened links with the council and invited civic leaders to inform their city-wide prayer gatherings.

Bath brings Christian charities and support agencies together across the city to strengthen their impact on issues like food poverty and homelessness. They have also brought Christians together in their different neighbourhoods to pray for where they live, irrespective of their denominations.

Coventry worked on an app so that people across the city could adopt a street and pray for it. Within half an hour of the app going live, half of Coventry's streets had been adopted. The

[118] www.experianplc.com (accessed 29th November 2021). Experian provides research and data analysis to enable individuals and organisations to make informed decisions.

city reported many breakthroughs and blessings as their prayers went local. In 2021, Coventry became the UK City of Culture. HOPE Coventry serves the whole Church and enables partnership working across the city, with schemes such as food banks, a prayer house and a good neighbours project serving those more than fifty years of age who feel isolated.[119]

Reading talks of increased favour and good working relationships with a variety of strategic groups, including the local authority, police, MPs and other people of influence. It makes no distinction between sacred and secular and embraces the Great Commission's 'go' call. 'We believe the gospel of Jesus Christ is good news to all and we see our ultimate mission as communicating and demonstrating this to all through our words and actions.'[120]

Southampton established Love Southampton. 'The network is developing a vision for the whole city, and not just personal and Church renewal. Links are developing with the city council and health authorities.'[121] One of the most exciting outcomes from the Southampton story was hearing the concern of council leaders about foster care across the city. The churches stepped in and have found many families and given hope to many children.

Churches in Bristol have worked together to address a range of issues like ending child hunger in the city, repenting of the city's previous investment in slavery, and working with the council on issues like housing. They have established networks across the spheres so Christians in health, education, business and other sectors can pray and support each other, because God wants His kingdom to come into every aspect of the city. Their focus became 'Bristol: A City of Hope', and they were thrilled when the city adopted this slogan and created a plaque with the words on the main entrance to the Council House. As Andy

---

[119] www.hopecoventry.org.uk (accessed 18th November 2021).

[120] Sutton, *A Gathering Momentum*, p130.

[121] Sutton, *A Gathering Momentum*, p40.

Street from Bristol puts it, 'The church is turning up with ideas, resources and energy – are you going to turn them away?'

This is a work that continues to grow. During the Covid-19 pandemic, leaders from business, the Church, charities, government across the UK met and learned from each other as Gather addressed key issues like grief and bereavement, food poverty, business and engaging civic authorities. Challenges like this raise questions such as, 'How do we deliver strategic change?' 'How do we lead in new ways?' 'How can we encourage entrepreneurship?' 'How can we pray for our cities with more authority?'

As lockdown began to lift, the Gather Network worked with the unity movements to ask the question, 'What happens next?' Aware that God's agenda was changing, it helped leaders think through their need to adapt and change. Christians were looking in new ways at how they related, and how they communicated with non-Christians, while recognising the new opportunities to spread the gospel. A new movement emerged: Movement for Recovery, where churches are working together with the elected mayors and other city leaders to help rebuild, renew and restore their cities. There is a growing recognition that local councils have an agenda to serve and restore, and churches must see what aspects of this restoration are best done by the people of God. As they look at this, they become more aware of the duplication, the lack of collaboration and the need for one united voice to engage the city leadership.

The Gather Network provides support and fresh thinking, but also links with fresh thinking and testimonies globally.

A global perspective

Let's look at some global stories, and as we do, let us just reflect – this is our God. He does the exceptional, He makes the impossible possible and He uses ordinary people. Some of these stories are driven by gifted, faith-filled leaders, but behind every one are people of prayer, people bringing wisdom and understanding, people bringing their pain and concerns, and people just getting on and doing small things that add to a huge picture. These are stories of the Ekklesia at work, and of God's kingdom being seen.

Toowoomba is Australia's second biggest inland city. Located in Queensland, it is known as the Garden City and is a regional centre for business and finance. The well-established unity movement has birthed many years of working with women within and outside the Church, addressing issues of abuse, bullying and lack of honour. Many thousands of women have spent weekends when the Church ministered to them and supported them through the hurts and trauma of mistreatment by husbands, fathers, brothers and colleagues. It was a deep work. From this developed a strong awareness of the huge damage porn was causing to families and relationships. They courageously stood against it and got their city on board, to the point where they declared Toowoomba a porn-free city.[122]

The South Bronx in New York had a fierce reputation for violence and murder. Crime was widespread and death a daily occurrence. The churches decided to redeem their city. They organised a prayer campaign on the streets to pray for peace, to declare that violence could not spread its roots into their city, to pray against the fear and intimidation of gangs and drugs. They began to see a change. When they saw one day without a murder, it was remarkable. When this became a week, they were astounded. Imagine the praise when they had a whole year with no murders, and then this became a year by year by year occurrence. The streets are Jesus' territory, and He is Jehovah Shalom. Here again, pastors may have led, but it needed others to join in and be proactive.

We can tell similar stories about Trenchtown in Kingston, Jamaica. Again, this was a violent neighbourhood with gangs and regular shootings. The Church took to the streets and

---

[122] www.citywomen.com.au (accessed 18th November 2021).

prayed peace. They praised Jesus as Lord of Trenchtown, and murders fell from triple figures to single figures.

Globally, there are many similar stories of transformation as leaders report the power of working in the opposite spirit – where there is greed, they bring generosity; where there is an independent spirit, they bring cooperation; where there are lies, they bring openness and integrity. They pray out corruption.

City projects start to arise – New Zealand tells of joint work with the police on domestic violence. Calcutta has a comprehensive work among the homeless and migrant workers. In Mumbai, the prison would only allow Hindu chaplains in, but over a long time the churches persisted and built a presence where they now work together to serve the prisoners.

Charlotte in North Carolina built a coalition of businesspeople, Christian organisations and church leaders to look at key issues in the city through an eighteen-month research programme, culminating in a highly impressive report and plan called the 'State of the City'. Businesspeople were key to each element, from the research to the detailed planning and to the highly professional report and recommendations. The depth of wisdom and understanding this gave about Charlotte has led to high-impact work to five key issues:

1. Raising aspirations and mobility;

2. Working with the most marginalised across their city;

3. As North America's youngest city, they want to focus on re-engaging millennials;

4. Helping the workplace better integrate faith and work;

5. Strengthening mission and discipleship.

The report is comprehensive, with recommendations to equip the Church across the city to better understand the issues, to pray in a practical and focused way and act.[123] This is business leaders, pastors and prayer leaders looking at how 'your kingdom come' (Matthew 6:10) can move from good intentions to very deliberate joined-up focus and action.

We see a principle demonstrated in the book of Revelation. Each of the seven cities is unique, some are struggling and others flourishing, but God's word for each one is clear and distinctive, whether it be a wake-up call to Sardis (Revelation 3:1-2) or an open door for Philadelphia (Revelation 3:7). We need to understand the primary call on our city – some have a regional impact, others an economic, political or creative impact. Others have negative influences that shape their reputations. Above this, Jesus looks at the spiritual health of the city, not what is seen on the surface but what happens in the heart. Jesus encourages cities where they should be commended and tells them to sort themselves out when that is necessary. What is the Spirit saying to your city or place?

God's city strategy

We have talked about understanding the pain of the city. As Charlotte demonstrates, this, in turn, gives us a united prayer, action and 'kingdom come' focus. Pretoria responds to the homeless and hopeless, Toowoomba to the pain of the women and the cancer of porn. Liverpool and Bristol both respond to their slave trading roots and the way this had shaped the cities. My city of Birmingham is responding to racial division and the need to be united as one.

Understanding the city needs depth if we are to understand the transformation needed. There are lots of elements, but some aspects will particularly resonate with you, given your experience and values. I have worked nationally and locally with

---

[123] www.forcharlotte.org/state-of-the-city (accessed 21st January 2022) for the 'State of the City Report', 2019. It is a clear, structured, well-researched document that has been the catalyst for action across Charlotte.

watchmen/watchers who think and pray about the city. One of the key things I have learned is no watcher sees it all; we all view things from our own perspective and understanding. It is when we work together as the Ekklesia, sharing our knowledge, that a complete picture emerges.

A city, town or region is incredibly complex. Here are some key city subjects – where do you bring expertise?

- The demographics – the age spread, ethnic and religious mix, etc.

- Health and well-being – key issues, health inequalities and challenges.

- Mental health – the rise in issues among young people, the issues of loneliness, creating supportive communities.

- Education across the age groups and neighbourhoods.

- The environmental challenges and greater sustainability.

- The local economy – the key areas for business growth and the areas of vulnerability.

- Housing – local provision and need, multiple occupancy, homelessness, new-builds and local provision.

- The broad cultural life of the city – in what ways is the city innovative and creative?

- Crime and safety issues, serious crime and gangs, crime 'hotspots'.

- The long-term vision for this place – its challenges and opportunities.

- Community cohesion – the ethnic mix, inter-community tensions; the level of unity.

- Political issues – the local government budgets, elections timetable, key city leaders.

- The history – the hurts and setbacks; how history has shaped reputation.

- The spiritual history – what and where God has blessed in the past.

- The third sector – what is it doing well, how does it contribute? Challenges.

- Church unity – where is the Church now? Where should it be?

It's a huge list. Again, no pastor, no denomination can tackle these things alone. The expertise is across the body of Christ. But a challenge this big gives remarkable opportunities. Can your city, or part of the city, your town or your neighbourhood ask groups of twenty- to thirty-year-olds to look at some of the issues above and come back with some clear recommendations? Can you allocate these issues to different small groups for research, discussion and prayer?

Sue Sinclair tells her story of getting to know her city of Liverpool. It started with prayer walking her neighbourhood and praying for different local organisations. She researched her community, looking at issues like the demographics, housing, crime and health. The research and prayer highlighted a key concern – people were dying prematurely from cancer, suicide, strokes, etc, and there were poor fertility rates. Sue and her team[124] felt they needed to cleanse the land from the slave trade and the way the city, including churches, had been built on its profits. The prayer team extended their walks and then led times of repentance. They recognised Liverpool was a gatekeeping city, bringing sin and death into the nation. As they prayed, they saw the death rate change and Sue was given details of ships coming into the city with drugs. She had credibility with the police, who raided the vessel Sue saw in a vision and took one

---

[124] www.cwmprayer.com (accessed 18th November 2021). Community Watchmen Ministries 'love, pray for and serve Liverpool'.

of the largest hauls of drugs seen in the city. 'Press into him for the strategy,' says Sue, 'and breakthrough for the people of your land.'[125]

God raises up people with a city-enabling call. It's not for everyone. Those who are real catalysts for change tend to be strategic thinkers and good networkers. They are skilled in bringing people together and facilitating discussion. They inspire people with hope. But the real work is done by people who are good at delivery – they organise and plan well, they listen well and understand what will work best; they build trust and credibility. One of the key things to embrace and rejoice in is that those enablers and deliverers can be aged sixteen or sixty, male or female, from any ethnicity or background or part of the city. Energy, drive and passion can come from anywhere. The skill of the Ekklesia is to recognise, release and honour that talent.

In 2011 we had riots in Birmingham and elsewhere in the country. In our city this led to the tragic event when three young Asian men were killed protecting their mosque. The city was a tinderbox. I was called to an urgent meeting with the council and police alongside other faith leaders. The rumour began circulating that the fury and grief in the Muslim community was going to lead to the killing of three young black men (it was believed that young black men had driven the car that killed the three Asians). There was a flame about to be poured onto petrol that would tear our city apart. Into this tension strode Tariq Jahan, the father of one of the three Asian young men. He eloquently pleaded for peace on the local and national news; he called the city to calm down. He was a figure of tragic nobility and he stood as a father and peacemaker to the city.[126] We need city fathers. Sometimes God raises them up for a reason, like

---

[125] Sue Sinclair, *Extravagant Breakthroughs* (London: Freedom Publishing, 2020).

[126] www.bbc.co.uk/news/av/uk-england-birmingham-58147894, for a BBC piece on the story (accessed 20th November 2021).

Tariq Jahan; sometimes they have an ongoing call and passion. Find them, encourage them, honour them: your city needs them.

In 2020, twenty-one-year-old footballer Marcus Rashford challenged the government on food for families during the school holidays. He spoke passionately about his own experience when his mum struggled to feed him and her family. He knew the cry of hunger and he wanted to use his celebrity to good effect. His campaign led to a significant change in government social policy.[127] I would categorise him as a catalyst. He is not a rebel, but he is simply asking that we do things differently. He not a city father, but as a young man of passionate beliefs he is getting things done. Keep praying for the fathers and the catalysts and for change to be released.

Andy's story

Andy Street lives in Bristol. He is an experienced business leader who has found himself as the key connector between churches and the public sector. He sees the big picture; he understands about creating alignments and joined-up approaches. He describes what he believes God has called him to: 'To be a connector across the city, to be an influencer, and to encourage collaboration and partnership.' In other words, unity. It is interesting to see how this has evolved. Now aged sixty-four, he still serves as a part-time director for a global environmental consultancy firm which he helped found in the 1990s. He describes his forties as when work was his identity. But then things became challenging:

> Our daughter was profoundly ill with ME for five years – over the period when I was between the age of forty-five to fifty. As I learned to pray properly for the first time and listen and commune with God, I felt that I needed to let go

---

[127] www.bbc.co.uk/sport/football/55338104 (accessed 20th November 2021).

of what had become my identity – my work! At fifty I stepped down from the Board of the company and went part-time. Over the period since then, work is no longer my identity as such – I love it, but alongside the other aspects of life. And since in effect letting go of the business, God has blessed it hugely – over the last fifteen years it's grown from a few hundred to 2,000 people.

Bristol is buzzing with Christian projects birthed in unity, and Andy uses his business expertise to great effect.

I know the city well and have invested a huge amount of time in getting to know people across all sectors – business, charity, civic life and Church. I've learned that leadership comes through influence and not position or title, and influence comes through investing in people and building relationships. It takes time, but it makes a world of difference!

He is a catalyst serving, guiding and enabling.

I chair seven local charities, I'm involved in three local social investment funds (chairing two), act as a key convener of church leaders across the city, connecting them with key areas of social need, and work closely with the elected mayor of Bristol.

In some ways, this is a surprise to Andy. It's not something he aimed to do, but by making himself – and, importantly, all his skills and experience – available, God uses him. There have been many changes in the city and a close working relationship between the Church and the elected mayor. Andy is at the heart of this. His business-honed skills are having a high impact.

We have looked in the book at how we all are shaped and driven by our values. For Andy, these are 'honesty, integrity, transparency and authenticity. I seek to live by those values in everything I do, including in the work environment.' He is integral in building a high-impact coalition of Church, civic, third-sector and business leaders across Bristol. A key player in his life has been a real city elder and father to the city, who saw something in Andy he wanted to encourage and has given great support and daily prayer for more than thirty years. Andy greatly values the support from his wife to partner him on this journey.

A longer vision

I have a vision for revival. This is when God does the extraordinary. Some will look at the demographics and future projections of church numbers and impact. They may argue the Church is increasingly irrelevant and marginalised. But I look at what God has done in the past and say, 'This is our God; He can do it again.' I look at what God is doing across the world now and the places where large numbers of people are coming to Christ. I read the stories of transformed cities in the New Testament where the Ekklesia grows rapidly. Why not here? Why not now?

I have lots of evidence that God is a better strategist than me! I have a hope that when God brings revival, it will not just rise up like a firework that fizzles and glows and makes loud noises for a minute and then is gone. I believe He will establish deep roots, so the revival impacts our cities, workplaces and families in a remarkable way. Revival is about people coming to Christ, which drives societal transformation in many rich ways.

Immediately before I started this book, I went on a revival tour. That sounds a lot grander than it actually was – it was just me and my satnav and some research on previous revivals. I wanted to get a sense of what God had done in the past because I believed He could do it again. In my mind's eye I kept seeing hundreds of feet – men, women, children, the old and the young – drawn to places where the presence of God was so powerful. Windswept, isolated Mow Cop hill in the Potteries, the very ordinary long streets and houses of Loughor, in South Wales, the chapels and churches of Lower and Upper Gornal[128] and

---

[128] Lower and Upper Gornal in the Black Country claims to be the last place to see revival in 1947 when a team from Cliff College came (then a Methodist Bible training college in the Peak District). Like so many

more. People were being called by God. They walked, often for many miles because they knew their lives needed a deeper hope, their hearts longing to know love and compassion.

We have looked at Isaiah 61 and the memorable call and promise to rebuild, restore and renew Jerusalem (Isaiah 61:4). The outworking of this promise is in Ezra and Nehemiah when God brings His exiled people back to Jerusalem. Not only that, but He brings them back into covenant relationship with Him – they have learned to love God again and they see Him do remarkable things. The starting point is rebuilding the temple, establishing the presence of God in the heart of their city. Restoring prayer, worship and adoration comes before the walls, gates and houses are rebuilt.

I believe God is giving our generation a similar call to rebuild, restore and renew His New Testament Church – the Ekklesia. As we seek God personally and corporately, we will see Him renew the power the early Church had. We make ourselves available by coming into His presence. We respond to Jesus' call for twos and threes to pray together and we grow as we learn to listen to God more deeply and see more happen. We will see God's holy strategy for city building as He appoints pastors, prophets, evangelists, teachers and apostles 'to equip his people for works of service' (Ephesians 4:11-12) in the workplace and in the city. We will see elders appointed and city fathers and mothers recognised and released. We will see the younger generation carrying the baton for change with a hunger to see God move. He is restoring authority to people like you and me to see God in the places where He wisely called us.

There is a lesson from John 17. Jesus is seen when we have unity. God is bringing us to a new unity. Unity and waiting on God birthed the Church/Ekklesia at Pentecost. Heaven is filled with every ethnicity, males and females with an incredible diversity of shapes and sizes. We are on an exciting journey as

---

places where God moved, there was nothing special about Gornal, but God's favour was there.

we broaden our networks and deepen our understanding and appreciation of each other.

Matthew 16:19 says, 'I will give you the keys of the kingdom of heaven'. We stand in our city and workplace with keys. They open and shut: you can stand against corruption, or tension, or antagonism to the gospel. You can stand to release a fresh revelation of Jesus, deep shalom and enduring hope.

Those keys include knowledge and understanding about our city and about God's heart. We can unlock that knowledge by prayer, fasting and dreaming with Jesus. As we listen, God reveals much about the present, the past and the future.

The keys give us authority. Our challenge is to use it. As we practise, and listen to testimonies of God moving, He builds our faith.

Call to action

Surely the Church is not called to dwindle in impact and eventually die! The New Testament picture is of city-changers sent across the known world. I am seeing change in my city. Christian leaders are uniting in ways we have not seen before. Our city has nearly 200 different ethnic groups and we must unite to be the gospel to them. We are seeing more collaboration. We are seeing businesspeople serving the whole city, some through the church but most by acting as school governors or working with local food banks or other organisations. In the 1870s, God brought together a powerful Birmingham coalition of business, politicians, Church and others. The city was transformed into a place of higher sanitation, increased healthcare and longevity and better housing. In 1896, local industrialist George Cadbury brought city and church leaders together to ensure every home in Birmingham was given a Bible. The stories of the past give us hope for the future.

Application

- What do you love about your town/city?

- What are you passionate about in your town/city? What are your hopes for the future?

- What skills, experience and insights do you have that can impact your city?

Each of us will have different levels of engagement – but as a minimum I believe we should all love our city and have a heart to continuously pray for it. What call is God making on you?

Prayer

I pray a blessing on the town, city, region where I live. I pray for a humble, expectant, united body of Christ. I pray for our calling to this city, that You will raise up people across every walk of life equipped to bless and bring Your kingdom. I pray for my call; guide me and use me, Lord. Amen.

Tim's story

Tim Fellows owns and runs a financial services company based in the Black Country. It provides independent financial planning and advice to businesses and individuals, working with investments, pensions and assurance. But Tim is also a key figure in bringing churches and Christians together across the four boroughs of the Black Country,[129] an area of more than 1 million people. This combination of business and spiritual leader has evolved over time. His drive and wisdom in building up his business has given him the skills and confidence to bring churches and Christians together. He often looks long term with clients at how they invest over twenty, thirty, forty years, and that same long-term perspective helps him to think long term

---

[129] Wolverhampton, Walsall, Dudley and Sandwell.

about his beloved Black Country. The key link between the two is Tim's heart for God: he has a passion to hear from God in both his callings, and a high expectation of what God can do.

Tim started in financial services in 1991 and became an independent financial advisor (IFA) in 1995, setting up his business in 1996 with himself and his wife as partners. They worked in a range of IFA networks until 2009 when the business became directly authorised by the regulator. They have about 450 customers/clients. Tim's business has faced a number of crisis moments.

In 2002, it was suspended prior to a six-week investigation. However, when they were fully cleared by the regulator, they were sacked by their business network. In 2009, the new network he belonged to contacted him and said they were closing their business the following day. Both events seriously threatened Tim's income and reputation. Integrity and trust are vital in the financial services industry, and Tim found it challenging to weather both these storms. It was scary, and he was angry and fearful as he went through situations he felt were unjust and dangerous.

As is so often the case, God was taking Tim deeper in His walk with Him. It can be hard to reach that point where you 'live by faith, not by sight '(2 Corinthians 5:7), because there were red lights all around him. However, Tim got to the point where he humbly trusted for the future and handed the business to God, believing God had Tim's best interests in His hand. There will always be challenges, but Tim enjoys what he does, he builds good relationships with his clients and he is helping them build a better financial future for themselves and their families.

In his early days in financial services, Tim was also the youth leader for a large Black Country church. The youth attended some regional events and from this Tim felt it would be good to pull youth leaders together from across the Black Country to dream about the future. This led to a series of events with 600 to 700 young people and, in 1997, as this work grew, Tim and others established The Net, a charity to support the regional youth work. Later he used The Net to pull Christian business leaders together, and then Church leaders.[130]

The Net developed a reputation and brand across the Black Country, and in 2000 they felt a call to bring people together to pray, and 250 people came. In February 2001 they had 1,100 praying. Numbers continued to grow; there was clearly a hunger to see God move. All-night prayer meetings attracted large numbers. In 2002, they had 2,200 people, 1,200 who were still there at 7.00am. God had his hand on the Black Country! Later they hit 3,000. Then they moved to a different pattern, with more focus on unity and prayer in the different boroughs. In 2020 they had 2,500 attend a meeting on 4th January to pray for the Black Country with an emphasis on unity, young people and the vulnerable, not realising God was preparing them for the coronavirus pandemic.

Tim describes the leadership as non-hierarchical, but he has brought a different culture to this unity movement because of his background and character. He is very quick to point to the importance of relationship-building and humility. A core team meet regularly and invest time in each other. There is a deep trust and respect and therefore a strong capacity for listening to God and seeking His vision for their region.

Tim stands as a bridge in the divide that often exists between Church and business. He turns others' eyes outward, so they are both looking to their community and asking how they can best serve the Black Country. My observation of Tim is that he carries a strategic clarity, not least because he 'gets' the whole of the Black Country. From a business perspective, it's his territory: he knows its people; he visits their homes. Added to that, God has given him 'divine downloads' and vision at some key times, which are clear words of direction for the whole Church and the people of God. He communicates well, and

---

[130] www.loveblackcountry.org.uk (accessed 20th November 2021). The Net is now part of the Love Black Country movement.

clearly, in a broad Black Country accent, with a twinkle in his eye. He has that great quality that all leaders need – he attracts followers who trust him for the long haul.

Tim's story shows you can bring your business skills and serve your community – locally within your neighbourhood or on a large scale with more than a million people! All is possible when God sees people willing to serve.

Chapter Twelve
The Call to Rebuild

I was leading the training element of a large-scale change programme in a financial services company and bumped into the sales director. He was one of the wisest leaders I have ever come across. We were discussing the extensive programme my team was delivering for his 400 financial advisors. 'Ah well,' he said, 'all this activity will quieten down shortly, and we should be able to get back to life as normal.' It made me question whether returning to 'life as normal' was ever going to be a reality, because it is quite obvious that in the workplace, we have to endure wave upon wave of change. When we add that to the changes happening in our own lives and in the community around us, many people may value stability, but it is not a frequent occurrence!

We have looked at some of the Bible passages on change – with Nehemiah's call to leave Babylon and rebuild Jerusalem, with the Isaiah 61 call to go out and preach 'good news to the poor', the 'broken-hearted', the captives and the grieving (vv1-3).

Clearly, the whole Covid experience in 2020 and afterwards was a time of intense change. It impacted how we worked; it impacted our travel arrangements, our families and our health. It changed the way many of us 'did' church. It led to a plethora of innovations and new ways of relating, retailing and communicating. For many it was distressing, stressful and traumatic. It reminded many of the value of relationships and the need to walk closely with Jesus.

Change and challenge should always cause us to ask, 'What is God up to?' I believe in the global sovereignty of God. Psalm 24 tells us, 'The earth is the LORD's, and everything in it, the world, and all who live in it' (v1). We recall verses 3 and 4:

Who may ascend the mountain of the LORD?
Who may stand in his holy place?
The one who has clean hands and a pure heart,
who does not trust in an idol
or swear by a false god.

History is filled with catastrophes, wars and devastations, but God remains sovereign, and His love takes us through these storms. More than that, He calls us to relationship with Him. In times of uncertainty, we can 'ascend the mountain of the LORD'; we can come into His presence; we can ask, 'What's happening, Lord?'

The psalm continues with the double announcement: 'Lift up your heads, you gates; be lifted up, you ancient doors, that the King of glory may come in' (v7). Are we at a time when the King of Glory is coming in – to our homes, our workplaces and our cities?

Rebuilding starts with me

Shakings and change call for a rebuild. During the coronavirus pandemic, people had to make many, many adjustments to the way they worked, their family life, their church life, their community life. It wasn't just the ferocious 'who can take home the most toilet rolls' competition. Much more seriously, it was the devastating grief across our communities with the removal or reduction of many bereavement rituals and areas of support. It was the uncertainty and the constant Covid-19 news updates. It impacted people of all ages, the new mothers and fathers, the frontline workers, the elderly, the vulnerable and lonely.

Many individuals and communities suffered a collective sense of fear. The fear bred suspicion, rumours and urban myths which then intensified the fear. For many, their normal Christian routines and support mechanisms changed or even disappeared.

I was once invited as a guest of the British Army to observe its officer selection assessment events. The process was to give the potential recruits a diverse series of tests, all of them leaderless, to see what leadership and character emerged during the challenge. Covid-19 seemed to have provided a similar process: how did we cope with the challenges it gave? Did we emerge as leaders making sense of the spiritual challenges, or did we get left behind?

God is in charge, shaking is painful, but He is looking to see what emerges. It takes us back to Psalm 24: 'Who [ascended] the mountain of the LORD?' Was it me? Was it you? Who took responsibility for their relationship with Jesus? Those who pushed through the challenges and built stronger prayer, deeper time with Jesus in their homes. Our homes became more holy places; the presence of the Lord was around us. If we went to work it was often by Zoom, but even if we were physically present it was different and constrained and we needed the presence of God with us. The coronavirus pandemic created a time for fresh thinking and new approaches.

God desires relationship; He desires intimacy. He wants us to flourish so that He can be seen in our character and our actions. 'We were made to live with God forever in this world and nothing less will ever satisfy us, so our only hope is to put desire back in its proper place on God.'[131] This is a time of refocusing; God is giving us a wake-up call; He wants us back.

God wants us back

Rebuilding starts with restoring and strengthening our relationship with God. We are all challenged by this – is He at the centre of my life? Do I spend time in His presence? Am I

---

[131] Comer, *The Ruthless Elimination of Hurry*, p146.

24/7 for Jesus? We are the distracted generation, and that distraction is at our fingertips. We can become obsessed with keeping up to date with the news and with Facebook, Instagram, Twitter, etc. We are concerned about what others think about us; we want to give the world our very own advertising campaign, showing them what an interesting and fulfilled life we lead. This in turn presents our lives in a rosy 'everything is fantastic' frame. We fall into the trap of a self-image that is not God-dependent but built on how many people like our post or share our Instagram. Allowing ourselves to come back to Jesus is a serious challenge for our times.

Can we get better control of our time? I used to run time management courses and would have all the time management tools. But the battle to control our time is in our heads. Stuff takes us over and we let it. We overdose on input from a vast range of sources. It might be entertainment, whether it be easily accessible sport, music or drama. We overdose on looking good. We can start to manage our time by reviewing how we spend it.

How do we manage our anger and our frustration? Our worlds are becoming more and more divisive. In some countries, the sharp contrast between my political views and your political views means we can annoy and frustrate each other at record speed. Generosity gets replaced by aggression, listening gets replaced by shouting, learning gets replaced by intolerance. Our little world has become self-absorbing; we find it hard to cope with delays, the broken printer, the slow driver in front, the wait for a GP appointment. This is a slippery slope and I want to get off.

Can we be less invested in wanting to prove our point or win our argument? Winning my point against someone with a different perspective, who is shouting at me because they think I am stupid, is not a good use of time. Breaking into cliques in the workplace or creating an 'us and them' feel between my department and theirs is not going to end well. Can the Lord of Shalom use us to be countercultural? Effective peacemakers go beyond, 'Can we stop yelling at each other?' to, 'Let's relearn how we can work together well.'

Can we give more time to Jesus?

A life less ordinary

In Luke 10, we read that Jesus sent out seventy-two ordinary disciples to the towns and villages. But He commissioned them to become extraordinary people who shared good news, brought peace and saw miracles happen. In Acts 2:42, we learn that the community of believers in Acts devoted themselves to:

- **'The apostles' teaching'** They were hungry to find out more about their faith from people who had spent time with Jesus.

- **'Fellowship'** They gave time to each other, to build relationships, to support and care for each other, to grow in unity. We know people responded to the gospel from all over the world on that dramatic Pentecost morning, and they learned to live together. More than that, they then worked together to bless the city, 'enjoying the favour of all the people' (v47).

- **'The breaking of bread'** Some people break bread – that is, take the Lord's Supper – every day and I think it is a good habit. It reminds us of the core of our faith: Jesus died to release us from sin, to build a new life, and He poured out His blood as an everlasting commitment to us. Regularly partaking in communion is good. I think it is good to do quietly in the workplace, to remind us that where we work is also holy ground.

- **'Prayer'** Prayer is the engine. It is the remarkable privilege we have not just to make our requests known, to ask and to seek, but also to hear and be guided. We 'ascend the mountain of the LORD' to converse.

The early Church focused on these four key things. Work consumes our energy and time. But our work becomes fruitful when we invest in making our lives God's instruments. The disciples devoted themselves to this. They understood the vital importance of hearing God's voice, letting Him guide their footsteps.

Let me tell you a story

I was on a phone call recently with one of the team behind the Eternal Wall of Answered Prayer. It's a vision to build a prominent sculpture in the centre of England that represents 1 million answered prayers. There will be 1 million bricks, and each brick will tell a story. Using digital technology, we will be able to access a contemporary story of answered prayer or prayer stories from our rich history of God moving in our nation and globally.[132] The person I was speaking to confirmed a key principle from this book: many of the answered prayers are from God sending us out – to our workplaces, neighbourhoods and family and friends.

I have provided a diverse collection of stories/case studies. They demonstrate that God is making His kingdom, my business. He is moving through us in our various workplaces.

- He is the God who guides and shapes our careers and where we work.

- He is the God who protects us when our businesses are threatened, and is with us if we lose our jobs.

- He is the God who gives us wisdom and compassion to be great neighbours in the workplace.

- He is the God who gives us dreams and fresh thinking.

---

[132] www.eternalwall.org.uk (accessed 18th November 2021), for more information on the project.

- He is the God who used the passion of workers to pray for their friends and families to shape a national revival.

- He is the God who heals.

- He is the God who gives us favour in our communities and cities.

- He is the God who walks closely with us, and is passionate about His kingdom coming to our workplace.

- He is the God who gives us the courage to be different and the grace to be a blessing.

- He is the God who calls us to mission and enables us to tell His story.

The stories are like gold coins in our pocket. Each one is an encouragement that Jesus has invested in us. He gives us the gift of prayer, He gives us authority in our prayer, He wants to see His kingdom come and He is roaring His encouragement for us as we complete the kingdom-building race.

Rebuild relationships

The Ekklesia thrives when the relationships are excellent, where people share perspectives and concerns, listen generously and then discuss what happens next. Prayer times should also be discussion times as we seek God's heart and purpose together. We see the power of relationships in Nehemiah as teams are appointed to first rebuild the gates that offer access and protection to the city and then rebuild the walls. They find their work opposed and eventually have to arm themselves and build at the same time. One will build, one will defend. As they look at the opposition to their call, they are told, 'Don't be afraid of them. Remember the Lord, who is great and awesome, and fight for your families, your sons and your daughters, your wives and your homes' (Nehemiah 4:14). The book of Nehemiah is, of course, about more than wall-building; it is the time God chooses to restore relationship with Israel and reconfirm His covenant. Historically significant events are happening, enabled by this commitment to stand together. This shared determination to succeed means that my contribution becomes stronger because I want to ensure my family and colleagues get their 500 yards of wall completed at the same pace as others.

So rebuilding relationships is essential if we are to rebuild elsewhere. I love the encouragers who text people with little messages. I wish I did it more. I love those who are very deliberate about their thank yous, because we all need appreciation and recognition. In a rebuilding time we need to ask some questions:

- Who can I help and support?

- Who needs encouragement?

- Who needs an audience, someone to listen to them, especially if they are lonely?

- How can we invest in finding out how people really are – getting past the initial 'I'm fine' response to, 'What are their concerns and anxieties?'

- Let's ask, 'How can I help you to flourish, to stand on God's call for you, to understand how God sees you and longs for you to grow?'

We need to make relationship-building deliberate. Using the diary is useful. Who should you contact next week, not because there is a task to be done, but because the relationship is important and needs more investment?

Rebuilding confidence in our call

I hope this book has reinforced the call you have to the workplace. We are many people's sole interaction with Jesus. We repeatedly pray for God's work to 'be done, on earth as it is in heaven' (Matthew 6:10). God's kingdom work is not confined to a synagogue, temple or church building. The kingdom touches the fishing boat, the marketplace, the city gates, the palace officials, the fields, the vineyards. We are servants. God wants to work remarkably through each one of us. More than that, if we are the servants, He is the master, and He ensures we can complete the task He has assigned to us.

We are in a time when God wants His people to rediscover their authority. We have talked about the authority He gives just two or three of us to spiritually bind and loose (Matthew 18:18-20). Is there bullying, harassment or malpractice in your workplace? You have the authority to see change. Work and practise with others to grow your spiritual authority. But this is not just for you – encourage, release and challenge others to discover their call and their authority so that God's kingdom can come in the workplace and in the community. Be an advocate for God's kingdom – our business!

Being out of work. I spent six months out of work and know how stressful and disorientating that is. It stretches our faith and reduces our energy. We question our self-worth and capability. This is a real challenge for many people. Making a career shift may be needed. I admire those who feel a call to wait even though this waiting period can be deeply challenging. I admire those who are also asking, 'What else can I do to bless and serve my community at this time, and maybe develop some new skills?'

There is one key message you need to cling to in times when redundancy is looming or in times when you are out of work. It is this: God loves you – and He is faithful. Stand on truth. Keep reading the Scriptures and hear what God is saying to you. 'God is our refuge and strength, an ever-present help in trouble' (Psalm 46:1).

> May the LORD answer you when you are in distress;
> may the name of the God of Jacob protect you.
> May he send you help from the sanctuary
> and grant you support from Zion [heaven].
> (Psalm 20:1-2)

I hate my job. You may work in a toxic environment, or it may just suck the life out of you every morning. It may provide no challenge or interest. It may be exhausting, with long hours and constant demands. You should not be alone. You are part of the Ekklesia, and you should have people standing with you. So many people feel the answer is to suffer in silence, but that is not God's kingdom plan. The body of Christ must be supportive, must give time to each other, must listen as you talk through your issue. If you need help, that's what the body does (it might not be your experience, but I think it is incumbent to ask for support: you might be surprised!). It may be that God wants you there to be countercultural, to choose life in the middle of hopelessness. But it can equally be the case that your prayer is to move on.

My wife, Carol, was working in an aggressive culture where fourteen- to sixteen-hour days were the norm and it was affecting her health. We decided she had to resign although she had no job to go to. We know it was the right thing to do, and in due time this led to the most fruitful role in her career. The secret is, 'What's God saying?' This is leading us back to Nehemiah, when people stand together, some with the trowel and some with the sword. We protect each other; we depend on each other.

Rebuild your expectations

Here is the voice of God speaking directly to us – this is like a trumpet call as we come to the end of this book. It is an inspirational passage. Let it speak to you and challenge you today. Let us be aligned with God's great plans and purpose. Here we can immerse ourselves in the prophetic words of Isaiah as he lets God speak very personally to you and me.

> 'Is not this the kind of fasting I have chosen:
> to loose the chains of injustice
> and untie the cords of the yoke,
> to set the oppressed free

and break every yoke?
Is it not to share your food with the hungry
and to provide the poor wanderer with shelter –
when you see the naked, to clothe them,
and not to turn away from your own flesh and blood?
Then your light will break forth like the dawn,
and your healing will quickly appear;
then your righteousness will go before you,
and the glory of the LORD will be your rear guard.
Then you will call, and the LORD will answer;
you will cry for help, and he will say: here am I.
If you do away with the yoke of oppression,
with the pointing finger and malicious talk,
and if you spend yourselves on behalf of the hungry
and satisfy the needs of the oppressed,
then your light will rise in the darkness,
and your night will become like the noonday.
The LORD will guide you always;
he will satisfy your needs in a sun-scorched land
and will strengthen your frame.
You will be like a well-watered garden,
like a spring whose waters never fail.
Your people will rebuild the ancient ruins
and will raise up the age-old foundations;
you will be called Repairer of Broken Walls,
Restorer of Streets with Dwellings.
If you keep your feet from breaking the Sabbath
and from doing as you please on my holy day,
if you call the Sabbath a delight
and the LORD's holy day honourable,
and if you honour it by not going your own way
and not doing as you please or speaking idle words,
then you will find your joy in the LORD,
and I will cause you to ride in triumph on the heights of the
land
and to feast on the inheritance of your father Jacob.'
For the mouth of the LORD has spoken.
(Isaiah 58:6-14)

This starts in the workplace. I know it is high-sounding poetic language, but the oppressed need setting free very close to you. These verses are as current as this morning's news. This is God's plan for how we relate with others. It might be that certain groups of people are treated unfairly or ignored. It might be that some colleagues have a great time in work but return to a place of oppression or difficulty. There are many who are physically hungry, all around us. There are others who are emotionally and spiritually hungry – they need our love, they need our time, they need our reassurance, they need our thanks and appreciation. Let's feed them. It's a challenge to see things change around us, but it is also a promise – God is with us, we will find joy in Him, He will guide us always.

'You will call, and the LORD will answer' (v9). Do we call enough? Do we ask or seek or knock enough (Matthew 7:7)? When we pray, do we pray specifically or vaguely? 'Your will be done,' or, 'Bless them, Lord,' are pretty low–faith investments. 'I pray they will sell their house in the next week;' 'I pray that Hanif's mother will come out of hospital, and that you will give her a deep peace and good health.' The more specific we are (as God guides us), the more clearly God is glorified. I want to see workplaces changed as people talk about specific answers to prayer. God is alive and dynamic in your workplace, and you have a power source maybe nobody else has!

'The LORD will guide you always' (Isaiah 58:11). Six powerful words. Six words that can change our lives, because when we are guided by God, He will work through us. We will indeed be 'like a well-watered garden' and a 'Repairer of Broken Walls' (vv11-12). Weave this into your prayers: 'Lord, You will guide me always. Let this truth shape my life.'

Rebuilding society

We are the difference society needs. *We are God's change-makers, lights in the darkness* (Matthew 5:15).

Our society is in a dangerous place. Nehemiah is following Isaiah 58's directions. He goes around Jerusalem with its broken gates and walls, the ruins and desolation. The city is insecure. It has been like this for many years; it must be a depressing place to see, let alone live in. Outside, others are actively working against Nehemiah's rebuild plans; they want to stop him by any means possible. As they begin to build, the city seems, if anything, even more vulnerable; the walls are hard to defend, the groups working on them are tiring and now they have to divide their duties between rebuilding and protecting those who rebuild (Nehemiah 4:16).

Isaiah also tells us to 'call the Sabbath a delight' (Isaiah 58:13) – it is about our relationship with God. He wants our time and attention through His holy Sabbath. Then we will 'find … joy in the LORD' (v14). Simply walking with God can seem extraordinary in a world full of fear and grumbling, insecurity and stress. A joy-filled person can make all the difference in our workplaces. Let us be the people who walk into the room and turn the 'can-do' light on, who energise our colleagues and put a smile on people's faces. We have caricatures of Christians being miserable and grim and self-righteous. But Isaiah calls us to 'ride in triumph on the height of the land' (v14). Ponder on that next time you are feeling miserable!

How are we rebuilding?

Our society is divided. There is a huge disparity between the rich and the poor. Deprived neighbourhoods see an accumulation of health inequalities, struggling and broken families, increased mental health issues, the ever-present menace of gangs and run-ins with the police.

We are called in Isaiah 58 to 'loose the chains of injustice' (v6). Liverpudlian Christians from many churches and movements saw this clearly when they fought for justice for the ninety-six victims of the Hillsborough Stadium football disaster in 1989. The fans were blamed; the city was shamed as it mourned the victims whose only crime was to love their football club. It took many years for the truth to come out that it was not the fans' fault and that the city had been unjustly treated. The hurt ran deep. I am so proud of those who stood with families, who prayed for breakthrough at the enquiries and continued to believe that justice would come through. This is what Christians do. We fight for justice.

Injustice brings deep hurt. It's the hurt of seeing a police officer choke the life out of George Floyd, and of a justice system that does not deliver justice. What happens to black people in the US has its impact elsewhere. Where people are treated unjustly in one nation because of the colour of their skin, it encourages and gives permission for that same ill-treatment elsewhere. The hurt is intensified when people feel that their plight is not understood. Letting 'justice roll on like a river' (Amos 5:24) starts in our workplace conversations; it impacts the way we do church and how we welcome people; it should drive us to listen intently to cries of those suffering injustices.

Isolated churches. This is a time for unity, to bless the whole city or neighbourhood. I find it hard to understand how churches can remain isolated when we hear Jesus' strong plea for unity in John 17; of course, our theology is important, but part of our theology should be about Jesus' heart for us to be one.

Disunity. Sometimes unity is the hardest thing. We have different views and perspectives. We can all be heading in the same direction and then something blows up. Honouring others is so important. Unity invests deeply and thoroughly in relationships. Unity is seeing someone else with God's eyes.

> How good and pleasant it is
> when God's people live together in unity!
> It is like precious oil poured on the head,
> running down on the beard,
> running down on Aaron's beard,
> down on the collar of his robe.

It is as if the dew of Hermon
were falling on Mount Zion.
For there the LORD bestows his blessing,
even life for evermore.
(Psalm 133:1-3)

Unity. The call to unity is, of course, Jesus' last word, as we see in the Upper Room discourse during the Last Supper. Psalm 133 is part of the Songs of Ascent; starting with Psalm 120 these psalms are a progression as we move closer and closer to the temple. 'Who may ascend the mountain of the LORD? (Psalm 24:3): Who may come into His presence? Brothers and sisters who dwell together in unity. Be a unity builder, repair the walls of broken unity. Let us release blessing. Unity is practical, it is kind, it is honouring, it is generous. It is ambitious for other Christians, churches and organisations because it longs to see God's kingdom come, as we stand together as one.

Rebuilding incorporates social justice. But in itself that is not enough. Isaiah 58 makes clear the need to see change in society, but we need to look at it in the wider context of the book of Isaiah, which is focused on God moving among us.

In Isaiah 9:6-7 we read:

For to us a child is born,
to us a son is given,
and the government will be on his shoulders.
And he will be called
Wonderful Counsellor, Mighty God,
Everlasting Father, Prince of Peace.
Of the greatness of his government and peace
there will be no end.
He will reign on David's throne
and over his kingdom,
establishing and upholding it
with justice and righteousness
from that time on and for ever.
The zeal of the LORD Almighty
will accomplish this.

The government, the authority, is on Jesus. Our workplace and communities need Him most of all. Where we work, He promises to be our 'Wonderful Counsellor, Mighty God, Everlasting Father, Prince of Peace'. These are powerful promises to change our work mindset. Real, long-lasting social justice comes when His kingdom comes. This, in turn, demonstrates the gospel. Here's a great promise: 'The zeal of the LORD Almighty will accomplish this.' We so often feel weak and of no consequence, but we need to let the zeal of God fill us, empower us and equip us.

Release the Ekklesia

It's simple. We have heard it throughout this book. Accept our position in the Ekklesia. At Caesarea Philippi, Peter has the revelation that Jesus is the Christ (Matthew 16:16), and in response the Ekklesia is called into place. So that's our starting point and our finishing point – Jesus is the Messiah. He has come to save the world, to change the world and to prepare us for eternity in His kingdom.

I believe these are times of divine shift. God wants us to stand in the knowledge of the Ekklesia. He did not call pew fodder; he called kingdom builders. He did not call us to be ordinary; He equips us to be extraordinary. He stands with us in the storms; He is our 'refuge in times of trouble' (Psalm 59:16), He walks with us in 'the valley of the shadow of death' (Psalm 23:4, ESV). This is a time for deeper faith.

Let us consider again those all-important 'last words'.

> Then Jesus came to them and said, 'All authority in heaven and on earth has been given to me. Therefore go and make disciples of all nations, baptising them in the name of the Father and of the Son and of the Holy Spirit, and teaching them to obey everything I have commanded you. And surely I am with you always, to the very end of the age.'
> (Matthew 28:18-20)

Then we read His promise made at the same time:

> But you will receive power when the Holy Spirit comes on you; and you will be my witnesses in Jerusalem, and in all Judea and Samaria, and to the ends of the earth.
> (Acts 1:8)

We have been commissioned, as members of the Ekklesia, and we have been given authority and we have been given power. More than that, we have been given people called to stand alongside us. One of the most powerful elements of the Ekklesia is this power we have in twos and threes. We are sent out in small groups. I encourage you to find your Ekklesia. Look for them in the workplace and build relationship; it will release power and focus where you are. I am so pleased I found mine in my network of friends and we saw God move.

If you are in a small group, encourage it to embrace the workplace, to understand the challenges we face and to stand with us. Many Christians in the workplace complain that their church does not 'get' them and does not support them. But the starting point is to not be embarrassed about our call, and not to keep quiet because others in the small group won't 'get' it – let us ensure we invest time in understanding and supporting each other well.

I think it is right that the church prays for people who go on missions abroad, and is interested in them, but most churches need a revelation that our impact in the workplace should be as great. Church needs to embrace the workforce because we are on the front line, but we need to be prepared to ask for prayer and to help others understand our situation.

God is rebuilding what it means to be Church/Ekklesia. He is reframing our understanding of His call on our lives. He is renewing our day-by-day intimacy with Him. He is restoring us to the New Testament picture of the gospel going out – into the home, the marketplace, the community – and seeing new people come to Christ daily. We are seeing His kingdom come, beautifully, often surprisingly, in the workplace, the community, in our schools and in hospitals and in many other situations.

Terry's story (continued)

We met Terry earlier in the book, with his story of turning a struggling school around and his faith journey as God led him to Eastbourne. In 2020, God led Terry in another unexpected direction when he found himself as team minister at Gateway Church. This gives him some interesting perspectives on the Church and workplace that I found very insightful. So here they are!

> The secular workplace, I believe, is where the gospel rubber hits the worldly road. It is a true mission field. Of course, it is tempting to focus on bringing non-Christians into our safe, for us, environment of the church, rather than supporting the troops fighting to bring the most amazing, life-saving news in the universe to the dirty trenches of the workplace. But it is in those dirty trenches that the gospel will attract others and transform lives. The Christian faith is of no use if it does not transform our workplaces, and needs to be there seen in its true power.
>
> I believe that churches need to see workplaces, not as places to while away the week waiting for worshipping God on a Sunday, but to take a real interest in them, and to understand and support them as a powerful mission field. Taking an interest in those workplaces and the Christians, especially those from one's own church, who work there, and praying for them, has huge power to bring about Christian change. Equally, giving those Christians in our own churches opportunities to share the challenges and opportunities for Christ in those workplaces can be very powerful.
>
> I have been fortunate throughout my time as a head teacher to have had those opportunities and, in doing so, was blessed by the prayers and support given. Through that, not through me, I believe that many, many lives were transformed.

His work experience now shapes Terry's church role:

As a multigenerational church, with a quarter of our congregation under twenty years old, we emphasise the development of young leaders and include young people in many of our leadership teams. Much of my time now is spent mentoring younger leaders and facilitating them to impact others, including our community and town, for Jesus. In addition, I have supported leadership in other churches, which again helps those churches in their missions in their communities.

When I took my first step with Jesus into teaching, leadership was not my skillset or my ambition. Yet it has become a key element of my gifting and ministry. Furthermore, my experience of working with struggling communities has helped me to shape a strategy at Gateway where we seek to bless our local community, which is in the top 10 per cent nationally in terms of the Index of Multiple Deprivation (showing disadvantages across a range of measures).

Could I have planned such an amazing outcome? No! Have I ever wanted to do this? No! However, by giving my work and career as an area of worship to God and allowing Jesus to lead me, albeit sometimes screaming and shouting, along His path for me, I have found fulfilment beyond my dreams and a joy in serving I could never have imagined.

Rebuilding our cities and communities

Our cities need rebuilding. I was with a group of leaders from Birmingham, and we were talking about the crud that has built up in our city around racial injustice. We made our wealth and grew into the UK's second city on the back of money generated through the slave trade. We were the gun manufacturers, and our guns were used as the key trading commodity to purchase slaves. In the 1950s and 1960s, many Afro-Caribbeans came to make Birmingham their home, and we put up signs on rented properties saying, 'No dogs, Irish or Blacks'. Black immigrants, wide-eyed at coming to the mother country, went to church to worship and were told to go away and find another place. Our emerging black churches in the city took rejected people and gave them a home. In the 1970s, 1980s, 1990s and beyond, there was racial discrimination on the job front, housing, the justice system, etc. Today, black people are treated with suspicion and prejudice and suffer from many barriers, including a wide range of health inequalities. Birmingham's Anglican bishop, David Urquhart, comments:

> We have before us the daunting task of eradicating personal and institutional racism. With Lord Jesus' humbling, forgiving power, we can each be transformed and so be part of making a truly diverse, free, and reconciled society.[133]

So we have these layers of crud across our city, reflecting the deep hurts we did to each other. Binding the crud together is a culture of suspicion, resentment and urban myths – a toxic mix that stops us from standing together. But now it is time to rebuild. We have other rebuild issues in our city too, but that is a predominant one for us. What are yours?

We can do so much more. Charlotte, North Carolina, has its joined-up plan to tackle four key issues in the city and to work together for mission. New York has seen remarkable growth and thousands of changed lives. Christian leaders are working together to rebuild the poorest neighbourhoods. Cities across the UK are praying together. In these challenging times they want the people of God to strengthen their focus on Jesus and release blessings on their city. In the Black Country, 2,500 gathered to start 2020. In Exeter, they used Zoom to gather 1,500 people for regular prayer. In Teesside, the different churches work together to joyfully tell their story of one church with different expressions. They pray together and work for their town together. In Nottingham, a series of very practical

---

[133] 'Churches take a stand against racial injustice', Birmingham Churches Together, 5th June 2020, https://www.birminghamchurches.org.uk/chu rches-take-a-stand-against-racial-injustice/ (accessed 20th November 2021).

projects brings hope to the city and country. In Bristol, they work so that no child will go hungry. This is God's people discovering the capacity to be change agents in their city, neighbourhood and workplace.

This work is growing globally. It is a movement of God. Covid-19 has accelerated the need to see our city from one perspective – God's perspective – and to unite so that the people we live alongside will see Jesus.

Yet again, Nehemiah gives us great clues on the way forward. The city walls and the gates to the city across Jerusalem need rebuilding. Only a few people need to have that big-picture perspective, and Nehemiah constantly seeks God for instruction. Most of us would be assigned to a specific task (Nehemiah 3:1-32). There may be a grieving in this as we remember what we have lost. Then we move to rebuilding – we may have a 500-yards assignment, but today we start with fifty bricks and a trowel. While I use the trowel you carry the sword; you are watching out for me, you want me to succeed, you pray for me. If needs be, you will put your body on the line for me. The practical and spiritual go hand in hand. Last week it was trowel-wielding, next week we go to attentively hear Ezra reading the Law of Moses (Nehemiah 8:2-3). Then we repent. We repent because we feel responsible for our cities' destruction. As we rebuild the walls, so we also are rebuilding our covenant with God. We are a renewed, holy people where the practical and the spiritual go hand in hand.

It is all about Jesus

Stop.
It is all about Jesus.
Stop.
It is all about Jesus.

These are those all-important last words. Your call, your life, your skills, your achievements are all enabled by Jesus.

I close this book with an eye on revival. Revival comes when people draw closer to Jesus. They hunger for more of Him. But it is not an empty hunger; it is a hunger for our lives to be turned around and our communities and workplaces to be radically changed. It's a hunger for our friends and family to find Jesus, and it's a hunger that says we do not want them go to hell and separation from Jesus; we want to see their lives filled with Him. It's a fresh perspective on that key phrase 'your kingdom come', because God's kingdom is glorious, releasing, empowering, eternal.

God's revival word to us is, 'You bring the fire and I will bring the wind.' What does your fire look like? It might seem small, or even a few flickering embers. But we can present our fire to Jesus and pray, 'Come, Holy Spirit.' Revival rescues. Revival restores. Revival brings hope to those struggling through hard and challenging times. Come, Holy Spirit.

I am praying for a deep and long-lasting revival.

It starts with one simple prayer: 'More, more, more of You, Lord.'

The nineteenth-century evangelist Charles Finney visited a factory and saw people touched by the Spirit as he walked by. The owner commanded that the mill be stopped and the workforce be given the opportunity to hear and respond to the gospel. The workplace experienced revival – a life-changing moment when people become very aware of God speaking to them and everything within them wants Jesus. Revival went through the mill with astonishing power. Could it happen where you work? This is what God does when revival happens.[134]

Across Wales, people started praying for revival; they were hungry for more of Jesus. Evan Roberts prayed for revival for

---

[134] Finney saw a great revival in Rochester, New York, when 100,000 people came to Christ, a remarkable turnaround for the whole region. He preached while others prayed and prepared the ground. An interesting footnote on Finney is that he accepted the Presidency of Oberlin College in 1833 on the condition that they would accept African–American students.

eleven years (from the age of fifteen). He studied revival history; he sensed this divine call that God wanted to move powerfully. This became a deep hunger, shared with many others for more of God; it changed churchgoers and those with little or no faith who felt this urge to get right with God. After four months of revival in Wales, 84,000 conversions were recorded – more than 5,000 a week. Shops closed early so people could get to revival meetings. God set Wales on fire. Swearing stopped, public houses became empty, theatres closed, police courts found their workload decreased substantially, family feuds were resolved, old debts repaid, and Welsh worship filled the chapels.

Evan Roberts, this twenty-six-year-old, was a facilitator of the Holy Spirit. Encouraged by older Christians, he asked God to use him. While people looked to him for a lead, he often just sat in meetings and let the Holy Spirit move as the crowded meetings spontaneously, with no choir leader or announcements, moved from worship song to worship song as the Spirit moved. Roberts said:

> Heads are bowed in folded hands. Shoulders are convulsed with emotion, and lips are moving from which no sound comes. Still the preacher gives no sign. Gradually a single low voice is heard in all parts of the chapel, singing sweetly the hymn, 'Have you seen Him?' in Welsh. For an instant there is time stillness of listening with bated breath; then slowly other voices join in singing until the building rings with thrilling melody. It is as if they have burst from prayer into song..[135]

He put his finger on it. This is our story for the workplace. This is our story for our community. Jesus can move powerfully through us, but first He must do a great work in us.

It is this simple truth. God does remarkable things through open vessels. Our workplace and our community can see His kingdom come. Revival is God moving through hungry people.

---

[135] 'Evan Roberts, Welsh Revival', www.thejesusgathering.org/evan-roberts.html (accessed 10th February 2022).

Jesus and Paul saw it in the marketplace, the workplace, through friendships and connections.

Prayer

Lord, You made me, You love me, You have called me to serve You.
I surrender to Your call and Your purpose; use me.
I am hungry to see more and more of Your kingdom, changing me and impacting others.
Your kingdom is my business; may more and more people experience Your kingdom through me. Amen.

Acknowledgements

I gratefully acknowledge the wisdom and support given by the team at Instant Apostle. As a novice in the book-writing game I am sure I was asking very naïve questions which they handled with grace and wisdom. More than that, they stuck with me on the journey from my overcrowded desk to the product you have before you.

I have the enormous privilege of walking with some wonderful friends and pay special tribute to my prayer triplet – Richard Nicol and Mark Billage: we have journeyed a long way together, always looking for God's best for each other and giving a grounding to each week. There are others who have been the iron that sharpened my iron from way back in university with my friends Ali and Wendy and Terry and Chrissie and Richard and Rachel – friendships that endure and bear fruit today. Others have come who have taken on that huge task of getting me to think! Paul Duncan, Matthew Gregory, Fred Rattley, Steve Ashton, Chris Crocker, Karamat and Sue Iqbal – let's keep walking this walk.

In 2015 God managed my diary and I got to meet a man called Roger Sutton. He sold his vision of God moving powerfully in our cities. It resonated with me; indeed, it resonated with me so strongly that I started 'stalking' Roger and travelling to global and national conferences with him. He was very tolerant! I was enthused by his vision and his network. Here were people seeing God moving in mercy and unity and practical actions in Bristol, and Stoke, and Pretoria, and Toowoomba, and Newcastle (the Aussie version!) and Berlin and Lincoln and Nottingham. I met people who became heroes to me because they loved to see Jesus move – Ian Shelton, Dave King, Sheena Tranter, Rick Prosser, Craig Sider and so many others. I took their big picture and put it into the workplace. It is simple – when God's kingdom comes, it changes everything.

Finally, I acknowledge the support of my family. I love them to bits, I am enriched by their company and protected by their wisdom. Thank you, Alice, Nate and Rachel. I would like my wife and best friend, Carol, to have the last word. She leads a team of 450 people providing a key service to the Home Office. She is approachable and kind, she is very sharp and wise, she creates breakthroughs in times of crisis. Most of all, she is a kingdom woman, walking very humbly with God, letting His shalom, righteousness and compassion shape what she does and the lives of those who work for her and with her. I believe God is very proud of her – as I am.